PRAISE FOR *A HEBRAIC OBSESSION*

"Riveting!"

— Kimberly Perel, Wendy Sherman Associates

"A gripping story, filled with suspense and a touch of the sexuality found in a Philip Roth novel."

— Tracie Dickerson, Author

A Hebraic Obsession is a real page-turner. Once I started reading it, I could not put it down. You don't have to be Jewish to enjoy this book. It was highly educational, as well as, entertaining. I learned a lot about the Holocaust from the point of view of a survivor and a survivor's son.

— Philip Reichert, Writer

A Hebraic Obsession reveals the deep emotions of the next generation of Holocaust survivors."

— Herbert Lerner, Jewish Activist and Attorney

A Hebraic Obsession

Mort Laitner

Transitional Press
Fort Lauderdale, Florida

A Hebraic Obsession

By Mort Laitner

Cover and book design by Dave Bricker.

ISBN: 978-0-9960369-2-4

Library of Congress Control Number.: 2014939475

TRANSITIONAL PRESS

FORT LAUDERDALE, FLORIDA
8679 SW 51ST ST
COOPER CITY, FL 33328
1.954.298.8178

Dedication

To the memory of my father, Dr. Wolf Laitner –
a great father, doctor, survivor, and my hero.

A Hebraic Obsession

Contents

Preface i
Acknowledgements iii
The Stairs 1
Questions 7
My Trades 23
My Dad 29
Old Spice 61
The Westerns 67
The Colonial Inn 77
The Eulogy 81
The Neighbors 85
Sitting *Shiva* 95
My Struggle 101
The Catskills 115
Our Town 141
Traveling Buddies 153
Tangiers 161
Toy Soldiers 177

Contents

American *Führers* 185
South of the Border 197
Tobacco 225
Law School 237
The Doctoral Dissertation 247
The *Seder* 251
The Computer 261
Barbarossa 265
Twenty-Six 267
Organization *Todt* 267
You Led a Good Life 279
Risk-Taking 285
Lists 291
The Photograph 309
The Arrival 315
Slave Labor 343
The Trial Transcript 359
About This Book 367

Preface

Since college, I have thought I should write a book about my father's wartime experiences. He was a doctor who survived Auschwitz. He failed to divulge much information about this period in his life. I did not dare to ask. I assumed that one day he would tell me his story. But as I grew older, I never got to hear my father's story. I built a career, a family and a comfortable lifestyle and that event never occurred. I would often say, "One day, when I retire, I will write my father's story."

I collected a small library of books that referenced the Holocaust and his life in the camps.

In 1989, one week after my Dad's death, I received his Holocaust audio tapes. Then I had the foundation for a compelling story.

From 2006 until 2009 I used a mixture of fact and fiction to write and publish short stories about him.

Then in 2010, I read a doctoral dissertation written by an Israeli Ph.D. candidate. The paper referenced his wartime activities in the occupied Soviet Union. Another important piece of his puzzle fell into place.

The doctoral paper rekindled the ember housed in my stomach. I knew the time for short stories had ended. The ember smoldered until my retirement in 2012. I then had the luxury of time to research and write.

In May of 2012, when I commenced writing this book, I intended it to be solely about my father, but it quickly morphed from a Holocaust story into a father/son tale – a father, who survived the Nazi horrors of being a Jew in Poland, Germany and Russia, and his American son who vicariously lived those horrors through written words, documentary films and a few hundred words which came from the mouth of my father.

My writing journey took me down two separate roads: Europe in the 30s and 40s, and America from the 50s to the present. These roads intersected into one compelling story of survival, filled with obsessions, discoveries and miracles.

Acknowledgements

I want to thank the following for their assistance in the creation of this book: my sons, Blake, Jason and Travis for their numerous edits and comments on the text; my wife, Shelley for her editing skills and her patience in allowing me time to write this book; my sister, Barbara Laitner Feldman, for her efforts in refreshing my memories about my father, editing and helping me select the photographs that appear in this book; to my Aunt Renia and my Uncle Mike Cukier, for their recounting many stories about my mom and dad; the Southeastern Florida Holocaust Memorial Center, Inc; and specifically, Paul Kaplan for interviewing my father; and Dr. Herbert Lerner his excellent comments and edits on the manuscript; two Healthy Stories senior editors, Philip Reichert and Tracie Dickerson; Dr. Bella Gutermann of the Shoah Resource Center, International School of Holocaust Studies, Yad Vashem, Jerusalem, Israel for her masterfully researched and beautifully written dissertation entitled, *Jews in Service of Organisation Todt in the Occupied Soviet Territories*, October 1941–March 1942, from which I learned so much about my father; Dr. Chris Mann, General Editor of *Great Battles of World War II,* Parragon Books Limited 2008, for his detailed analysis of Operation Barbarossa; Professor Thomas Childers from the University of Pennsylvania, author of *A History of Hitler's Empire,* 2nd Edition to *Healthy Stories,* A Miami–Dade County Health Department publication, for having published some of the short stories that are incorporated in this book; Wolf Gruner, for his enlightening book, *Jewish Forced Labor Under the Nazis, Economic Needs and Racial Aims,* 1938–1944; To Geoffrey Roberts, author of *Stalin's General, The Life of Georgy Zhukov;* Ann Kirschner, author of *Sala's Gift, My Mother's Holocaust Story,* for information about my father's activities as a doctor in the labor camps and for the 1942 photograph signed and dated by my father which graces the cover of this book; Mel Laytner for providing my father's testimony at the trial of Erich Hoffmann; Jewish Review of Books, *Cri de Coeur,* by Amy Newman Smith, Volume 4, Number 2 Summer 2013 for her review of *The Short, Strange Life of Herschel Grynzpan: A Boy Avenger, a Nazi Diplomat, and a Murder in Paris* by Jonathan Kirsch; *The Collaboration: Hollywood's Pact with Hitler* by Ben Urwand and *Fritz Kuhn and The Rise and Fall of The German-American Bund: Swastika Nation* by Arnie Bernstein.

Mort Laitner

A Hebraic Obsession

A Hebraic Obsession

One

The Stairs

As a ten-year old, I eavesdropped on my father telling his harrowing story of almost being gassed to death. In darkness, I sat on the top of the stairs, my legs hung over the first two steps. I pushed my head forward to be better able to hear him. I listened to my father's somber voice as he sat with his friends in the living room below and spoke in his thick Germanic accent. I sat within a few yards of my father but totally out of his sight. If anyone started to climb the stairs, within a second I could escape to the safety of my bedroom.

I listened, concentrated, and memorized his words as if I knew one day after he was gone it would be my duty to pass them on. He spoke them in English, Polish, Yiddish or a mixture of all three depending on the audience's language preference. His old friends quietly sat, as silent as falling snow. Many had not seen my father since before the war. Many were fellow survivors with numbers tattooed on their arms and memories permanently burned into their brains. As invited guests, they allowed my father, the doctor, to speak first. He captured their minds with unimaginable horrors. They never interrupted him, being too polite or afraid to ask questions for which they may not have wanted to hear the answers.

I also sat in silence, listening, fidgeting, and wondering. My father never told his story directly to me. I thought he wanted to protect me. But, I believed he knew I was perched on top of the steps.

Thirty years later, I again heard my father's voice tell the story, this time resonating from the speakers of a cassette recorder. My dad died of a heart attack, one day before his unedited Holocaust Memorial tape arrived via mail to his Boca Raton home.

I ripped open the manila envelope. I popped open the cassette player window, pushed the tape in the slot and pressed the play button. For the next three hours I sat transfixed. I listened. I remembered. I cried.

The interviewer asked, "Doctor, when you were a slave at Auschwitz, what was your most harrowing moment?"

My father said, "There were too many frightening moments to count. I don't know how or why I survived. But here is one miraculous moment that I have often told my closest friends.

"It started during morning roll call, on a cold, rainy day. My constant pangs of hunger retreated as the metallic taste of fear washed across my bleeding gums. An SS doctor determined that I was no longer fit to work. Therefore, I had to die. At gunpoint, several other men and I were marched into a group of new arrivals.

"Mothers held onto their babies and young children. Elderly couples walked hand-in-hand. Crowded into a large courtyard, I faced what the Nazi's termed the 'delousing showers.' Having lived in, or better said, survived in the extermination camp, I knew that all of us were going to be gassed to death in those showers. I had been told by men who brought the bodies to the ovens. I smelled the putrid odor of burning human flesh. The stench permeated my nostrils as well as the entire camp. Smoke rose from the chimneys of the crematoria. Ashes of the silenced snowed down upon those selected to live.

"I knew most of my family had been murdered. Death stopped appearing to be my enemy. Having already descended to Hell, I wondered if there was a heaven.

"I, with over a thousand other people, was ordered to strip. I unbuttoned my blue and gray striped camp shirt. Sewn on the pocket was a yellow six-pointed star. In the middle of the star, as if the star alone was not a sufficient symbol, one word pointed out my religious identity. JUDE. The reason for enslavement summed up in one four-letter word.

"I dropped my trousers which were encrusted with filth and stains of death. I folded my soaked so-called 'pajamas' on top of my wooden-heeled shoes. As my fingers grazed the Star of David, a sharp, burning, electrical jolt shot through my body and clutched my heart.

As the pain subsided, I used my hands to cover my privates. I was surrounded by the naked. I wept as I listened to the cries of babies. As I shuffled toward the gas chamber, I looked into the dark smoke-filled skies as rain battered my face. I prayed the *Shema Yisrael* as I wondered about the existence of the Almighty.

"I glanced over at the perimeter of the crowd and saw a Nazi guard holding his rifle in the direction of the throng. The guard talked to my fully clothed lover, my girlfriend.

The guard screamed and pointed his rifle at me, 'You, vermin! Get out of line! *Raus!*'

"I had known that if I paused for a second it would be my last.

"I hurried to find my clothes and shoes among a thousand piles.

"Miraculously they appeared.

"I questioned my luck. I would be allowed to survive in hell for another day.

"In seconds, I dressed, stepped out of the formation and turned my back on a thousand naked people being led to the gas chamber. I feared looking back."

As I sat at my father's table, in his Boca home, my ears felt the Interviewer's silent pause as he absorbed what he had just heard.

Trembling, I gently pressed the off button. I had heard enough.

I shut my eyes and returned to my tenth year. I found myself in my childhood home, in the hallway, hunched over on the top stair, wishing my father had been less protective.

Two

Questions

My father failed to transfer much of the weight of his past onto my shoulders. I always believed he did this out of love, to protect me. As his only son, I learned much in dribs and drabs from his wartime friends and acquaintances. From his mouth came a few horror stories. We had an unwritten "Don't-Ask-Don't-Tell" policy. I thought this policy even applied to my mother – who was a fellow camp survivor – having never remembered them discuss their lives in captivity in Polish or in English.

After his death, I listened on a number of occasions – approximately once every five years – to his Holocaust tapes. From those tapes, I learned of his luck, courage, and intelligence. I learned of his bravery, calculated risks, and his generosity.

On the tape, he said to the interviewer, "This session only tells one percent of my wartime experience. I saw cruelty 1,000 times worse than I describe to you today." Based on that statement,

I guessed that I only knew about one tenth of one percent of his story.

I learned from those tapes why he thought he had survived the camps.

> "People often ask me, 'How did you survive?' I would tell them I was lucky. I was not so smart but I had alert eyes and ears. I knew how to behave. I knew when to work. I knew how to steal. I knew how to go two or three days without a meal. Those without hope perished. Something kept me going. I looked for signs, for the magic in numbers, for any good omen. These superstitions kept me alive for an additional day. But if the war had lasted an additional two weeks I would not be here to make this audio tape."

I understood these acts of human nature. We all look for signs, especially in times of crisis. However rather than quenching my thirst for his story, he left out details I craved to know.

I wanted to know what his girlfriend said to that Nazi guard to get him pulled out of the gas chamber.

I wanted to know why his Jewish girlfriend was clothed while the remaining 1,000 were naked.

I wanted to know if my father said anything to the Nazi guard who pulled him out of the line.

I wanted to know how he had a girlfriend in a concentration camp.

I wanted to know for how long this woman and my father were lovers.

I wanted to know why my father was sent to Auschwitz.

I wanted to know if, as a doctor, he was granted any privileges.

These questions were not answered on the audio tape.

I realized that the more I learned about his wartime experiences, the more questions rose to the surface.

On the tapes, I learned of one of his biggest mistakes. He believed that Germany would never attack Poland. The two countries would never go to war. He thought Hitler would demand some territory, Poland would surrender some land, and Hitler would be satisfied. He, like British Prime Minister Neville Chamberlain, thought Hitler's desire for territory could be satiated. This was one of the few times I heard my father say, "I was wrong."

Seven months before the German invasion of Poland, Hitler told the world his prophecy concerning the fate of European Jews. He gave his speech in front of the Reichstag on January 30, 1939:

> "I have often been a prophet in my life and was generally laughed at. During my struggle for power, the Jews primarily received with laughter my prophecies that I would someday assume the leadership of the state and thereby of the entire Volk and then, among many other things, achieve a solution of the Jewish problem. I suppose that meanwhile the then resounding laughter of Jewry in Germany is now choking in their throats. Today I will be a prophet again: If international finance Jewry within Europe and abroad should succeed once more in plunging the peoples into a world war, then the consequences will be not the Bolshevization of the world and therefore a victory of Jewry, but on the contrary, the destruction of the Jewish race in Europe."

My father and his family, most likely, read those words in the Yiddish paper. My father, like a majority of Jews, thought that even if the Nazis invaded, the Jews would adapt like they had done for the past thousand years. Hitler was an insane braggart. He loved to threaten the race he was obsessed with. My Polish relatives knew that Jewry had survived the Black Plague massacres, the Spanish Inquisition, and the Russian pogroms. The Jews were negotiators, not fighters. They were more than capable at fleeing to new nations. They would work around this modern devil. They were history's survivors and would find a workable solution. His people failed to grasp the meaning of the adage, "Know thy enemy." They had three options: fight, flight, or negotiate with their lives. They would somehow survive this tough new reality. The whole world knew that Jews were internally programmed to look for signals and once learned how to cut a deal.

Even Hitler in *Mein Kampf* (his manifesto) understood this:

> "In hardly any people in the world is the instinct of self-preservation developed more strongly than in the so-called 'chosen' ... Where are the people which in the last two thousand years have been exposed to so slight changes of inner disposition, character, etc., as the Jewish people? What people, finally, have gone through greater upheavals than this one – and nevertheless issued from the mightiest catastrophes of mankind unchanged? What an infinitely tough will to live and preserve the species speaks from these facts!"

The "chosen people" could never picture death factories where SS guards poured Zyklon B over a chamber filled with children, the disabled, and the elderly. When the Zyklon B crystals hit the floor they exploded into a poisonous gas. The gas killed its victims within 10–30 minutes. How many of the millions imagined this process would be the German solution to the "Jewish problem?"

Through his book, Hitler smeared his blood-soaked philosophy across Europe. Those barbaric words were not read by his victims. Those written words came from the mouth of a madman. No civilized nation would elect such a paranoid man.

As a child, my dad told me how he used his medical training to help other prisoners, how sometimes for a massage he was rewarded with a crust of bread. But as a ten-year old, I sensed that I only knew a small part of these frightening chapters in his life. I asked myself, "Did my dad do anything in the war that he was ashamed of? Would he have done anything differently if he could?

While he was alive, I never had the courage to ask him such a question. I dared not bring up the past for fear of causing him pain. In my eyes and heart, Dad had suffered enough. Bringing up his past would open doors that needed to remain shut. What good would come from asking such questions?

To avoid discussions and protect my dad, as a fourteen-year-old coin and stamp collector, I hid my Nazi coins or stamps from my father's eyes.

I held stamps bearing Hitler's image or swastikas wondering who had touched them. Was Hitler's DNA on the back of these stamps? Had this man who sealed a deal with the devil licked these stamps?

I studied a stamp in which Hitler wore a general's military hat, a white shirt, and a dark tie. The hat's visor reached over the bridge of his nose. He stared into the sky as if he was the messiah. He displayed an aura that spoke to his disciples, "I know the path to glory and victory."

This stamp honored Hitler's 53rd birthday with the date 20 April, 1942 imprinted above his hat. The words *DEUTSCHES REICH* frame the bottom of the stamp.

I pushed my index finger across Hitler's paper face, pressing down on his Charlie Chaplin mustache trying to suffocate his image. I loathed his unmistakable face. This murdering son-of-a-bitch received compensation from his government for his likeness appearing on this stamp.

A year after my bar mitzvah, I became a coin collector, a numismatist. It was a hobby where I could learn about the Nazis and the Japanese. Unlike baseball cards, I saw a financial future in this hobby. These coins seemed to have value. On Sundays, I religiously read the *New York Times* coin and stamp section. I scoured *The Times* as if I were reading *The Wall Street Journal* for stock tips.

Once a month, my dad would drop me off at the Middletown Coin and Stamp Shop. With a dollar allowance in my pocket,

I was perplexed over whether to buy first-day covers or Indian-head pennies.

In this shop, I purchased my first stamp album. It was appropriately titled, *My First Stamp Album.* It claimed to be ideal for the beginning collector with its "historical and geographic descriptions of each country." It had world maps in full color for my study of geography. Four years after I purchased it, I used the book to meet the requirements for my stamp collecting Boy Scout merit badge.

One day upon our arrival at the coin and stamp shop, my Dad said, "Son did you know that President Franklin D. Roosevelt was a stamp collector from when he was your age, and he collected until the day he died?"

"No Dad, I had no idea he was a collector." I replied.

Then he reached into his jacket and pulled out a newspaper clipping. He read aloud a Roosevelt quote: "The best thing about stamp collecting is that the enthusiasm which it arouses in youth increases as the years pass. It dispels boredom, enlarges our vision, broadens our knowledge, and in innumerable ways enriches our lives. I also commend stamp collecting because I really believe it makes one a better citizen."

"Dad, FDR really understands my passion for the hobby."

I agreed with Roosevelt's opinion. I only wished he held the same passion, or at least interest, in saving European Jewry.

I found one small example in which he did. In June of 1944, Franklin signed an executive order which helped 892 non-Italian Jewish refugees leave Italy and come to the US. They were placed on a Liberty ship, the *Henry Gibbons,* and transported to the Port of New York. They were taken by train to Oswego, New York, a town just 200 miles north of Woodridge, where they were housed in a refugee center, a refugee center that was surrounded with a barbed-wire fence and guards.

I wondered why our stamp-collecting President did this humane act after years of not giving a shit about the six million. Why rescue Jews who were living in territory under the protection of the US Army? I never found out his motive.

Years later my Dad gave me his opinion of FDR. "Son, I have little respect for Roosevelt. He was a son-of-a-bitch when it came to caring about European Jews. He did so little to stop the slaughter in the camps. The bombers could have destroyed the rails entering and exiting the camps. Roosevelt's minions made it really difficult for European Jews to escape to the States.

Dad pulled out a newspaper article from his coat pocket. "One of those minions was Breckinridge Long. He worked in the U.S. State Department before and during the War. He was in charge of the European refugee desk."

Dad started to read from the article, "In June of 1940, Long wrote an intradepartmental memo which read:

> We can delay and effectively stop for a temporary period of indefinite length the number of immigrants into the United States. We could do this by simply advising our consuls to put every obstacle in the way and to require additional evidence and to resort to various administrative devices which would postpone and postpone and postpone the granting of visas.

My Father continued, "190,000 people could have escaped the Nazis if not for Long's obstructionist policies. I don't think FDR's face deserves to be engraved on the dime or on any postage stamps.

"Well I'm going to up you one, and invite you to drive down to Maryland with me to take a piss on Long's grave and tombstone. I think it is so fitting."

I smiled when I heard my Dad laugh. "Dad, I don't know if you knew that in January of 1944, FDR took the refugee rescue effort from the State Department and gave it to the War Refugee Board. That board did assist in the rescuing of up to 200,000 Jews."

"I still don't think Roosevelt should be honored on any stamps."

At home, I closely examined pages 37–39 of *My First Stamp Album.* These were the pages dedicated to Germanic stamps. With my magnifying glass, I studied each Nazi stamp illustration. One bore a large swastika and multiple hands raised in a

"Heil Hitler" salute, or the *Hitlergruss.* All good Germans were required to salute and those who did not were looked at with distain or given a beating. Another stamp displayed a proud medieval sword and a shield-bearing helmeted German soldier. Here the Nazis associated themselves with the glory days of ancient German empires. Another showed a worker and a farmer marching in front of an unfurled swastika flag. There was one with Hitler's portrait and many with the eagles clawing wreathes that surrounded swastikas. In examining the designs, I realized the value of stamps as propaganda. These stamps became my miniature picture stories.

On another trip to the shop, I observed a glass case filled with foreign currencies. I focused on two German bills, a twenty and a fifty-mark note. The fifty note bore a picture of Moses holding the Ten Commandments. There were actual words written in Hebrew on the bill. The twenty-mark note bore an attractive German woman's face. Next to her face stood an eagle holding a swastika. I shut my eyes and pictured lighting a match to the note. A smile cut across my face as I imagined the swastika and the woman burning into a tiny pile of ashes.

I asked the coin dealer, "What's the history behind the note with Moses holding the Ten Commandments?"

"That bill is quite rare. It was used in the Theresienstadt Ghetto or Concentration Camp. The Nazis wanted the camp to have an appearance of autonomy and normalcy. They wanted to camouflage their intentions. It was one of their many methods of deceit. They created a Jewish currency to trick foreign visitors, like the Red Cross. It was an attempt to mask their real intentions. The German/Jewish money made the Nazis look reasonable."

Holding the note I asked, "Do you know how to translate German on the note into English?"

"*Ein wenig,* a little bit. I think the note says that it is a receipt for 50 crowns and anybody who falsifies or imitates such a note will be punished," the coin dealer proudly proclaimed.

"Thanks for the info," I said as I thought how devious and cruel the Nazis were in their quest for the final solution. Even their Hebraic currency referenced punishment.

One year later in the same shop, I held a *Deutsches Republic pfennig* coin. I rubbed it between my fingers trying to erase the eagle, the wreath, and the swastika. Two thoughts came to mind: Had Hitler or some other big shot Nazi touched this coin? As an egomaniac, why didn't Hitler put his face on German coinage? I never learned the answers to these questions nor discussed them with my father.

Who was I to ask him such questions? The privileged son of a doctor, a hippie who studied at a private university and became a lawyer.

Was it not the Biblical admonishment to honor thy father, not to cross-examine him? Was it not Moses who held the commandments on that concentration camp note? The only word that came to my mind about asking these questions was, *"chutzpah."*

How dare I, a man who never walked one second in my father's holocaust shoes, ask him any questions?

How dare I ask any questions of a man who watched his life and family obliterated, and in silence rebuilt them.

How does one atone for the sin of curiosity?

At our Depression-built Woodridge Temple, on every Yom Kippur, the congregants beseeched the Lord for forgiveness. They repented from their yearly crop of sins and transgressions. Our teacher, Rabbi Goodman, was a slender man who wore a manicured moustache and a black *kipa*. He read the Biblical text in English and Hebrew. He educated us on the sins of greed, avarice, and gossip. We thought about our sins of the flesh as well as our sins of omission. We wondered which sins were venial and which sins lead to major consequences. Luckily for the congregation, the rabbi did discuss all of the violations found in the 613 commandments. Rabbi Goodman listed our sins and then the congregation in one resounding voice responded with their requests to the Almighty for forgiveness.

As a ten-year-old staring at our temple's rafters, I imagined G-d sitting in a Greek or Roman temple in Heaven. His left hand pounded his chest as he looked down at the city of Jerusalem. I watched as his lips quivered. *Who do I repent to? Who forgives me for allowing six million of my 'chosen children' to perish at the hands of the Nazis.*

Can G-d sin? Can he transgress? Can he atone? Does he know how to repent?

Sure, he is G-d, isn't he?

Near the end of the service, members of the congregation, who brought their own shofars to temple stood next to the Rabbi, holding their ancient trumpets. These curved horns of the ram reminded me that Abraham sacrificed the ram instead of his son Isaac. Today the shrill sound leaving the horn hurts my inner ear and reminds me of my need to repent. As the Rabbi's voice intoned, *"tekiah, shevarim, teruah, gadolah"* four different sounds boomed from these ram's horns, I listened intently to each sound, as my head fired round after round of questions.

Had I ever gone three days without a meal?

Never!

Had I ever amputated slave laborer's frozen fingers and toes?

Never!

Had I stolen a crust of bread to survive for one more day?

Never!

Had I lifted and carried 50-pound sacks of cement for ten hours a day?

Never!

Had I entered a Russian *shtetl* in which the town's inhabitants were evacuated *en masse?*

Never!

Had I witnessed babies murdered by being thrown against walls?

Never!

Had I ever been ordered at gunpoint to move boulders from one side of the road to the other side and on the next day to move them back to their original positions?

Never!

Had I ever had to sleep on a frozen brick factory floor watching my fellow prisoners freeze to death?

Never!

Had I ever had to hide in a concentration camp after being ordered to be a feces commando?

Never!

Had I ever seen cattle cars filled with dead and dying bodies?

Never!

Had I ever watched people starve to death and die like flies while lying on four-tiered wooden planked bunk beds?

Never!

My father had!

I then posed the question, *What would a mensch do?*

I knew the answer. No mensch would ever ask a survivor, no less a parent, a question that might cause him pain or discomfort.

Not being a believer in happy endings – we all die – and all lives possess an urn full of fear, sorrow, pain, and discomfort – I feared that some day, I would learn something that would ruin or tarnish the heroic image I had created of my dad.

Three

My Trades

Who was I to ask such questions? I had never experienced war other than on a movie or TV screen. I had never been jailed. I was never subjected to beatings, torture, threats and starvation. Well that last statement is only partially true. I have never been tortured or starved but in high school I took two minor beatings – bloody noses, punches in the stomach and busted lips. I once even had a knife held against my throat.

I speculated that some of those punches were thrown by an anti-Semite. My aching gut said this "scooper" – a local term for a person who shovels horse shit – hated Jews but I lacked proof to back it up. I heard no anti-Semitic taunts or slurs as the punches fell. As for threats, they were not uncommon but hardly ever fulfilled. Most of the time in the village where I grew up, tranquility ruled.

However, on and before my thirteenth birthday, fear ruled my life. As I studied, learned and memorized my *haftorah,* a

Hebrew reading and cantillation from the Book of Prophets, I dreaded my *haftorah* and the blessings before and after it. I feared reading it out loud, not only reading it out loud, but singing it in a chant. As the *maftir,* the last person called up to the Torah scroll, I would be standing in front of my family, all of my friends and the whole congregation on the hardest day of my life.

G-d cursed me with a reading-aloud disability. I did not hold my problem against him, figuring all humans were given obstacles to overcome – crosses to bear.

Streams of words babbled out of my mouth. My hands trembled as if I faced a Nazi firing squad. I choked on words as if my father had stuck a tongue-depressor deep down my throat. Moving my index finger over every syllable of every written word gave no relief to my anxiety-ridden brain.

I tried to hold back my tears, while stutters and stammers flew out of my mouth. All the while my classmates laughed their heads off at my weakness, causing me to choke back my tears. Continually I fought and failed to enunciate even one lousy sentence until my exasperated teacher moved on to the next student.

My problem was never properly addressed by my parents or my teachers. I continued to suffer humiliation and ridicule every time I was called upon to read aloud. Therefore, I sought the assistance of a higher power. *G-d please remove this cursed reading aloud disability from my shoulders.*

As my Bar Mitzvah approached, my prayers became more urgent. I knew with G-d's help I would survive. I felt like Tevya in *Fiddler on the Roof,* with my nightly prayers consisting of begging and bargaining with the Almighty. *Please G-d, if you allow me to survive this ordeal, this rite of passage into manhood, and not be publicly humiliated in the eyes of my parents, friends and neighbors, I promise to believe in you forever.*

I thought G-d got a good deal, allowing me to read one page of Hebrew and one page of English aloud in exchange for a lifetime of belief.

He accepted my offer. I knew my prayers were answered, when I heard the sounds of bags of candy hitting the floor, the yelps of joy bellowing from the mouths of women tossing the bags from the second floor and the footsteps of children scampering to find the bags. The reason women were seated on the second floor was to prevent the male congregants from becoming sexually aroused during the act of prayer. I understood this traditional concern having attended services in temples where the men and women sat together.

My ordeal was over. I survived. I could walk down Broadway with my head held high. I was a Jewish man in the eyes of the Lord and my community.

As proof of my commitment to the Lord, almost every morning, I put on tefillin.

Tefillin or phylacteries are two, one inch by one inch, black leather boxes holding scrolls of parchment inscribed with Torah verses. Religious Jewish men wear them during morning prayers.

I placed the hand-tefillin on my upper arm, wrapping the strap around the arm, hand and fingers. I secured the head-tefillin on my forehead. During my Bar Mitzvah lessons, I learned that the Torah commands Jews to wear Tefillin to serve as a "sign" and "remembrance" that G-d brought his children out of Egypt. I pictured my bearded forefathers following this ritual for hundreds of years.

I wondered until what age my Father participated in this obligation. I never saw him lay on tefillin. I do not think he owned them. I did not ask him and he never told me. He knew that I did – but I do not recall him ever praising my efforts.

At my Bar Mitzvah party, I relaxed sipping glasses of sweet Manischewitz wine. I got high enough to the point where I heard a voice say, "Son, the deal is sealed."

Starting in ninth grade, I also feared the end of semester tests known as the New York State Regents Examinations. As I lay teffillin in the morning, I prayed to the Almighty. I offered him no grand bargain. I only beseeched him, "Please let me pass the chemistry regents so I can go to a good college and make my parents proud."

Again my multiple regents' prayers were answered in the affirmative. I implored and he granted my requests. We were on the same page.

Four

My Dad

Wolf Laitner loved to: spoil his wife and children, garden, dress in tailored suits, appear well groomed, take care of his patients, eat Italian food, drive fast, own expensive cars, wear Omega watches, make money, feed winter birds and tend to his pigeons and tropical fish.

Wolf Laitner stood five feet, ten inches. I matched him in height but little else. In my eyes he was larger than life. He was the type of man that women craved with eyes dark and piercing, thick black eyebrows and Hollywood looks. Women gave him much more than that casual glance, they turned their heads in the same manner men do when they spot a women with a gorgeous backside.

G-d marked him with one imperfection, a large raised, hairless, brown mole. This misplaced beauty mark grew on his left shoulder blade. It stood out and I always had an urge to touch it. I didn't have to touch it because I had one of my own. As I matured an identical mole appeared in the middle of my chest. This genetic sign proved to me that I was my father's son. After my father's death I had it surgically removed.

G-d had blessed him with a personality that equaled his looks and intelligence. He showed no evidence of a protruding gut until late middle-age when G-d, pizza and pasta gave him the gift of a "spare tire."

Wolf Laitner believed in G-d in as much as any survivor can believe in the existence of the deity. He prayed hard on the High Holidays. I witnessed it. I stood next to him watching his lips reading the Hebrew texts. His eyes, voice, and facial muscles confirmed he was a believer. I doubted that he was acting for the sake of his patient community or for the sake of his children. He did not need the prayer books for he had all the prayers memorized. He prayed at all three of my sons' circumcisions. He chanted *Kaddish* at funerals and when he sat Shiva. He lit and said the prayers over the Hanukkah candles. He said "Amen" at my wedding, in thanks to G-d that his nerdy son was able to catch a woman.

In our home we always had a Passover Seder where in Hebrew he blessed the wine, the matzo and the family. He did not wear his religion on his sleeve or on his head but his tattoo was there for all to see. If he questioned G-d he did so privately. He stood in Temple as a modest man, looking like any of the other congregants. He did not outwardly show his feelings toward the Lord. I questioned if the Lord ever asked him about his Holocaust experiences. I doubted he ever opened those discussions.

He was a modest man with all the reasons to be immodest. He possessed that rare combination of brains, looks and a good sense of humor. His demeanor gave him a presence in any crowd. He was a quiet man who did not take himself too seriously. But he still possessed an ego which he fed with better things in life: Hart, Schaffner and Marx and Hickey-Freeman suits, Countess Mara ties and an assortment of Arrow shirts. He wore no jewelry, not even a gold wedding band.

Every morning in our bathroom he had a three-exercise ritual. Toilet-bowl coughing ,vigorous teeth brushing – in an attempt to remove tobacco stains – and the combing and slicking back of his thick black hair. He never let a hair fall out of place.

Cupping a hand, he shook and dispensed perfume into it. Then he doused his body with a liberal dose of 4711 Eau de Cologne; Dad always smelled good.

As a ten-year old, holding the 4711 glass bottle, I admired its shape, its blue and gold label, its gold metal top, its 1.7 fluid ounces, its assertion of high-quality ingredients and essential oils and how it professed to having a "secret formula."

Twisting the stopper off of the top of the bottle, I inhaled and found the fragrance a little too sweet for my taste. On that label, I read: *ECHT KOLNISCH WASSER ORIGINAL EAU DE COLOGNE.* With my limited Yiddish I knew that *"wasser"* meant water. I wondered how many Nazis it took to produce this *wasser.*

In 1792, a monk created this "miracle water" as a wedding gift for a merchant. The merchant not only obtained a sample of the perfume but its secret formula. With that formula he built a perfume factory in Cologne, thereby establishing the world's first *Eau de Cologne.* The monk's "miracle water" was sold for internal and external use. I could not image anyone taking a swig of this stuff. But miracles must be partnered with sacrifices.

Years later, I wondered why my dad bought and used the same cologne issued to submariners in the German U-Boat fleet. Why a German perfume, when there were so many great American colognes, like Old Spice? I rationalized his usage, thinking he used the 4711 cologne before the war. Old perfume habits die hard. I still use English Leather as I did when I started college.

I figured out that 4711 did add up to that magical number 13. Dad said he had a thing for the interpretation of numbers. I doubted that his belief extended to the claim that the perfume had miraculous powers. Maybe the cologne brought back memories of the days when he was lucky with Italian or German ladies. But I never bothered to ask him any of these questions.

Wearing his faded-out, bell-bottomed blue jeans, a plaid pearl-buttoned cowboy shirt and the fragrance of 4711, Dad thrived in his Woodridge garden. Whenever he had free time from the early spring, when the tulips broke through small patches of snow-covered ground, until the late fall, when he drove his riding lawnmower over the now brown-grass. He loved every minute he spent in his garden. He loved getting his hands dirty. He religiously fertilized, mulched, and watered his plants and shrubbery. He hired a gardener to assist in his obsession. Unlike the perfectionist gardeners of Woodridge, he did not mind seeing his lawn peppered with dandelions. He understood his labors would pay off with patches of flowers: irises, geraniums, daisies, butter cups, Queen Ann's lace, mad-dog skull caps, white baneberry or doll's eyes.

He loved pruning his roses as they climbed up freshly-painted white trellises. When the rose buds fully blossomed he'd watch me pull the flower to my nose and deeply inhale its fragrance.

"This year's roses smell better than last year's," I told him. He'd smile, nod his head and keep clipping the vines, knowing I was just trying to make conversation – like I really cared about gardening.

Unlike my dad, my thumbs were not green. They were black, the color of the moist soil mixed with rotting vegetation, my digits ran through in search of night crawlers. These earthworms were used as fishing bait. These tube-shaped, segmented hermaphrodites which I lanced on to my fishing hooks were still able to wiggle their bodies in their vain attempts to escape the hook.

My love for plants extended mainly to the greens I ate, and to marijuana. I thought about growing the illegal plant, wanting to save the cost of purchasing it. But my risk-taking skills had not fully developed. I could see the police pulling my plants out of the ground. It would have been my time to plant and the cops' time to uproot what was planted. Then they'd carry these five-foot giants to my parents' house. "Dr. Laitner we are sorry to inform you that we are here to arrest Mort. He's a marijuana grower and distributor."

My father would ask, "Do you have any proof?"

The cops would hand my parents photographs of me tending the crop, "Look at these photos. They tell the whole story."

As they would handcuff me, lower my head into the squad car, and begin to drive away. I'd yell out the window, "Mom, Dad I'm sorry! Please hire me a lawyer!"

When it came to large-scale crime operations, I was as yellow as a sunflower.

But I appreciated the beauty of flowers: the tulip's vibrant reds, pinks, and yellows, the rose's perfumed blossoms and silk pedals. However, I found limited enjoyment in the labor required to harvest the crop.

This emotion briefly changed in the spring of my twelfth year. I formulated a plan to get closer to my dad I wanted to spend more quality time with him. At breakfast, I asked, "Dad, how about you allocating a portion of your garden to me? I'm ready to learn the art and science of farming."

"Sure, son. After you finish your milk, we'll tour the garden for a place to start your new profession. Have you decided what you are going to plant?"

"Not yet, Dad. I'm going to the hardware store to study the seed catalogue. Do you have any recommendations?"

"I'd try peas and string beans. They grow pretty well in our soil and once they sprout they don't require much work."

Side by side we walked to the northeast corner of his garden as if we were farmers heading to the back forty. He pointed to a small corner plot and said, "This spot gets plenty of sunshine and I fertilized it about week ago, so the soil is ready for planting."

"Thanks for the land and the recommendations," I replied.

"Let's go to the shed, I'll teach you what gardening tools to use."

We strolled to his metal barn-shaped shed. He proudly pulled open the shed's doors. He handed me a trowel with its stainless steel blade, ash wood handle and leather-hanging strap as if he was holding a newborn infant.

"This is a great tool for breaking up the soil. So is that spade sitting in the corner, and that planter's shovel. Here are my weeding gloves. Use them and they will protect your hands. If you need more fertilizer, there's a bag in the corner. Take good care of these tools. Clean them and put them back in the shed when you're done with them. I have had them for years."

"Thanks again, Dad. I'll use all of this stuff and I promise to keep your farm implements clean before I stick them back in the shed. By the way, can I get an advance on my allowance to buy the seeds?"

He smiled, pulled his wallet out of his pants pocket and handed me a crisp new dollar bill.

That afternoon, I ran up the Main Street hill to Hechtman's Hardware Store. For years I had studied the Burpee's seed packages but today with my allowance in hand I'd make a purchase.

A small plaque on the display rack read: "Burpee Seed Company founded in Philadelphia in 1876 by 18-year-old Washington Atlee Burpee." Washington had a passion for seeds and a mother willing to lend him a lot of "seed money," By 1915, Burpee Seeds mailed out one million catalogues to North American gardeners.

The seed-display rack pulled me in like a horse-shoe magnet attracts safety pins. The display lit up the hardware store. The plant photos showed the greenest peas, the yellowest corn cobs, and the reddest radishes. Like a fly stuck to flypaper, I stood paralyzed next to riveting vegetable and flower photographs.

Now faced with one of a farmers hardest tasks, I'd have to decide which seeds to plant. On the back of each package, in small print, were the all important growing instructions: days to germination, seed germination temperatures, days to harvest, harvesting instructions, the average number of seeds per packet, the direct seeding rate, and sowing depth. My respect for farmers and my father grew as I realized there was a lot more science in gardening than art.

On that unfenced, 15 x 15 foot lot, I planted and grew my home garden. In a few months I tasted the fruits of my labor. The pulled-from-the-plant-and-placed- right-into-your-mouth peas and beans tasted as if they were cultivated by G-d. They were the best vegetables I had ever eaten.

I had read Job1:21 in Hebrew school, so I knew the Lord giveth and the Lord taketh away. Most August nights the Almighty's rabbits devoured most of my crop.

As my garden was consumed, Dad worked on making his garden look like a European park. A park filled with: Canadian-flag sugar maples with their helicopter seeds, balsam firs, weeping willows, dogwoods, white walnuts, native birch, and apple trees. A park littered with sheets of slate – to walk on so as not to crush the blades of grass; a park where moss grew on flat slate plates, surrounded by mistletoe and northern maidenhair ferns.

I wondered if my grandfather created such a park in Poland. But I did not ask.

To accomplish the creation of a park, my dad purchased – or we stole – stone masonry: statues, bird baths, fountains and cement urns. My favorite two statues were the ones we found abandoned on our car rides through the mountains. A statue of a chubby five-year-old naked boy gripping his penis. In Belgium, this statue is called *Manneken Pis* which is translated into "The Peeing Little Man of Brussels." To the joy of tourists and locals, he has appeared in Brussels since 1619. He is often dressed in costumes of the world. The boy's left hand holds his manhood while his right rests on his hip. His head is covered in tight curls, the type of curls my son, Blake, possessed as a five-year-old. This boy of Brussels partially shuts his eyes as if he is enjoying the act of urinating as a steady stream of water falls into a scalloped basin. I contemplated, "Why do I love this statue?" Was it the memory of holding and controlling my stream of pee as a five-year-old, or years later writing my name in yellow in the pristine white snows of Woodridge?

The other naked-boy statue was of Hellenistic origin. Here the boy clasped two hands around the neck of a goose. He tightly held the bird against his body. The goose and the boy were almost eye-to-eye – the boy being a few inches taller than the goose. The goose's eyes bulged out of his head as its open beak screamed for help. The boy displays a sadistic smile as his penis and testicles dangle toward the ground. As a teenager I asked, "Is this curly-haired boy struggling to control or strangle the goose? Did he have the strength or the desire to kill the goose? In my mind he wanted to strangle and kill for the boy was a sadist and the goose represented the weak.

At the age of 15, I felt like that goose, for the fear of failing my driver's license test constricted my airways and the blood vessels flowing to my testicles. I had easily passed the written portion of the examination. My wallet proudly held my driver's learning permit. Dad spent hours teaching me to drive his Cadillac. While I nervously sat behind the wheel, trying to avoid running off the road, he'd smoked his Marlboros and acted as if my driving met with his approval. As I kept my eyes fixed on the road, he scoured the scenery for cement relics. When we passed an abandoned hotel, he'd crush out his cigarette and calmly state, "Son, slow down and pull into the driveway on the left. Do you see that white statue of the naked boy peeing. Pull up next to it, so we can lift it and lower it into the Caddie's trunk."

"Sure, Dad," I replied, contemplating whether this 50 pound cement artifact was worth going to jail for. I rationalized it was abandoned property but feared our antics would besmirch the Laitner name. In silence we lifted, lowered, and rolled this pisser into our backyard.

In the Laitner backyard park, near the naked boy fountains and next to the tool shed, my dad built a pigeon coop. The coop housed around 25 homing pigeons. Twenty-five pigeons with short necks and stout bodies. They bobbed their heads as if *davening* in *shul.* These were not pretty birds due to their dull plumage, but both of us enjoyed watching them fly. They flew in quilt-like patterns over our house as if they were a squadron of RAF Hawker Hurricanes bombarding a German military base. Dad said, "Mort, when I was a kid in Poland we raised pigeons." I wondered if he knew that the Nazis forbade German Jews from owning pigeons, but I didn't ask him.

In the summer, these pigeons feasted on the ivy berries that grew on the side of our house. During the winter, when I purchased coins and stamps in Middletown, Dad drove to Lloyd's to buy 50-pound bags of birdseed. A Lloyd's employee lifted the sack and dumped it in the back of the Caddy. These 50-pound sacks lasted a week or two, feeding the pigeons, the non-migratory wild birds – those who somehow survived the bitter New York winters – and a scurry of bushy-tailed squirrels. Through our glass kitchen door we were entertained watching the squirrels and the birds fight over the seeds.

My father never competitively raced pigeons as most of the other Woodridge pigeon enthusiasts did. He let them fly over the town and loved when they returned to the coop. This affection for birds surprised me because he showed no interest in my parakeets. One cold winter morning, he walked into the kitchen to feed his birds. I was eating Aunt Jemima pancakes as he returned wearing the most somber face I had ever seen.

"Dad, What's the matter?" I asked.

"A fox or a raccoon got into my pigeon coup. It's a bloody massacre. They are all dead. I failed to protect them."

I looked for a tear in his eyes and found none. I did not know what to say to console him. So I blurted out, "Dad you can buy another flock."

He did not reply. I wondered if he had not heard me or was he just ignoring my insensitive comment. He staggered out of the house to take a long walk. As he left, I thought I hear him say, "Why me? Why always me?"

Dad never bought another pigeon. The pigeon loft stood empty for years as if a memorial.

My Father loved practicing medicine. He loved taking care of his patients. He loved his medical office and when he was not using it, I pretended it was mine. I sat in his large brown leather chair and admired his collection of paraphernalia housed on the shelves opposite his dark hardwood desk.

On an upper shelf, I studied his 18 inch high, white glass Leaning Tower of Pisa. He bought it on a return trip to Italy in the sixties. I wondered what thoughts ran through his head on his return to the school he attended before the outbreak of the war.

On the walls hung his medical degree from the University of Genoa, his licenses to practice medicine from the states of New York and Rhode Island and an Albrecht Dürer print. Dürer, a German artist from the town of Nuremberg, engraved the print entitled *Knight, Death and the Devil* in 1513. Nuremberg is the city which held the massive Nazi rally of 1934. Director Leni Riefenstahl made the infamous film *Triumph of the Will* at that rally. This film that enthralled the German people made Hitler look like a knight in shining armor.

As a ten year old, this Dürer masterpiece mesmerized me. I studied each character for hours. I wanted to be the bearded knight riding his magnificent steed through a heavily forested valley. He wore a helmet with a visor and armor across his body. This knight in shiny armor was the picture of courage and bravery. He rested a ten-foot long spear across his shoulder with the tip of the his spear covered with a fox's tail. A sword rested on his waist. His eyes stared straight ahead as he ignored his adversaries. A white-bearded Death, with snakes growing out of his head, sat atop his horse holding an hourglass. A swine-snouted devil stood at attention with a spear resting on his shoulder.

A road leading to the castle appeared to give the devil a large curved horn. The knight's hound dog scampered between the legs of his horse. At the top of the engraving I saw a castle which I assumed was the final destination of the knight. A skull rested on the ground near Dürer's initialed monogram, which took on the appearance of a gravestone.

As a ten year old, I wondered if the Satan and Death really looked so scary. Why had my father selected this German print to hang on his office wall? Was it his reminder that he faced death and the devil and had survived? In my eyes, he was the knight. For four years in the camps, he had walked through the valley of the shadow of death and feared no evil.

As a sixty year old, while reading Erik Larson's *In The Garden of the Beasts,* I learned the mayor of Nuremberg, at one of the town's choreographed Nazi Party rallies, had presented Hitler with a print of *Knight, Death and the Devil.* I pictured Hitler standing on the platform, studying the print and picturing himself as the knight, in an alliance with Death to rid the world of the devilish Jews. I doubted that he realized or cared that to the Jewish world, he was the offspring of that Satan and Death.

Dürer became one of my favorite artists because of his attention to detail.

I studied the knick-knacks the pharmaceutical companies plied him with so he would prescribe their medications. They ranged from Japanese-silk Geisha dolls sewn on white cardboard to plastic block calendars adorned with the name of a drug to small marble cubes covered with bronze plaques with his name and a caduceus imprinted on them, (the concept that two snakes wrapped around a staff represented of the field of medicine always seemed odd to me) to a heavy pewter statuette of an elderly doctor standing and wearing eye glasses, a headlamp and lab coat. He holds a stethoscope in his right hand aimed at his invisible patient while his left rests in his pocket. The hand in the statuette's pocket and its lab coat reminds me of my father's slave labor photograph, the one where he holds the plastic baby doll.

One whole shelf was dedicated to old medical books. They were written in many languages. I searched for copyright years in his collection of medical books. A German text dated back to 1513. I studied its anatomical charts picturing a German physician practicing primitive medicine learned in this book.

On the top shelf, a large white-marble owl perched. The owl represented my father's quest for knowledge. The owl's white eyes glared at me. I heard him speak, "You'd better study hard or you'll disappoint your parents, and I'll fly off the shelf and bury talons deep into your neck."

On the lower shelf sat the three monkeys. I had seen these monkeys before in the auction houses on Lincoln Road. My dad said they were wise monkeys and as a ten year old I asked, "Why?"

Each brass monkey was two inches wide and three inches high. They had a motto: "See No Evil, Hear No Evil and Speak No Evil." Each monkey's hands were placed on their ears or mouth or eyes. Trying to rub the tarnish off of their bodies, I knew they represented a life lesson cast in brass. I loved monkeys. On TV, chimps made ideal pets. These so-called "wise monkeys" made me laugh, to the joy of my family, I mimicked their behavior at the dinner table. As I matured, they taught me how to avoid punishment and stay out of nasty entanglements. They became my risk-avoidance idols.

What possessed my father to purchase and display these three brass monkeys? Was it his sense of humor? Was he trying to tell me something? Did this statue represent his concentration camp survival kit? Didn't this threesome formulate the survival motto of all prisoners and the politically oppressed?

Dad said on the tapes that he knew when to talk and when to act invisible. As a teenager, I learned that in some cultures the trio symbolized the Golden Rule, while in others they stood for the lack of moral responsibility by people who refused to acknowledge wrongdoing. By covering their eyes, they looked away from danger and sorrow, by covering their mouths they said nothing about injustice, by covering their ears they heard no screams of pain. They deprived all of their senses and obtained the ability to feign ignorance. These "see no evil" monkeys epitomized the Germans after the Second World War. They saw nothing, heard nothing, said nothing, and most of all, they *did* nothing to prevent the Nazis from committing their crimes against the Jews, the Gypsies, the homosexuals and the Jehovah's Witnesses. I pictured the three monkeys perched on top of the Brandenburg Gate as a reminder to the German people of their complicity. I never bothered to ask my dad why he bought the monkey statue or what it meant to him. I was the wise monkey with my hands covering my mouth.

As a ten year old, on cold winter nights, I snuck into my father's medical office to monkey around. I secretly spent hours scrutinizing the contents of his desk. Pulling some items out of it for closer examination, I searched for answers to what made my dad tick. One item that intrigued me the most was a six-inch bullet. I clutched the shell in my decade-old hands warming it to the touch, while fanaticizing about its use on the battlefields of Europe. This projectile I imagined belonged in a American-made machine gun. Since Dad never owned a rifle, I wondered why he possessed this deadly cartridge with its copper jacket and pointy lead nose.

How did he get this Freudian symbol of manhood?

Who gave it to him? Or did he buy it?

Why was it housed in his middle desk drawer? The drawer he'd pull out many times a day looking for his pen and prescription pad.

I never asked him these questions. Was it any of my business?

After my Father sold his medical practice, I never again saw the bullet nor his desk. I wondered what happened to this live-piece of ammunition, knowing that I would have cherished it as a memory.

My father and mother wanted me to go into that medical practice, to study medicine, to pass the New York State Medical Boards and to take over his lucrative practice. Being the obedient son that I was, I started the process by declaring my intent to be a pre-med student at the University of Miami. I only lacked one thing: the ability to pass a chemistry course.

As I prepared to go home for Spring Break. I knew I would be breaking my parents' hearts with the announcement that I was giving up my pre-med studies. To prepare for this endeavor I sought the assistance of a Gestalt therapist. In a group session with about 20 students in attendance, many of them voiced the same concerns of having to tell their parents news they did not want to hear. The therapist, a man in his mid-thirties with a thick black beard and shoulder length hair advised us, "When you go home, tell your parents the news they do not want to hear. They will curse you and your decision. They may do this directly into your face. They will yell and cry for hours as if they were spoiled children. They will do all of this in hope of you changing your mind. But you have stuck to your guns. When you wake up the next morning, they will greet you with love."

I knew if I followed this therapist's advice, I'd be taking a big risk, a risk that could affect my relationship with my parents for years. However I saw no other options; I was a risk-taker.

On the first night of my return home at around 9:30, I met my parents at the kitchen table. I thought to myself, "Get rid of this anxiety, the sooner the better."

"Dad… Mom… please sit down." As they sat I continued, "I have some news about my career. I have decided to give up on my pre-med studies and go into a pre-law program."

They both looked at each other as if I had stabbed them in the heart with a Bowie knife. My Dad asked, "What's happened to you becoming a doctor and taking over my practice?"

"Dad I'm not suited to be a doctor. My grades in chemistry prove that."

"Is this your final decision?"

I nodded affirmatively and mumbled, "Yes."

"As a favor to us, can you think about it during you break and go back to school and try again?"

"Sorry, Dad; my mind is made up." I paused to look at the tears in my mother's eyes.

"Dad … Mom … I'm so very sorry. I know I'm destroying one of your dreams. I know how much this decision is hurting both of you. But, I have no choice. With my chemistry grades I won't get accepted into any American medical school. With tears flowing down my cheeks I continued, "I'm sorry. I'm not cut out to become a doctor. I'm going to do my best to become a lawyer."

Before I left the kitchen, I saw my mother wiping away her tears. My father's hand's trembled and his eyes glazed over. This was as close as I ever saw him come to shedding a tear.

I left the room and headed upstairs. As I walked toward my bedroom, wondering if the therapist's advice would be right, in a low tone I repeated, "I'm sorry, I'm sorry, I'm sorry."

I lay in my bed for the next three hours unable to fall asleep. My parents' weeps and screams made sleep impossible. Their bedroom was one door away from mine. I heard every word they said. Insults were hurled in my direction in Polish, Yiddish and English. My room echoed with their voices. This was drama for the Broadway stage and I had a front row seat.

I prayed, "G-d please make that psychologist's predictions come true. Please give my parents the wisdom to accept my decision. Please let them understand that my umbilical cord has been severed. Lord give me the strength not to curse them – *and tell them to shut the fuck up and go to sleep."*

That night I became a man. My parents had not yet realized that their Buber I-IT relationship with me had died."

I silently prayed in rhythm to the hum of the room's fan. My parents' voices bombarded my ears. Their words cut to pieces by blades of the window fan, still managed to sting as if a wasp had found its way into my ear. I asked, "Were these the two people who in an act of love created me?"

My mother: "We should have never sent him to that damn southern school! We should have sent him to school in New York State. We would have had more control over him."

My Father: "He must be smoking a lot of dope in that college. It screwed up his sense of ambition. It killed his drive. Who knows how many brain cells he has murdered smoking that weed."

My mother: "I didn't think he was that stupid or lazy!"

My father: "He'll come to his senses and change his mind in the morning."

My mother: "Where did we go wrong in raising him? We should have sent him to a private high school or to a military school. They would have toughened him up."

They repeated these statements using many different variations, but always in an angry tone loud enough to split my eardrums. They knew I was in earshot and they didn't care. Their tone, their words and their anger tightened like a coarse noose around my neck.

I had never, in my whole life, heard them so loud, so mean or so crazy. G-d, there was a wealth of energy hidden deep inside their bodies. My father who hardly ever cursed did so in three languages. My father who hardly ever raised his voice now gave me a headache. I touched a nerve and his brain exploded.

He had control over his medical practice, his garden, his pigeons, his tropical fish, but he had lost control over his son. He had planted a seed within my mother and now I was uprooting what he had planted.

I knew with G-d's help I possessed one powerful edge over my parents. While I prayed the *Shema,* my declaration of faith in the unity of G-d. "Hear O Israel, the Lord our G-d, the Lord is one."

They cursed me. They never intoned the name of the Lord in their tirade. They failed to ask G-d to get me to change my mind. While my prayers were filled with the Lord's name. They only spoke the language of hate. It was their time to throw stones.

I listened carefully to my parents' words and began questioning their unconditional love toward me. I had had my time to speak and now it was my time to keep silent. I realized that at this early juncture, the Gestalt therapist's predictions were 100% accurate. I hoped he would keep up his average.

By 12:30 A.M., they lost their voices. Silence reigned. I fell asleep.

I don't remember if I dreamt that night but I woke up feeling refreshed like a burden had been lifted from my neck, back and shoulders. I heard the sounds of chirping robins. Powerful rays of sunlight streamed through my oscillating window fan. I thought, "These are positive signs." I quickly dressed and joined my parents for breakfast. We hugged. We smiled. We kissed. It was as if the night before had never happened. The therapist was right. All was forgiven. All their poisonous words were quickly forgotten.

I have never forgotten the day my father said, "Son, I'm proud of you." I'm pretty sure he only said it once in his life but I could be mistaken. I said it to him on a few occasions but he never understood the concept of reciprocity. I wondered if he thought, "Who is this little squirt to say to me that he is proud of me?" Dad was quick with a pat on the head or a touch on the shoulder. He praised me for making the Dean's list and passing a Bar examination. My reward was a manly handshake and a "Good job! Congratulations!"

However it was not until my 40th year that he bestowed the "P" word on me. I had gotten a call from CBS News that a segment they taped on me discussing illegal adoptions in America was going to air that night. This was going to be my 15 seconds of fame so I advised friend and family. I called Dad from Miami. "Dad, be sure you and Mom watch Dan Rather on the CBS News tonight; I should be on the air."

"Sure, son; we wouldn't miss it."

After the show aired, I called to see if they had seen me on the show.

"Son that was great. Your mom and I were just going to call you to congratulate you. You did a fine job."

Thanks, Dad. Just called to see if you saw the piece. Love you. Good bye. About one week later, after my father had received calls from friends, family and patients from around the country congratulating him on his son's appearance did he give me a call. "Son, you won't believe it. I'm getting calls from across the nation concerning your appearance on that CBS program from people I have not spoken to in years. I just called to say how proud of you I am."

Those words sounded like a Beethoven symphony to my ears.

"Thanks Dad," I replied,

My Father loved the smell and sound of expensive new cars. I speculated that he developed this habit from his father. When his medical practice began to thrive, he purchased his first Cadillac. Every two years after that first purchase he bought a new one. They were always painted black and had long sleek rocketship fins. The Cadillac was the car of choice of all of the physicians in the Catskills. It was his sign that he had reached the level of success associated with the medical community.

In his Caddy, he sped around the mountains, from our home to the Monticello and Hamilton Avenue Hospitals, to his patients' homes, and back to his office. These were the days when doctors made home visits and charged the outlandish fee of five dollars for their services. Every two years, like Swiss clockwork, a new Caddy found its way into my dad's garage. From 1959 to 1973 my dad never changed his preference. However when I returned home from law school in 1973, the car sitting in the garage was a spanking brand new Mercedes Benz.

On my trips through Europe, I had boycotted Germany. On my way to Scandinavia as the train stopped in German cities, I bought no snacks or souvenirs. I did not even get off the train, and now my Concentration Camp-surviving father had spent thousands of dollars purchasing a German-manufactured car.

My friends asked, "How could your Dad, a survivor of Auschwitz, buy a car made by former Nazis?"

With a puzzled look on my face, I replied, "I don't have a clue. I have never asked him. Maybe it was his way of ridding himself of hatred, in an attempt to find happiness."

This ended their questioning as they thought about what I had said. But for at least a year, whenever I rode in the Mercedes,my stomach turned with the thought that I was betraying my dead Laitner relatives and the rest of the six million.

Growing up I observed that the Laitner name was spelled differently in books and papers: Lajtner in Poland, Leitner in Germany, and Laitner in the United States. My father said he wanted the pronunciation to remained the same as it was in Poland so when he came to the States he spelled it Laitner hoping it would be pronounced like "light- ner." For most people, his idea did not work. The letter "a" would not remain silent. They pronounced the name "Layt-ner."

Wolf Laitner was born on March 23, 1914 in Niemce, Poland. In the tradition of his faith, my Father acquired his first name from a deceased relative. His great, great, great grandfather was named Wolf.

Niemce is and was a small town in western Poland, located near the city of Krakow and the Czech border. Thirty-to-forty Jews resided in Niemce when my Father lived there. Jews lived in the area since the late 13th Century. Many Jews were represented in the town's developing industries in the 19th and 20th Centuries.

My grandfather, Mordechai Hirsch Lajtner, was born in Dabrowa Gornicza, Poland in 1872 and was murdered in Faulbrueck Concentration Camp in 1944. My grandmother Bacia, born in 1886, was also murdered in 1944. My sister Barbara was named after Bacia and I after Mordechai. Bacia was murdered in Auschwitz in 1943 when she was 56 years old.

At the tender age of five, my dad was sent to live with friends of his parents in a nearby town because it had a *chedar,* an elementary school where students studied Hebrew and the Bible.

Dad, Wolf (Bobik) had three brothers, Abraham (Adek), Jacob (Januk) and Lazar (Lolek), and two sisters, Renia and Lola. Lola died before the war. The Nazis murdered Jacob and Lazar in the death camps. After the war, Abraham lived in Poland and Renia (Rivka) lived in the States and in Israel.

After graduating from the *chedar,* my dad attended high school in Krakow. Upon graduation, he aspired to become a doctor. He first applied to attend the medical school in Warsaw. He was rejected because Polish medical schools had strict quotas on the number of Jewish students allowed to attend. He was later accepted into medical school in Italy. My dad said, "There was no way I was getting accepted into the Polish medical school even with the connections my father had." In a way he was lucky. The Jews who were accepted were required to stand on the left side of the classroom while the Polish students sat. After class, Polish students would attack the standing Jewish students with razors inserted in their shoes.

Dad personally observed that anti-Semitism was growing stronger in Poland to the point that when Hitler came to power in 1933 many Poles were happy. They wanted to emulate the conditions the Germans imposed on German Jews in Poland. They commenced boycotts of Jewish-owned stores, built and operated concentration camps (not death camps), filling them with Jews. My dad heard Poles chanting and yelling, "The houses are yours but the streets are ours."

My father knew that life in Poland had become too dangerous. Jews had limited rights. To my father, Poland had become country without a future. Once on a trip with a friend to visit a Polish coal mine, a Polish policeman, waving a billy club, chased my father down the streets of the town screaming, "Dirty Jew! Hitler will get you! Go back to Palestine!" I wondered if my father had told this event to my grandfather.

I had only known my grandfather from a single photograph. I remembered holding that photo and realizing that here was a man who I would never get to kiss, touch, see, or love. I shivered as I studied his middle-aged facial features and his moustache on this two-inch-by-one-inch passport-type photo.

He owned a foundry in the town of Neimce. He was one of the richest men in the town, if not the wealthiest. His family was one of the few Jewish families that lived in the town, and that led to problems.

When my dad and I drove by the Woodridge Laundry, he'd point to its fifty-foot high chimney that cut into the sky. "my Father owned a number of buildings with chimneys attached to them that were just as tall as that one."

I'd then ask, "Was my grandfather a millionaire?"

"Yes he was. He owned a fancy car, lots of acreage, and factories. Many men worked for him."

"Dad, whatever happened to your grandfather?"

"His name was Jeduda Leib Laijtner and he was born around 1830. I forgot the year of his death." He grew silent and I stopped asking questions.

I knew little more about my paternal grandfather other than that he conceived five children and that he was wealthy.

One of my cousins traced the family roots to France in the 1750's, Germany in the 1800's, and then into Poland. I wondered if they were forced out of France and Germany. My cousin speculated that our forebearers might possibly have come from the Alsace region of France. The French spelling of the name, "Laitneur" may have come from the French word for milkman.

My grandfather's foundry employed many Polish (Christian) workers. My dad appreciated how his father chose his employees. The story was, "My father invited the prospective employee's to join him for a meal. While they ate, he observed the prospective employee's eating habits. If the man ate in a leisurely fashion he was not hired. His thought process was: if they ate slowly, they would work at an even slower pace."

I have always gobbled up my food and I wondered if that story influenced my eating habits. My dad ate at a slower pace, savoring each morsel of food.

My father had many negative memories of these workers. They hated Jews. Even the life-long employees of the foundry had the nerve to voice their hatred. With a mixture of hate and joy resounding in their voices, they spoke right into my Father's face, "When Hitler comes to Poland, you Jews will be finished."

These foundry workers never bothered to read *Mein Kampf*, the book Hitler penned while he was in prison in 1924 and 1925. If they had, they would have learned their status under the Nazis was only one step above that of the Jews. The Jews would be exterminated. But as Slavs, they would be slaves of the Germans. Upon the Nazi arrival, they too would be finished.

My father predicted peace, not war, between Poland and Germany. He said war would be too devastating to both countries. But these racist Poles knew and wanted it occur. As I listened to my father's words on tape, I recalled one of my favorite quotes, "Never underestimate the power of denial." Millions of Polish Jews lived and died in this state of denial.

Five years before the war, even with my grandfather's connections, my father never got accepted to a Polish medical school. So from 1934 to 1939 he studied medicine in the Italian cities of Pisa, Naples and Genoa.

These years were my father's "happy time." The Italians, unlike the Poles, treated him with respect. In Italy he did not fear beatings, threats, or imprisonment.

In July of 1939, after graduating from medical school, he returned home to visit with his family. After this family vacation he was to commence a medical residency in the Belgian Congo.

In my father's words, he was "not happy" in Poland. Even if he could get licensed as a Polish physician, he had no future there. He was right. On September 1, 1939. Hitler invaded Poland from the west and sixteen days later the Soviet Union invaded Poland from the east.

The Nazis overran the town of Bedzin.[1] In the town there is a cemetery where Laitners are buried. Bedzin is one of the oldest towns in the Upper Silesia coal-mining region. It developed as a center of mining and heavy industry. It is located 12 kilometers from Katowice and four kilometers from the center of Sosnowiec. Before the war, my maternal grandparents Toby and Rose, my mother and my aunt, Renia, lived in Sosnowiec.

1 Until World War II, Bedzin had a vibrant Jewish community. In 1897, of a total population of 21,200, Jews constituted 10,800. In 1921, the town had a Jewish community consisting of 17,298 people, or 62 percent of its total population. In September 1939, the German Army (Wehrmacht) overran this area, followed by the SS commando units (Einsatzgruppenn), who burned the Bedzin synagogue and murdered many of the Jewish inhabitants. These death squads were following the "Commissar Order" which instructed them to eliminate all "political commissars, guerrillas, partisans and Jews."

The Bedzin Ghetto was created in 1942. Eventually, in the summer of 1943, most of the Jews in Bedzin were deported to the nearby death camp at Auschwitz. Since Bedzin was one of the last Jewish communities to be liquidated, two thousand Jews managed to survive while twenty-eight thousand perished.

Five

Old Spice

Fifty years after the destruction of the Bedzin Ghetto, I stood in my bathroom lathering my face. I glanced in the mirror and observed my first grey eyebrow hair. It stood out like a seagull flying over a dark sea. I wondered if I should pluck it. Would two new grey hairs replace every one that tasted the metal of my tweezers?

This sign of aging made me reflect on the three items resting on the sink, the roll-on deodorant, cologne from Kenneth Cole's Black collection, and Old Spice shaving cream. All three products seemed to have lasted for well over two months. They showed no sign of graying. I wondered which would be the first to go.

I remembered smelling Old Spice for the first time in 1960 in Rashkin's Pharmacy. I bought a dollar bottle of Old Spice aftershave for my dad. I pulled the plastic grey stopper and inhaled the unmistakable sweet odor of Old Spice. It came in a buoy-shaped white glass bottle with a drawing of a clipper ship. On the bottle a strong wind filled the ship's large sails. I recalled the TV commercial where a handsome sailor wearing a blue jacket and a cap swaggers off the ship with a duffle bag flung over the shoulder. His destination is an attractive woman. As I picture the sailor meandering through the streets. I started whistling the catchy nautical Old Spice jingle and remembered the first birthday present I ever gave my dad.

For a month, I saved my meager twenty-five cent weekly allowance. My dad seemed pleased when I handed him the Old Spice. I said, "Happy Birthday Dad." He replied with a firm hug, a kiss on my cheek and a twinkle in his eye and said, "I love your gift." I nailed it.

That Old Spice year my dad decided to send me to Camp Alamac. I questioned his selection, but he knew the camp was within walking distance of our home and it served the campers the same hot lunch the Catskill hotel guests received. The summer was my father's work-like-a-madman season. Our community grew from a few thousand to over twenty thousand. As one of the town doctors, he rose at six, was in the hospital by eight, back in his medical office seeing patients by eleven and then he did intermittent house calls until it became dark at nine. Camp would keep me out of his hair except for a quick dinner.

So every morning at 7:30, I sucked in the crisp mountain air and walked ten city blocks to camp. I strolled across the railroad tracks whistling, *Someone's in the Kitchen with Dinah* while observing the beauty of small town America. My mind wandered as I daydreamed about fishing while listening to robins chirp and watched them wrestle worms from the ground.

Down Broadway toward the Glen Wild Road, I skipped with my only stops consisting of meeting and greeting fellow campers until I reached the camp.

Life was simple with no worries about satisfying the opposite sex. My goals were limited to pleasing my parents, friends and counselors. I never thought about school.

My daily camp activities were well organized: dodgeball, baseball, soccer, shuffleboard, football and punchball. There were color wars and arts and crafts. With pride I braided my own lanyard key chain. On rainy days, we played knock hockey or ping pong. Life was fun. Camp Alamac had nailed it.

The Alamac was a fancy Catskills hotel with a small day camp. From June first till the day after Labor Day the hotel and day camp were packed with New York City tourists and Woodridge campers. The hotel consisted of a large three-story guest house with an Olympic-sized pool. The grounds were landscaped with fifty-foot maples.

A smattering of white Adirondack chairs rested on the green manicured lawn. The smell of the freshly cut grass filled one's nostrils as quickly as an opened bottle of Old Spice. The property gave the appearance of wealth and class, a look desired by those tourists from New York City. They also loved the food. The three C's meant nothing to them. Cholesterol, carbohydrates and calories were "future speak" and their average life span was 65 .

A typical Alamac dinner menu read :

Hotel Alamac

— DINNER SELECTIONS —

Please make one choice from each course.

First Course

Chopped liver appetizer............ with a freshly baked challah or bialy

Gefilte fish.. with purple horse radish

Second Course

Chicken soup

Bowl of borsht..with sour cream

Third Course

Boiled chicken

Brisket

.... Both entrees served with carrot *tzimmes* cooked in honey

Fourth Course

Homemade Apple strudel

Homemade Babka

Homemade Rugelach

Beverages

Soda or Iced Tea

Orange, Prune, Cranberry, or Apple Juice

Loose Leaf Teas

House Blend Coffee or Decaf

No one ever left the table feeling hungry.

When it came to food the Alamac Hotel nailed it.

Forty years after I attended Camp Alamac, my dad passed away. Under his sink, I rummaged through and examined his toiletries. There stood his shaving cream, his deodorant, and to my surprise, my gift, the Old Spice aftershave. I gently picked it up as if it were a valuable antique. I pulled out the stopper and inhaled a whiff. Memories of my father danced in my head. Based on the weight of the bottle I realized it was full. My Dad had never used the first present I ever gave him. I remembered the twinkle in his eye as I gave him the gift, and smiled realizing that my dad had kept my gift for over forty years.

Six

The Westerns

With my father's love of cowboy movies, I should have bought him some Stetson cologne, with its pictures of cowboy's wearing John B. Stetson's hats. As the advertisements said, "a cologne for the man of the American West." He may have at least removed the stopper and given it a whiff.

As much as Dad loved watching westerns on TV, I can only remember going to a few movies with him. I think we saw some films in Radio City Music Hall, but I cannot recall a single title.

Neither can I recall him tossing me a baseball, a basketball or a football. He never attended my high school cross-country, track or wrestling matches. This hurt a little, since watching wrestling on TV was one of my father's greatest thrills. In fact, Dad died sitting on his favorite chair watching his favorite wrestling program.

We never attended a football game at West Point, or a basketball game in Madison Square Garden. My friends' fathers fulfilled that role. My dad was the town doctor. His business was saving lives. He was too busy practicing medicine and making a livelihood that put sirloin steak, fried potatoes and baked pork and beans on my plate. This Friday night family culinary ritual became my favorite cowboy meal. I devoured each morsel as if I were cowpoke returning to the chuck wagon after riding the range. I did not own a horse – I did get to ride on a rental once a week – but I had the Stetson cowboy hat, the cowboy boots and the cowboy meal. My dad did fork over the five dollars a week for my horseback-riding experience.

Dad never taught me to ride a two-wheel bicycle for which I did question his parenting skills. But I don't remember ever asking for a bike even though all my friends owned one. I don't ever remember feeling neglected for not owning one, but I hated chasing after my friends as they rode their bikes.

On the positive side, the memory of him pulling me on my sled in late December on Main Street in Middletown still warms my heart.

We did have one passion in common: watching television. We spent hours in front of the tube. Except for the summer months when he was too tired or too busy working, our family time was spent staring, laughing and commenting on TV. We watched and trusted Walter Cronkite on CBS. After the news, we laughed our heads off to Jack Benny and Rochester, The Three Stooges, Laurel and Hardy and Abbott and Costello.

But on nights when we had to choose between comedies and westerns, the westerns always won out. We watched hundreds of them a year. We even watched the rebroadcasts. We loved the action, the smoking pistols being fired from charging horses, gunslingers dueling it out in the OK Corral, stagecoaches being chased by Indians, settlers hiding behind mule-drawn Conestoga wagons as Apaches on horseback circled the wagon train shooting at the pioneers, and the U.S. Calvary charging to the rescue.

These westerns influenced my career choices. I wanted to become a cowboy, while my father told me to follow in his footsteps and become a doctor. A successful medical practice awaited me. From his life experience, he knew doctors were always needed.

We loved the old-West scenery: the high plains, the mesas, the Rocky Mountains and Death Valley. We loved the John Wayne classics, John Ford's, Stagecoach as well as the nightly western onslaught that we viewed on the seven channels broadcast from New York City.

After I finished my homework, we relaxed in front of the TV. I sat on the couch and Dad reclined in his Castro Convertible. We wore matching wool sweaters my mom had knitted for us. When the theme song introduced the show, we listened and basked in the glory of a father-son moment. We ate westerns for dessert.

We memorized the lines of the classic western movies.

We watched classics, like *High Noon* on WOR Channel Nine's, *Million Dollar Movie.* Like any parent with multiple children, and we had no favorites. We loved them all: *Gunsmoke, Rawhide, Bonanza, The Lone Ranger, The Roy Rodgers Show, Gene Autry, Hopalong Cassidy, Wagon Train, Have Gun – Will Travel.* We even tested each other's memories on the names of their horses: Trigger, Buttermilk, Scout, Topper, Champion and Buckshot.

We knew the good guys wore white hats and the evil-doers wore black ones. On our small silver screen, honor and respect for the law was clear. In the fifties and sixties the black and white westerns showed no shades of grey. The Indians were savages who deserved to die and the U.S. Calvary were heroes. In John Wayne's genocidal words, "The only good Indian is a dead Indian."

On television I watched Hitler saying something to the same effect about the *Juden.* The Nazis, before they commenced full blown genocide, even considered setting up Jewish reservations in occupied Russia. I remembered Hitler's knowledge of tobacco and American Indians. He knew the success the white American had in snuffing out the red Indian populations on reservations. The Germanic mind understood that during the war resettlement of Jews would be too costly. Hitler's Hebraic obsession mandated a "final solution," an act of "genocide" to solve the Jewish problem. The world needed a word to describe the crime of intentionally destroying a group of people and a Polish Jew, who escaped the Nazis to find a new home in America coined the word "genocide." It perfectly described the plight of the Jews in German-occupied countries.

With the use of one word, a word previously used so successfully on Native Americans, "resettlement" Jews were tricked into cattle cars for their final trip to the death camps.

While attending Fallsburgh Junior High, I could no longer identify the bad guys or my heroes by the color of their hats. The bad guys now wore: heads of skin covered with SS lightning bolts, swastika tattoos, white sheets and *keffiyehs.* Life had become a bit more complicated.

As a member of the Fallsburgh Central Cross-Country team, I ran two-and-a-half-mile races to uncomplicate my life. I ran to try to forget my neuroses and my acne. Sometimes it worked, sometimes it did not.

Our team competed against neighboring, rival high schools. Our toughest annual race against a field of runners from multiple schools was held at Bear Mountain. The runners ran a tortuous mile and a quarter up Bear Mountain and then reversed the process running back down the mountain.

As I ran this pain-inducing course, I scanned the other mountain tops. Seeing castles resting on estates, I pictured Bavaria,

Germany. My father had a photo of the Bavarian mountains in his office. I remembered reading about a small group of American Nazis who in 1940 practiced rifle shooting not more than twenty miles from where I raced. The FBI arrested them but failed to win convictions. I wondered were these castles the homes of German-American Nazis.

Each step hurt as I climbed toward the peak. I thought about Yorkville, New York, the headquarters of the German-American Bund. This town populated with German-Americans was less than 50 miles from where I now raced. Before the war, this was a town filled with goose-stepping, Hitler saluting scum.

Bear Mountain was located about 60 miles away from Madison Square Garden. The midtown Manhattan sporting venue, named after our fourth president—James Madison, was also the site of political rallies, wild-western shows and circuses.

On March 15, 1937, this venue was packed to the rafters with 20,000 Jews and Christians rallying for the boycott of Nazi goods. The rally was sponsored by the American Jewish Congress and attracted speakers like CIO's John L. Lewis, New York City Mayor Fiorello LaGuardia, and Rabbi Stephen Wise. The arena was plastered with American flags, bunting and two large banners which hung in front of the speakers platform. One read: BOYCOTT NAZI GERMANY. The other showed a virile white male holding clipping shears cutting into a swastika.

On February 20, 1939 the same venue held the largest German-American Bund rally. Twenty thousand Bundists cheered every anti-Semitic word spewed from each speaker's mouth.

The Bund's rally's poster read:

PRO-AMERICAN RALLY
– MASS DEMONSTRATION FOR
TRUE AMERICANISM –
FEB. 20th, 1939 MADISON SQUARE GARDEN –
GERMAN AMERICAN BUND.

The poster pictured a serious-looking, Nordic-Aryan warrior holding a spear and a shield. On the shield were the stars and stripes. In front of the shield appeared a coiled snake ready to sink its fangs into the American nation. The head of the snake bore a hammer and sickle. The tip of the spear, that pierced the body of the snake, bore a swastika.

The rally was held in honor of George Washington's birthday. In the arena two swastika banners waved next to American flags. A giant banner of George Washington hung in front of Fritz Kuhn, the founder of the German-American Bund. On that night, he was the keynote speaker.

It came as no surprise to me that Fritz, this Munich born, naturalized U.S. citizen had been a chemist working for the American king of anti-Semitism, Henry Ford.

Kuhn, like Hitler, earned the Iron Cross First Class for bravery in World War I. Kuhn, like Hitler, spent time in prison. Kuhn admired the *Führer* so much that he wanted to be his American clone. He gave himself the title *BundsFührer.* But Hitler treated him as if he was a pimple on the *Führer's* ass.

Twenty years later, as a ten-year-old, I sat in the same venue with my Mom and Dad, cheering Rin Tin Tin, Rusty, Lt. Rip Masters and Gail Davis as Annie Oakley, not knowing American Nazis once packed this arena to the rafters. On September 27, 1959, I sat in the Garden mesmerized watching the cast of my favorite TV show, *The Adventures of Rin Tin Tin,* a story about a boy, a German shepherd, and the US Cavalry posted in Fort Apache. Rusty, the ten-year-old boy, was being raised by the soldiers because his parents were killed by the Indians. Posters of my western heroes lined the walls of the arena.

Eight years later, as a 17-year-old, I ran up and down Bear Mountain with sweat burning my pimples. The beads ran across my face and back. My oily-skin canvas looked like an early Jackson Pollack—a collage of blackheads, whiteheads, and reddish pustules. These scar-causing pimples disfigured my face. With worry I asked, "How am I ever going to attract a member of the opposite sex burdened with this teenage curse?"

A dermatologist advised me that my condition was part of puberty, part of growing up. He said, "Stop eating chocolate." For one year I did, only to find out that my chocolate consumption made absolutely no difference in the number of pimples attacking my face.

My dermatologist said, "Your nervous system produces oil in your pores and if you do not scrub it all out, your pores get clogged and infected."

But as my lungs inhaled the cold air of Bear Mountain, I wondered if my Holocaust obsession accelerated the production of oil on my face. Was my family's history causing me to suffer as a teenager without a love life? Were my abnormalities due to the Nazis and their abhorrent treatment of the Jews. So as I became near sighted at the tender age of 10, and bore cataracts at age 47, and had two detached retinas in my fifties, the Nazis took the blame.

Seven

The Colonial Inn

In the year my nearsightedness required me to wear glasses, my family wintered on Miami Beach. We flew on National Airlines from LaGuardia to Miami International. Upon arrival in Miami, we hopped into a cab to get to our final destination, the Colonial Inn Motel on Miami Beach. The appropriately named Colonial Inn was easily identifiable. The cab parked in front of its Gone with the Wind columns and its cement white horse pulling a black carriage. Little did I know then that in five years, I would be attending college in Miami and my grandmother Rose would winter on Miami Beach.

On this vacation, my family strolled up and down Lincoln Road with its high-class shops. My dad was proud of his beautiful wife, who wore her new mink stole, and his two good-looking kids. Dad dressed to the nines and looked like a Hollywood actor. He was happy, and it showed in his smile and in his stride. His life had taken a turn for the good.

During this Christmas break, I basked in the sun, swam in the ocean and stomped on Portuguese men-of-war. The lifeguards had posted their signs:

WARNING!
MAN-O-WAR STINGS ARE PAINFUL
STAY OUT OF THE WATER

As a teenage risk-taker this signage was an invitation to dive right into the ocean. I knew that these "blue bottles" got their name because they looked like the sails on 16th Century Portuguese warships. Wearing my beat-up Keds, I ran up and down the beach stomping all the jellyfish I could find. I would solve this headache for the Miami Beach Tourist Bureau. I killed hundreds of them. I relished hearing their blue bells pop. I was the U.S. Infantry landing on the beaches in Normandy and these Portuguese men-of-war were the hated Nazis.

During the afternoon, I spent an hour floating on my dollar blow-up raft. I tried to avoid the jellyfish blooms which surrounded my raft in an attempt at retribution for my morning beach stomping. I feared their venomous tentacles knowing the toxicity of their stings. As vigilant as I was, I got stung. The left cheek of my buttock swelled and for the rest of the day I remained in pain in my motel bed.

The next day I returned to the sea and back on my yellow raft. I lay on my back peering skyward. A low flying Piper Cub towed a banner advertising the Newport Motel.

"Come to The Seven Seas Lounge and See our Waitress's Treasured Chests."

I fantasized entering the lounge and seeing these huge-breasted pirate-garbed babes. But not being of drinking age, I would have to do with the women in their bikinis who surrounded the Colonial Inn pool. I searched for excessive exposure of cleavage or pubic hair. But what I observed most were women basted in *Bain De Soliel* Orange Gelee holding silver-foiled metallic UV reflectors under their chins, trying to get deeper, darker tans. They knew the status that a Miami Beach tan carried in the winter in Northern states and none of them feared skin cancer.

On windy days, choppy waves splashed salt water directly into my mouth. The taste reminded me of the Passover table with its boiled eggs to be dipped in saltwater. On other afternoons, the Atlantic was as flat as a Catskill Mountain lake in August. On one of those tranquil days, my mind landed on the Kenilworth Hotel which was within walking distance of the Colonial Inn.

At the pool, a kid mentioned that the Kenilworth had a policy that forbade Jews to be guests. I knew that Arthur Godfrey owned a piece of the place. He talked about it while playing on his ukulele during his mid-morning TV show. The rumor went that the Kenilworth posted a sign at the front desk that read: NO DOGS OR JEWS ALLOWED. I was tempted to visit the hotel to ask for a postcard while scanning the front desk for the sign. I thought the sign might be possible in the twenties but not in 1959, not after the Holocaust.

I never walked the three miles to the Kenilworth to find out if the sign existed. But I wondered, "Had Dad heard the story and if he had, how it made him feel?" I never asked.

At night I walked Collins Avenue, collecting postcards from neighboring motels. I scanned the front desk of each for any verbiage dealing with dogs and Jews. Having found none, I questioned the validity of the Kenilworth story. I figured that if someone had a Jewish sounding name or a nose which was a tad too large, the management would politely say, "Sorry, Mr. Greenberg there are no rooms available tonight. May I call a cab for you? There are some excellent establishments located within minutes of our hotel." This thought-process reminded me of a movie I had recently watched on TV. The 1947 Academy-Award winning film was called *A Gentleman's Agreement.* It starred Gregory Peck as a Christian reporter who pretended to be a Jew to learn what anti-Semitism felt like. But that was America in 1947, and not 1965.

Eight

The Eulogy

At my father's funeral I wore a black skull cap. I stood gripping the podium and looking into the crowd. My father's family and friends had gathered in the sanctuary. They waited for the eulogies. In the front row sat my crying mother, my sister, Barbara and her husband Jeff, my wife Shelley and Dad's five grandsons.

I paused, I waited, and I held back my tears. As silence engulfed the room, I raised my voice:

"My father, Dr. Wolf Laitner, was a saint. He was a saint so righteous that he did only good. Not just an ordinary saint but one of the 36 righteous people mentioned in our Talmud. He was a *Lamed-Vav Tzadikim.* The *lamed* is the Hebrew letter for the number thirty and the *vav* the letter for the number six. Our Biblical tribe's mystics declared that in every generation 36 saints roam the earth. Like Superman or the Lone Ranger they must mask their identities. They are collectively known as the "concealed ones." No one knows who they are. Some think even they do not know that they are part of this select team.

"Why hide their identities you may ask?

"The answer is because this group's role in life is to justify the purpose of mankind in the eyes of the Almighty. Let me say that again. They must justify the purpose of mankind in the eyes of G-d.

"Who in this sanctuary would want such a responsibility?

"Not I. For if anyone of these 36 saints fails to meet G-d's expectations, human life on this planet will come to an end. On their shoulders rests a burden as tough as the one Zeus forced on the mighty Atlas.

"According to the *Hassid's,* if my dad figured out that he was a member of this select group, he might die and another saint would immediately replace him. I wonder if one day long ago he came to that conclusion. But for those of you here today, who knew him, you knew he was way too humble to ever make such a proclamation.

"There is no tougher job on earth than the one my dad held and my father never received a grade below an "A" on his *Lamed-Vad Tzadikim* job evaluation.

"You may ask why my father's life journey justified the 'purpose of mankind' test.

"Well my father was tested as Job was in the Bible – not in the belly of a whale but in a Nazi concentration camp. My father, like Job, was a righteous man. He had many of his family's lives stolen in the camps. His faith, like Job's, was repeatedly tested. Somehow he remained a believer... just like Job. And just like Job he was rewarded with a new family.

"My father was starved, beaten, and tortured and yet he kept his faith in the divine presence. He inspired all who knew his story to have faith.

"Therefore, today I pray that his soul be kept among the immortal souls of Abraham, Isaac, Jacob, Sarah, Rebecca, Rachel, Leah, and all the righteous men and women in paradise.

"Therefore, today in your presence, I bestow the title 'Saint' to my father's name... Saint Wolf Laitner, one of the righteous 36 and on his behalf I challenge all of you in this Holy sanctuary to lead your lives as if you were tasked with the duty of justifying the purpose of mankind in the eyes of the Lord."

As I left the podium, the room remained silent. Walking with tear-glazed eyes and trembling hands, I sat next to my sobbing mother. I reached for her hand and tightly held it.

Turning my head toward the assembled crowd, I noticed many with tears running down their faces. They remembered my Dad.

Nine

The Neighbors

A year after reading my father's eulogy, I met one of my father's friends. He told me a disturbing story. "After the war, around 1946, your father had a German girlfriend."

This statement bothered me because after all my father went through at the hands of the Germans, he could still touch the flesh of a German women.

My father never discussed any of his paramours to me. The most he ever said was, "Son, when I was a medical student in Italy I had a sports car and great time with the local gals."

A parade of thoughts marched through my head: "How could he possibly get aroused by a German woman?

"She must have been beautiful?"

She must have known he was a Jew with that tattoo burned into his arm.

"My dad must have had one fucking insatiable sex drive to fuck a *fräulein* one year after the end of the war – one year after his liberation.

Did he douse himself with that miracle water?"

Was this acquaintance pulling my leg?

If I were a survivor, could I have screwed a German woman?

I had read about how tough the times were for the Germans in the Allied occupation-zones. Hungry people sell their souls for food, and sex becomes a common commodity. Someone with food could easily buy sex in Germany. I had seen enough movies and read enough books about the post-war black market.

I assumed this woman was at least single. But I was wrong.

The friend continued, "In her apartment, your father found two hidden photographs of her SS officer husband. One in which he shook hands with Heinrich Himmler, the leader of the *Schutzstaffel,* (protection staff) who were also known as the 'black-shirts.' You know, those were the bastards who ran the concentration camps. In the other photo he was clothed in full Nazi regalia, wearing a soldier's smile as he tightly held his new bride in his arms. When your father learned that her husband was still alive and visiting her, he reported the information to the occupation authorities who promptly arrested the bastard."

In a matter of seconds, thoughts crossed my brain like credits at the end of a movie:

"How could he… WOW! He must have felt great watching the SS officer being dragged off to jail.

Did the *fräulein* ever learn of my father's betrayal?

Did she care?

Did my father ever make love to her after her husband's arrest?

If so, how intense an orgasm did he have after the betrayal?

And most of all I wondered if any part of the story was true.

Dad was gone and I doubted, if he were alive, whether I would have the *cojones* to ask about this liaison .

I never discussed my sex life with him. What right would I have had to ask about his secret life? A secret life was meant to remain just that, a secret.

Not long after the *fräulein* story, a couple of naturalized, German-born Americans moved into our Cooper City neighborhood. Heinrich and Eva grew up in West Germany. They immigrated to the States in their twenties for better job opportunities. Now naturalized citizens in their thirties, they had no children. Heinrich was a tall, muscular, blond garage mechanic. He would have made a good poster model for an Aryan soldier. He loved dark Germanic beers and Lowenbraü. When he drank a good number of them, his mouth detached from his brain lowering his inhibitions, and his hands started to move freely to any woman who sat next to him.

Eva was his opposite. She stood five-foot-four inches, with short strawberry blond hair and a prominent large ass. Her backside was her center of gravity, a good counterweight holding her body in an upright fashion. It was the type of ass meant to be grabbed or pinched or kissed. I saw her as the classic German farm girl, grabbing the teats of a cow and squeezing milk out of them. If she was a bit skinnier, she could have appeared in a Nazi propaganda poster for German farm production. Hitler, with his desire for more members to be added to the master race, would have loved her large child-bearing hips. Her physique spoke to the male observer, "I understand what nature wants you to do with my body. You'll find no virginal orifices left in it."

My wife and I became friends with these neighbors. We went out to dinner together. We had barbecues and drinks at their pool as well as ours. We invited them to our annual parties. They knew we were Jewish. I told him I was born in West Germany and that my parents had survived the camps. They didn't appear to have a problem with it.

I never asked what their parents did during the war and they never said. They never divulged their parents' pasts except Heinrich once told me, Eva's mom had been raped by Russian soldiers during their conquering of Germany.

They took summer trips back to Germany to visit their families. One August day, when Eva and her daughter were in her homeland, Heinrich confided in me. "Mort, I cut a small port-hole in my garage door so I can sneak my Cuban girlfriend into my house. That way I can make sure there are no neighbors snooping around when I take her back to Miami in the morning."

As I examined the small garage-door opening, I replied, "Wow, I didn't know you had a mistress. Then my brain rattled off a number of voiceless questions:

Why is he telling me this?

Was this his way of bragging?

How many other neighbors had he told this to?

How many of my neighbors had peepholes in the garage doors?

Is this guy paranoid?

Is he bullshitting me?

That summer our Polish/American neighbors had a pool party. For some odd reason, none of the Jews on the block were invited. I remembered my dad's admonishment on his Holocaust tapes. "The Poles are even more anti-Semitic than the Germans." I didn't think that was possible.

What our Polish neighbors and Heinrich did not know was that one of their female guests was half-Jewish. After six Lowenbraü's, Heinrich's mouth became liberated from his brain. In front the half-Jew women and her Irish/American husband, he spouted off the following, "You know Hitler's only problem was that he didn't finish off the job."

The Irish/American pulled his fist back to punch Heinrich in the nose, "You son-of-a-bitch; my wife's mother is Jewish."

One of the men in the crowded living room grabbed the Irishman and pulled him back, "Cool down buddy, it's Heinrich's liquor talking. He only meant it as a joke."

When the block's four Jewish families heard the hateful tale, our attitudes quickly changed. Heinrich's utterance led to his being blackballed. A cone of silence hung over Heinrich's head. Our cold shoulders chilled him as if he was buried in the snows of Stalingrad.

One year later, Heinrich approached me as I mowed the lawn. He announced, "Eva and I are moving to Nashville. We lucked out and sold our house for a good price. I got a better-paying job up there. I bought a home in a neighborhood that is free of Blacks. All my neighbors are good all-American rednecks. I'm leaving on Monday and Eva will follow me in a week."

I didn't ask Heinrich, but I bet the area was also *Judenfrei.* My facial muscles relaxed with the knowledge that this fucking racist was leaving Cooper City. I wanted to tell him, "Good riddance!" but I chickened out and wished him and his wife, "Good luck."

The next week Eva approached me as I retrieved my mail. She asked, "Why don't you put on a bathing suit, come over to my pool, and get some sun. She causally touched my arm and cooed, "I'd love to talk to you for a while before I move. You know, I am leaving Florida for Tennessee next week."

I knew Heinrich had already left for Nashville. "Sure I'll change into my swimsuit and be there in fifteen minutes."

I met Eva at her kidney-shaped pool. From the outdoor speakers mounted to the walls of her patio porch, my ears caught the sounds of the theme from *A Man and a Woman.* I hummed along, ba da ba da da da da da da da, thinking how much I'd like to make love with that beat in the background.

She greeted me with a warm smile, the aroma of 4711, and a cold Lowenbraü. She looked hot as the cement surrounding her pool. Eva dressed in a bright yellow bathing suit which barely covered her ample bosoms and derriere. She possessed the type of ass that men like to tattoo love notes on with their spittle. She had already taken a dip in the pool and her short-cropped, wet, blond hair glistened in the sunlight.

While taking a seat in the lounge chair directly across from Eva, I sipped my beer. Glancing at her crotch my eyes focused on a patch of pubic hairs. I did a quick count—three, six, nine, twelve, fifteen, eighteen. A cluster of eighteen strands freed from the confines of her swim suit. I studied this mass of sandy-brown curls as if my life depended on it. While my animalistic desire for a whiff and a lick grew within my swim trunks.

My first thought: "Manna from Heaven."

My second thought: "A gift from the Gods."

My third and fourth thoughts: "How do I look – without staring? How do I keep my manhood down?

I watched these exhibitionist hairs dry in the sun.

A barrage of additional questions bombarded my brain like the *bratatat* of a machine gun:

Had she created this sensual display just for my visual pleasure?

Did she even know that this cluster had sneaked out of her bikini?

Was this her way of asking me to fuck her?

If I did, would I get to hear a screaming unintelligible German orgasmic moan exit her mouth?

Was this my time to embrace and my time to plant seed?

Did she have any sexually transmittable diseases?

Was she setting me up for a later confrontation with her husband?

Isn't Heinrich at least 1,000 miles away from us?

Would she tell my wife if I propositioned her?

Should I tell her about the peep hole in her garage door and her husband's Cuban lover?

Was this her way of screwing her husband for his infidelities, by making love to a Jew?

Had she ever made it with Jew before?

The machine gun paused as if jammed. One last absurd question burst in my brain.

"What would my dad do under these circumstances?"

We both drank another Lowenbraü as *Me and Mrs. Brown* played in her boom box. We both continued making idle chatter. For the life of me, I cannot remember one word of the conversation. I continued to gaze. Eva continued to act in a nonchalant manner. Every other second I pulled my eyes away from her patch. I wanted to ask her to go back in the house, bring me a pair of scissors and a Baggie. At the very least I wanted to snip off those wanderers, place them in the clear cellophane bag and hide them as a treasured memento.

I waited for a hint to fly out of her mouth. But none did.

Eva had sent me a blatant message and I was too timid, or wise, or chicken, to make a move. After swallowing my last sip of beer, I stood up, handed Eva the empty glass bottle and as our fingers touched an electrical current flowed through my body.

Standing next to her I said, "Eva thanks for the brews. I'm glad we had this last opportunity to talk before you left town. Have a safe drive to Nashville. I wish you the best of luck."

Eva craned her head in my direction. I kissed her on the lips as we hugged. We closed our eyes. Another bolt of current electrified my body. Her breasts massaged my bare chest as those much observed strands rubbed against my inner thigh. I became aroused.

We separated and I knew that this golden opportunity had been lost. I tottered back to my house.

Entering it, I berated myself, "You pussy! You wuss! You total failure! You're lower than a wuss. You're not a risk-taker. When opportunity knocks, you run from the door. Shame on you! For once in your life, follow your smaller head. Go back to her. There is still time."

But I did not return to Eva and all I had left was fodder for future jaw-jutting, toe-curling masturbatory fantasies.

Ten

Sitting *Shiva*

Three days after my dad's death, I sat *Shiva* in my mother's Boca Raton home. In her villa, a group of ten adults – our *minyan* – stood, talked and waited for the Rabbi to make his appearance.

Alone, I stared out the kitchen's glass doors at the lake and the golf course. I flashed back at how happy my father was when Jason, his grandson, caught a large bass in that lake. I smiled realizing that picture had become one of my unerasable Kodak moments.

Each day of *Shiva*, I sipped flavorless coffee as my reddened eyes noticed that the lake appeared a paler shade of blue and the golf course a browner shade of green. I recalled the sweet taste and rich aroma of my dad's freshly-brewed coffee, how it ran over my tongue and ignited my taste buds, how in this kitchen I sat looking at him and at this lake.

Walking into the living room, I found myself surrounded by acquaintances, family and unknown friends of my parents. My father had touched all their lives. They shook my hand, expressed their condolences and said how much they respected my dad.

Lining the living room walls were impressionist paintings. I scanned them and realized they represented my blurred life. In this living room, on these couches, next to these paintings, my dad and I had talked for hours. He was a master storyteller – a male Scheherazade. We discussed wars, history, and how life was treating us. He told off-color jokes and I laughed. I loved his sense of humor and he knew it. Those days and those laughs were now gone forever.

The rabbi's appearance broke my daydreaming. He instructed the *minyan* to stand and face east. He led us in prayer. He helped my mom, my sister and I recite the Mourner's *Kaddish.* As the three of us searched for meaning and comfort in this spiritual ritual, I silently prayed, *G-d walk through our house and take away our sorrow and please watch over us and heal my family.*

After the Rabbi left the villa, two elderly men cornered me in the vestibule. "Hi, I'm Saul and this is David. It is our pleasure to meet you."

They appeared to be in their late sixties or early seventies… short, balding men with protruding stomachs. They both wore white cotton short-sleeve shirts and like my father, bore tattooed numbers on their forearms. I shook their hands and glanced into their eyes. I sensed they were messengers, sent to tell me a story, sent to hand me another piece to the puzzle that made up my father's life.

In a thick Polish accent, Saul said, "You know you look an awful lot like your father."

"Thanks." I replied. "Many folks considered him a handsome man."

David piped in, "Many women loved the way he looked and dressed. He told us many stories about the time he spent in Rome before the war, when he was in medical school, about those beautiful Italian women he knew. Boy could he tell a story – so descriptive, down to the minutest detail."

Saul interrupted, "Your father befriended us during the last days of the war... in the death camp, just days before we were all liberated by the Soviet Army."

"We wanted to tell you that he saved our lives." David continued as he rubbed his tattoo.

I remembered hearing those words before. Usually from my father's patients or their family members who told me how he pulled them away from death and back to the living.

"Thanks for telling me. How did he do it?" I inquired as I pulled on the small piece of black cloth pinned to my jacket.

"He gave us the most important gift of all... the will to live," Saul said.

David continued, "Well it was near the end of the war. We were all imprisoned in a concentration camp... inches away from death. We were ill and starving. We were skin on bones. We heard the bombs exploding in the distance, but we didn't know how many days it would be before the Russian Army liberated us. Every minute, prisoners died all around us. Both of us were sixteen years old, and your father knew we were virgins. He kept telling us to keep struggling, not to give up on life, your father said we should stay alive, because making love to women was something we had to experience. He told us one story after another about his sexual escapades."

As David talked, my mind wandered. "Did my dad know that by telling these stories to these young men he was also saving his own life? Was storytelling his salvation, his medicine of hope and love? Would I exist if not for those stories?"

I observed tears forming in David's eyes as he whispered, "He kept our minds off of food and death. He gave us hope in our darkest moment. Your father, without medicines, used the only tool left in his medical bag...his brain."

Saul jumped in, "A brilliant strategy. It worked! We fought death and we won. I doubt that without those stories we would be talking to you today."

Hugging both of them, I replied, "Thanks so much for telling me your moving story. My dad never did."

Alone, I stared out the kitchen window, feeling proud of my father. I now noticed the brilliance of the lake's blue waters and the sharpness of the green radiating off the golf course.

Eleven

My Struggle

My father never read *Mein Kampf*. He spoke German so he would not have needed a translated version of the book. So for years I followed in his footsteps and never sought out this bible of hate. I was curious but I did not want to touch the ink of an obsessive anti-Semite nor hear the words that vomited out of his mouth. I am a Jew, and a Jew does not handle the filth of the devil incarnate.

The year I realized that G-d gives you many signals on your way to death, like my eyebrows turning grey. My struggle was over. I decided it was time to read the maniac's words. I learned that Hitler dictated his book in 1925 and 1926 in Landsberg Am Lech Fortress Prison to his fellow crony prisoners, a book that became the bible of the National Socialist German Workers'(Nazi) Party, a bible that equated the inferior race, Jews, to the status of snakes, vermin, parasites and maggots. "Was there any form of filth or profligacy, particularly in cultural life, without at least one Jew involved in it? If you cut even cautiously into such an abscess, you found, like a maggot in a rotting body, often dazzled by the sudden light-a kike! Jews are" always only a parasite in the body of other peoples."

They are the "the great masters of the lie." I laughed at the master of the greatest lie pointing his finger in the face of the Jews.

In his spiritual doctrine, Hitler prophesied that Germany may not have lost World War I "if some twelve to fifteen thousand of the Hebrew corruptors of the people had been poisoned by gas before or during the war." Here was an early precursor of the destruction of a people with gas and fire.

I read *Mein Kampf* with a particular interest on Hitler's fanatical views and thoughts about the Hebrew race. I was surprised to find portions of the book to be highly readable. He understood how to slowly suck the reader in. For years I had heard that this text was so poorly written that it made reading it intolerable. Sections of the book on history and economics were tedious but to paint the book as unreadable was a falsehood.

Hitler presented his: parents, childhood, upbringing, education, and career as an artist and soldier. And from his humble beginnings he was transformed into a role model and an educator on how all parents should raise their children to be "good Germans."

He presented himself as a man who knew hunger. He was poor and starving. These experiences gave him the insight to understand the economics of the world. He had lived life. He had learned its lessons and now it was his duty to teach them to his people.

He mocked Jews as not a water-loving people. They stank and their odor made him ill. Even with his eyes shut he could identify them by their stench. On top of their body odor, they wore dirty, smelly clothes.

Their clothes, physiques, and facial features gave them a "none-too-heroic appearance."

But they did have skills. He sarcastically said "one did not know what to admire more: their glibness of tongue or their skill in lying."

As for people he hated, like J.P. Morgan, he libeled them by saying they were endowed with Hebrew blood. He played the same trick on President Roosevelt after he declared war on America.

On Biblical matters he commented: "The Old Testament is nothing but a collection of stories about prostitutes and cattle traders," "The personification of the devil as the symbol of all evil assumes the living shape of the Jew," and "I believe that I am acting in accordance with the will of the Almighty Creator: by defending myself against the Jew, I am fighting for the work of the Lord."

Hitler's mentor, Dietrich Eckart pounded anti-Semitism into his head. Together they studied and discussed the history of the Jews to find out what made the Jew tick. This morphine-addicted poet and playwright participated with Hitler in the Beer Hall *Putsch* of 1923, a failed revolution that landed both of them in Landsberg Prison. Eckart believed a German messiah would rescue the nation after its loss in World War I.

When Eckart heard Hitler speak, he found his messiah. It became his role to convince Adolf that not only was he a genius and an Aryan superman, he would become the German Messiah. He built on the ideology of the "genius superman." Eckart became the spiritual father of National Socialism. Hitler so admired Eckart that he dedicated the second volume of *Mein Kampf* to him and named an arena after him.

The more I learned about Hitler's rise to the top, the more I realized he was groomed, mentored, and tutored in all things Nazi from how to give a speech, to how to raise funds and, with great particularity, how to hate Jews. His personal development was as programmed as the IBM computers he used to keep track of Jewish possessions.

I kept searching in *Mein Kampf* for the portion of the book where Adolf meets the devil. Hitler failed to mention this encounter. I wanted to read the exact words of the pact he cut with Satan. I imagined the two in deep discussion.

I figured this meeting with Mephistopheles took place in the filthy trenches on the Western Front. On this cold rainy night, Hitler slept curled up in his mud-soaked blanket. Throughout the day, he had run messages through those trenches. He reeked from lack of bathing and having worn the same uniform for months. But in his dreams, he basks in all his soldier's glory, for he fights a war for the Motherland and is awarded the Iron Cross for his actions.

Adolf awoke from a deep sleep as a hand touched his shoulder. He opened his eyes to see Satan standing above him, Satan dressed in a clean tweed three-piece suit with polished and manicured fingernails. His well-groomed auburn goatee framed his white face.

"Don't be alarmed, young man. I am here to bring you the gift of joy and happiness."

Hitler stared in disbelief into the Devil's fiery red eyes and listened.

"My name is Mephistopheles and I have spent all night searching for you – my comrade-in-arms. I have a deal for you that will make you the ruler of Europe.

Hitler smiled in silence, rubbing his eyes as if thinking he was still asleep.

The Devil removed a typed sheet of paper from his coat pocket. He unfolded it and handed the document to Hitler.

"Here is the contract I wrote especially for you, my beloved, Adolf. Read it carefully. Before you sign it, please pay close attention to all of the details.

Hitler rose to stand near a lantern hung on a piece of barbed wire. Under minimal light he read:

STANDARD EXCHANGE OF SOUL FOR

TOTALITARIAN POWERS AGREEMENT

Between Adolf Hitler and the Prince of Darkness

Paragraph 1– In exchange for services rendered and your soul being placed in eternal damnation and as consideration for my granting you the following diabolical favors, Adolf Hitler shall receive the authority to:

Murder millions of innocent men, women, and children from the following groups: Jews, Gypsies, Russians, Poles, Jehovah's Witnesses, homosexuals, the mentally infirm

In addition, the undersigned will receive:

- Personal protection from bullets, shells, poisonous gas, artillery and/or brief case bombs;
- Access to your rightful place in history;
- The leadership of a great Germanic nation including its army, navy and air force;
- Absolute control of most of Western Europe and a large portion of the Soviet Union and Africa;
- A totalitarian state in which your subjects will adore, fear and believe you are their Messiah.

Paragraph 2—In exchange for the above, you shall act as my emissary on earth for a minimum of 12 years, and with your minions shall:

A. Murder people in the most despicable manner possible;
B. Torture and starve those prisoners that you do not murder;
C. Succeed in psychologically injuring generations of survivors and their offspring;
D. Cause the destruction of most of the European Continent.

I sign this contract in my blood, freely and with the full understanding of its terms.

I consign my soul unto his ownership to be rendered at the end of 37 years from the date this contract is executed.

____________________ ____________________

Adolf Hitler Satan

Hitler blurted out, "Hand me your pen so I may sign, my darling Mephisto? I love this deal."

The Devil stares at Hitler knowing he has chosen well.

"My dear Adolf , slow down. There is one exclusionary clause you must carefully read. It is a suicide clause. We provide no protection from death by your own hands."

Adolf gripped Satan's gold-tipped fountain pen, and jabbed the pen into his index finger. As a droplet of blood appeared from the dirt-covered finger, he dipped the pen into the cold blood and scribbled his signature on the contract.

"The deal is sealed." Adolf yelled as he handed the agreement to the Devil.

Satan neatly folded the document into three sections, placed it in a white envelope and tucked it away in his suit-coat pocket. They shook hands, hugged and bid each other farewell. As Satan climbed out of the trench, Hitler examined his hand, remembering the intense electrical current that ran through his body as their flesh touched. He knew his destiny had been secured.

Not finding this Faustian bargain in the text, I thought about Adolf and how after every close encounter with death he must have thought divine intervention was keeping him alive to fulfill a greater purpose such as his war against the Jews.

First, during the First World War on the Western Front, he was a soldier/messenger running communiqués through battle line trenches. Bullets and shells avoided making contact with his body. In the trenches Hitler tasted the enemy's poisonous gas. It filled and choked his lungs. But poison gas proved insufficient to cause his death or permanent injury. He was hospitalized and won the Iron Cross for his efforts. Had some Valkyrie decided this soldier would not die in battle?

This alone would have been enough to lend credence to the belief that the hand of the Almighty or the Devil protected this madman.

Second, in 1923, Hitler lead a group of his followers from a beer hall (The Beer Hall *Putsch*) to a government building to take control of the city of Munich with the intent to continue on to Berlin. Hitler stood in front of crowd with his fellow revolutionaries. They were confronted by armed policemen. When the shooting commenced he stood in the line of fire. When the shooting ended, 16 National Socialists were dead – gunned down by Bavarian police – but not Colonel Adolf Hitler.

This close call alone would have been enough for him and his believers to think he had celestial body guards (Nazi angels) who had given him invisible body armor.

Third, on July 20,1944, in the Wolf's Lair Conference Room, Lieutenant Colonel Claus von Stauffenberg of Operation Valkyrie fame, placed a briefcase with two bombs inside it under a large solid oak table. Approximately six feet away from the brief case stood Adolf Hitler. He conducted a war-planning meeting with 20 officers and some staff. Then the fates took over. One officer kicked the brief case away from Hitler and only one of the bombs exploded. The room splintered into a million fragments. Four of the Nazis died in the room. Hitler's pants and ear drums were badly damaged but his luck crept out of the room intact.

This fact alone would have been enough to convince him and his followers that bombs could not kill their Messiah.

I returned to reading *Mein Kampf* where Hitler spent thousands of words on the Jewish relationship to Marxism, to Bolshevism, to trade unions and to the press. As a paranoid, he saw conspiracies everywhere. He knew his enemies were the "Judeo-Bolsheviks."

A master propagandist, he commenced his story by portraying himself as an innocent. Then he skillfully set his hooks in the reader. He did not jump to the conclusion that the Jews should be eradicated from the face of the earth. He traveled a long tortuous journey to find his solution.

"I gradually began to hate them." He remembered how happy he was when he figured out that the Jew was not a German.

He remembered his moment of clarity, his total metamorphosis. "This was the time in which the greatest change I was ever to experience took place in me. From a feeble-cosmopolite I had turned into a fanatical anti-Semite."

As with Ahab's monomania for the whale, Hitler was totally fixated on the Jews. Before his doctors injected drugs into his veins, he was addicted to a substance more powerful than heroin, hatred of the Jews. I wondered why G-d did not make sex or women his addiction.

After reading *Mein Kampf* I doubted that he could spend a waking hour without obsessing on the Hebrew Tribe. His obsession was so strong that he believed that "no crime, no act against morality" lacked the hands of the Jews in it.

He feared the idea of Hebraic hands on the breasts and vaginas of Aryan women. He loathed the sexual mixing of the Aryan race's pure blood with the infected blood of Jews. He painted his fears in words: "For hours the black-haired Jew boy, diabolic joy in his face, waits in ambush for the unsuspecting girl whom he defiles with his blood and thus robs her from her people." Those defiled women would pay a heavy price for their desires when Hitler came to power.

In 1935, the German legislative body, the *Reichstag* adopted the Nuremberg Laws. These laws addressed Hitler's fear of the insatiable sex drive of the Jewish male by prohibiting extra-marital intercourse between Aryans and non-Aryans. Further, German women 45 and under were prohibited from working in a Jewish household. This law served two racial purposes, halting the defilement of their women, and the protection of the purity of German blood.

One of the most popular of *Mein Kampf*'s covers contained the author's picture and name as well as its title in a bold white font surrounded by a blood red banner. An artistic portrait captures the monster, with his scowling face; eyes staring hypnotically at the reader. I marveled at his cover selection. I realized the psychological effect the jacket cover had on the weak-minded.

This book which Hitler originally wanted to title, *Four and a Half Years of Struggle Against Lies, Stupidity and Cowardice,* written while Hitler sat in prison brought in royalties that were large enough to buy him a Mercedes-Benz. When he became the leader of Germany, millions of copies were bought. These sales made Hitler a wealthy man.

Why would my father buy this hatemonger's book. What self-respecting Polish Jew would spend a *zloty* on this madman's writings? However, five to ten million copies were sold. If my dad had purchased the book, he would have learned that Hitler craved *lebensraum* (living space) for the German people. Hitler detailed his belief that Poland fell into the "living space" category. My father was not alone in those mistaken beliefs. Many Jews lived in the land of denial. After the enormous loss of life in World War I, who would have thought the Europeans had the stomach for more bloodshed? Who could have predicted that such mortal enemies as Stalin and Hitler would sign a pact dividing up Poland? Even the wisest political scientists failed to make that prediction.

Twelve

The Catskills

I grew up in a small Catskill Mountain community, in a village called Woodridge. The village made up part of the Township of Fallsburgh, which was part of Sullivan County. It was located in the southeastern portion of New York State, approximately 90 miles northwest of New York City. One of the town's claim to fame was its ski resort. A ski resort called Big Vanilla at Davos. I lived at the bottom of the mountain next to the road that lead to Davos. As a teenager, on almost every winter weekend, I skied on the trails of Davos Mountain. As I skied, my eyes hunted for deer or rabbits. But more often, I found that I had bonded with nature and tasted the beauty of G-d's creations. The winter scenery rushed past my eyes, the cold wind hit my face, and for a few minutes on that trail I knew life was good. At the end of the day, as I stood next to the lodge's fireplace, sipping a hot chocolate and warming my frozen hands, my life's obsessions seemed as distant as the stars.

My family moved to Woodridge when I was five. One of the town's general practitioners, Dr. William Fernhoff, had died in a car crash. At the time my father's sister, Renia, resided in the village. When she learned the news of the car accident, she immediately telephoned her brother.

"Wolf, this is a golden opportunity. There is a small house you can rent in the center of the town on Broadway. That building can be set up to house the family and your medical office. The rent is cheap. I already inquired. Within a year you'll acquire the doctor's patients and your practice will be doing so well that you'll be able to buy the doctor's large medical building and his house."

She paused to catch her breath, "You know the village is covered in Jews. In the summertime you won't have time to breathe. Thousands of them spend June, July, and August in bungalows. You'll be so busy making house calls, you won't have time to count your money. The locals and the city folk will hear what a great doctor you are. They will flock to your office. You'll become a big fish in a small pond. This is a great place to raise a family."

I watched as my father kept nodding in agreement. He replied, "I have been to the town's synagogue. I know the town is filled with Jews. This is opportunity knocking. Even my mental patients are not making much progress and my state salary is so low."

Dad paused, "Anyway I don't think I'm cut out to be a psychiatrist. This may be *bashert* (destined). I'll talk to Henia and get her opinion. I'll sleep on it for a night and call you with my decision. Thanks for thinking about me."

Renia replied, "Brother, don't think too much. Another doctor may move into town before you and steal this opportunity.

"Love you.

"Good-bye."

My father followed his sister's advice. We moved thirty miles west from Middletown to Woodridge. A year after living in a small three-bedroom house in which my father used two rooms for his medical office, we moved into the large two-story Fernhoff house. Dad also purchased the adjoining Fernhoff medical building. Dr. Fernhoff was one of Woodridge's two Jewish doctors from the 1930s to the 1950s. He was also the town's health officer.

For the next 57 years, I knew almost nothing about Dr. William Fernhoff until my sister, Barbara, emailed me some articles he had written in April of 1938. Dr. Fernhoff wrote them in a publication I had never heard of, *The Woodridge Community Club Bulletin.*

In March of 1938, Austria was annexed into German Third *Reich* – the *Anschluss.* Hitler predicted this union in *Mein Kampf.*

In 1937, Dr. Fernhoff went to Austria to see relatives and spent three months in Austria. Years earlier, he experienced anti-Semitic riots as a student at the University of Vienna. He said the Austrians he spoke to never thought the Nazis would take over their nation. There was an anti-Semitic regime in Vienna which copied Hitler's ideas and had driven the Jews out of most government, law and faculty jobs. Jews were still allowed to attend medical school but appointments for internships were nearly impossible to obtain. "So the unfortunate ones, whom I met daily, kept on living in starvation and hoping for some miracle, little imagining that it could be still worse, and the word Hitler was taboo to them."

In his second installment Fernhoff warned Woodridge Jews, "They are being bled, first robbed of their possessions, and then the borders will be opened and the Jews driven out." He ended on an ominous note, "It can't happen here." I wonder if the democracy in America is strong enough to withstand this raging pestilence, which is called fascism."

Fernhoff tried to convince his relatives to leave for America. He had visas for them. They only promised they would follow him later on.

I wondered if Fernhoff's family made it out of Austria and kept their promise to follow him.

While I lived in the Fernhoff house, I learned what country life was all about – cloud-covered mountains, verdant forests, crystal-clear streams. A bounty of white-tailed deer, squirrels and rabbits inhabited my world, but so did a thousand humans. They all knew my name and almost everything else about me. This small town thrived on gossip and rumors like a Hebraic version of Peyton Place. As I matured, I could not wait to leave. I needed anonymity. I wanted freedom from the locals' snooping eyes and vicious tongues. These townies cherished tattling on me. My indiscretions flowed into my parents' ears. I needed to have readily available excuses. I wanted out. I wanted space between my family and my neighbors, so I applied to colleges at least one thousand miles away from home.

Before moving to Woodridge, I attended kindergarten in Middletown, New York. I was the only Semite in the class. My Christian classmates were well-behaved and I followed their lead. Our teacher never raised her voice, and quite often smiled and lavished us with praise. All her five-year-old minions respected and loved her.

Upon my arrival at Woodridge Elementary School, I went into culture shock. Here the class was predominately made up of Jewish kids. These children's voices were as loud as crows. In class, I sat cupping my hands over my ears to protect my eardrums. The decibels rose to headache level. I prayed for my return to Middletown Elementary. The teacher shouted threats, raising her voice to compete with the screeching sounds emanating from classmates' mouths. I soon followed suit and within months my classmates converted me into a member of the tribe of the unruly. I had become a monkey.

During recess we played on the school's monkey bars. The girls acted like rambunctious chimps swinging, hanging, and sitting on the iron bars. The girls, who wore dresses, often allowed me and anyone else who sat on the bottom metal pipes, to catch glimpses of their underwear. My kindergarten buddies and I were developing into *voyeurs.*

Riding on the lowest rung, I spied upward and saw green, yellow and blue cotton panties. As my manhood rose, I knew I was not to blame for my arousal, these kindergarten cuties were undergarment exhibitionists. At this early age, my mind photographed these pastel colors and cotton became my favorite fabric. How I wanted to touch that soft material and learn the mysteries of what lay beneath it.

My day was made if Nancy, a strawberry blonde, spent a few extra seconds on the top of the monkey bars. I praised the inventor of this playground cage while stealing peeks of her covered treasure.

"Nancy, whoever came up with the idea of monkey bars was a genius or a monkey."

She looked down at me and only smiled. Nancy loved the attention my eyes paid to the patch of cloth that clinked between her legs and covered her hairless genitals. Every day

I prayed Nancy would forget to put on those cotton panties under her shirt.

Before moving to Woodridge, we lived in Middletown, a city of around thirty thousand. One of my first and best memories entailed my dad pulling me on my new red sled through downtown Middletown at six o'clock in the evening. This past vision brings a longing for my father and for the simpler days of childhood.

Middletown's Main Street was dark except for a yellowish aura emitted from the town's street lights. Large icicles hung from every gutter as if ornaments were attached to trees. Three-foot high mounds of snow, created by snowplows, gave the town a miniature alpine landscape.

Bundled in a woolen sweater and a winter coat, and with a checkered scarf running around my neck, and black mittens warming my fingers, I was protected from Jack Frost. Black clip-on rubber boots kept my feet dry.

As Dad pulled the rope tied to the sled, this nylon umbilical cord deepened our relationship. Riding on my sled, I smiled at him and he returned the smile. In below freezing temperature I was blanketed by the warmth of his love. He loved making me happy and I knew it.

With the snow dancing around us, I stared into the streetlights and observed the descent of the flakes. On those snow-covered sidewalks, the sled glided past the storefront windows aglow with blue, green, red, and yellow Christmas lights. The sound of *Jingle Bells* rang from mounted speakers above door frames. In these, I studied Nativity scenes, gingerbread houses, candy canes, silver bells, sparkling trees, and Santa Claus riding in his sled, being pulled through the sky by Rudolph and his fellow reindeer. My dad was my reindeer and I was Santa Claus, bringing joy to my family.

The Nativity scene was still a mystery to me. Who was that child in a cradle surrounded by his parents, and their friends dressed in biblical robes? The manger's donkey and sheep caught most of my attention. I thought they would make good additions for my toy collection. I wondered if this nomadic group moved into the gingerbread house on blustery nights. I feared for them thinking it may have been the witch's house from Hansel and Gretel. I knew if I tasted the white icing or the yellow, blue, or red gum drops that rested on the roof of the house the witch would grab me into her clutches. Would the witch make them into those cookie-shaped people with frozen smiles and three buttons running down their bellies?

The toys filling these Christmas displays made my eyes light up as if they were the stars on top of the tree. The list I sent to Santa now appeared before my eyes: FBI cap gun, Hopalong Cassidy lunch box, a green feathered Robin Hood hat with bow, quiver and arrows and U.S. Army Tommy gun.

I had watched the Christmas TV specials – Chanukah TV shows were nonexistent in the Fifties – so I knew the holiday rules. I displayed no pouts, shouts, or cries during December. I understood Santa's toy-giving powers to the "good" kids – even though our apartment had no chimney and we were Jewish – because of my exemplary behavior and on Christmas Eve I left him a glass of cold milk and a sugar cookie. Santa did not fail me and I repaid his kindness 30 years later when, as a Cub Scout pack leader, I played his role to 100 cheering Cub Scouts.

On Chanukah, we lit the candles on the menorah, sang the prayers and *I Have a Little Dreidel,* spun the dreidel, clapped our hands on winning, ate hot *latkes* covered with sour cream or apple sauce and chocolate coins melted in our mouths. The festival of lights and family always surrendered to the glitter of Christmas.

My father worked at the Middletown State Mental Hospital. This hospital opened in 1874. In 1870, the legislature established the state lunatic asylum for "the care and treatment of the insane and inebriate upon the principles of the medicine known as homoeopathic."

In 1955, the hospital still had the original main building with its imposing Gothic towers. Here my father worked as a resident, studying to become a psychiatrist. Dad had already acquired the skill of being a great listener. However he loved healing. He said, "Working with the mentally disturbed is challenging.

I need to see my patients get healthy, and at this state hospital it is a rarity."

I loved Middletown for two reasons. The first being, that in this *Leave It to Beaver* town, I fell in love with my first blond-haired *shiksa* (a gentile woman). She was so beautiful that my pupils dilated every time I saw her. Not being quite as naïve as the Beaver, I knew the meaning of the gold band on her finger. She was married to the handsome young doctor who worked in the same hospital as my dad.

I could not take my eyes off of her. The way she sat in her tight blue jeans on our apartment building stoop, with her silky blond hair tied in a ponytail begging to be tugged. Her short-sleeved white blouse was knotted above her belly button. I wanted to kiss that midriff section of her body and run my fingers through her hair.

When she smiled at or spoke to me it was like manna from Heaven, a gift from the Almighty. Life was good.

I remembered how this Blondie proved to me I was a heterosexual, by causing my five year old penis to stand at attention.

She was a perfect ten. I would later use her as a standard against which only four other *shiksas* ever measured up. I was a categorizer, a maker of lists, a person who put people into boxes so that they could be easily understood.

Just as the Nazis had created discriminatory guidelines based on one's Jewish ancestral heritage, they boxed people into categories, and so did I. They had their *mischling* scale I had my *shiksa* scale.

A *mischling* in German means a mutt, a mongrel or a half-breed. I recalled reading about the signs posted in the twenties and thirties at the front desk of hotels in Germany, as well as in the States: NO JEWS OR DOGS ALLOWED. In Germany they added an extra two words: ARYANS ONLY.

Many German Jews converted to Christianity, thinking it made them as German as any of their neighbors. Hitler did not agree. If a practicing Protestant German had two Jewish grandparents, he or she was designated as a *mischling* of the first degree. A German with one Jewish grandparent was a *mischling* of the second degree. The 1935 Nuremberg laws did not care about what religion a person practiced. The laws applied to blood lines.

I realized the blood flowing to my little head had been manipulated by Madison Avenue and Hollywood. The pop culture idolized blondes. They brainwashed me to draw the dividing lines on degrees of *shiksas*. They bombarded me in weekly issues of *Life* and *Look* with blonde models hawking all kinds of products. If I drove my car, billboards extolled their beauty, cleanliness and sexiness wrapped in one package. To entice my proclivity toward blondes, *Time* (or was it *Newsweek?*) plastered Twiggy's elf-like face on their cover.

Hollywood rendered a plethora of magnificent *shiksas*: from Harlow to a naked Cybill Shepard standing on a diving board removing her bikini top and bottom in *The Last Picture Show*. *Playboy* magazine filled my eyes with topless-blonde-virginal-girl-next-door types as well as America's favorite blonde bombshell, Marilyn Monroe.

Monroe posed on a rumpled red velvet sheet, and her nude picture catapulted the magazine (called *Stag Party* at the time) into a financial success. In the photo, her eyes were almost shut and her mouth slightly opened as her fingers caressed the red velvet as if she was touching herself. Hugh Hefner had paid five hundred dollars to place that photo in his first magazine. That edition sold out – seventy thousand copies!

Who could forget the virginal purity of Laura Dern in *Blue Velvet* or the grapefruit-sized breasts of Jane Mansfield almost falling out of her pink satin dress? Every decade of American movies had those blondes who I would pray for. From magnetic bombshell Jean Harlow with her silky platinum blonde hair to Betty Grable, the number one pin-up girl for American GIs during WWII. Betty's legs were insured by her movie studio for a million dollars by Lloyds of London. Grable's

1943 bestselling bathing suit poster hung wherever American soldiers were stationed. With her blonde hair curled on top of her head, she posed wearing a white swimsuit which showed off those million dollar gams and her two million dollar butt. Her tight butt flew off the glossy photo and landed squarely in my eyes. Throughout my life from West to Fawcett to Anderson to Rodgers to Madonna to Dickinson to Deneuve, these blondes created a tableau of Western beauty.

I knew why these Jewish producers and directors favored blondes. They, like I, craved the taste of forbidden fruit. These assimilationists obsessed on hot *shiksa trafe,* loving its non-Kosher flavor as much as King Kong desired Fay Wray snatch. They knew their mothers would disapprove of the lustful habits and their insatiable desires but they acquired a taste for lobster, shrimp and bacon. A well-prepared pork chop became their culinary treasure. These *trafe*-eating movie creators repelled their religious beliefs as readily as King Kong swatted airplanes from the top of the Empire State Building. Their fixation was well known but hardly ever discussed with the possible exception of the Roth household.

Phillip Roth presented Alex Portnoy's mother as a complainer, a *kvetch.* "What did their Jewish mothers do to them to cause such acts of rebellion? Were they the less-loved sibling? Did their mothers drive them into the clutches of these women?

Did their mothers make them into self-loathing Jews? Did their mothers push them too hard to find success, to become a "doctor" and to make a good living so that they would be able to take care of them in old age? "

Portnoy fancied blonde *shiksas* because he was a child of Hollywood, Madison Avenue and American television and so was I.

Googling the issue I found that no research papers have been written on the subject of the unholy alliance between Hollywood Jewish big shots and their irrational preoccupation with beautiful blonde Gentile women. I did find some racial nationalist (Neo-Nazi) websites voicing their hatred of Jews and their blonde Christian girlfriends. The propaganda sounded as if it was written by Goebbels. Even Marilyn's death was blamed on the Hollywood Jewish crowd.

Little did I know that these CEOs of Hollywood were more interested in making money than in protecting their religious brethren in Europe. In the thirties, they had cut a deal with Hitler. The Nazis would let them distribute their movies in Germany in exchange for Hollywood not producing any anti-Nazi movies. I wondered why the major studios never made a movie about *Kristallnacht* or the plight of the Jews in the camps or the destruction of Jewish life in Germany. I thought they feared an anti-Semitic backlash in America. I was wrong. They feared the loss of profits. While money was rolling into their wallets, they were unwilling to rock the boat. They allowed a German official in Los Angeles to decide what films to make for American movie audiences. They created their unholy trinity: money, hiding their identity and blondes.

I pictured the faces of Jack Warner, Harry Cohn, Louis B. Mayer substituted in that infamous Nazi photo taken in Berlin where a pretty, young blonde Christian women stands next to her large-eared, short Jewish husband with a paper sign hanging around her neck. The sign said something like, "I am a pig because I married and sleep with this Jew."

Perhaps, subconsciously, these Hollywood moguls injected their fatal attraction for blondes into the blood of young Jewish-American movie fans. Maybe King Kong was not a metaphor about Black males but a moral lesson for Jewish men. You mess with *shiksas* and the world's armies will hunt you down and shoot you.

Now I knew why *King Kong* was one of Hitler's favorite films. Ben Urwand, author of *The Collaboration* said, "He spoke of it often and had it screened several times." Here we had something in common. I had often spoken of *King Kong* and had watched it multiple times on the *Million Dollar Movie.* He and I both liked some Laurel and Hardy films as well as Mickey Mouse cartoons. Adolf obsessed about movies. Almost every night before going to bed he watched a film.

Did Adolf think the gorilla represented the Jews? Did he not understand that anti-Semitism had not killed off the religion for over two thousand years but that blonde beauties were much more deadly? My grandmother, Rose, said it best in Yiddish, this situation represented a real *shonda*, a real shame and a real pity.

My shame was that these blonde bombshells all made it to the top of my *shiksa* scale. To reach this top tier, my ideal blonde needed: a head covered in curls, her triangle wrapped with a growth of silky hairs, a 36/24/36 inch figure, armor-piercing blue eyes, dimples, a Donna Reed smile, the talent to pout, flirt and climax on cue, the knack to release a torrent of sexually-charged filthy words as she reached orgasm and a cute Betty Boop bubble butt.

This model of my desire wears no tattoos, not on her ass, nor on her breast. She has allowed no man to incise any marks on her body – a biblical ban that I obey based on the concept that G-d's creations need no artistic improvements.

When I observed such *shiksas* strolling in the Broward Mall, dressed in knee-high black leather boots, I pictured them naked, except for the boots. Their hands partially covering their triangles, which left their breasts and some pubic hairs exposed for my viewing. I rotated around them to view their protruding butts, imagining my hands cupping the curvature of their butts and then my fingers digging into their fleshy derrieres.

I shut my eyes and refocused. I remembered a blonde experience. I sat with my a black-booted blonde in a small dark café. Across from each other we whispered words of love. She had already blessed me with my favorite type of kisses, stolen ones. And, not just any ordinary stolen kisses, but those deep-probing ones where tongues craved for the taste of tonsils.

My ears captured every word that floated from her hot lips into my welcoming ears.

In our eyes, we viewed the reflections of our images like convex lenses in a Kodak.

As our eyes flirted, I slipped out of my loafers, extending a sock-covered foot between her legs and I touched her soft inner calves and thighs. My toes crawled from her ankle to the space just below her pubic patch. They ached to reach her Venus fur.

Wishing my feet were bare, I repeated these movements as she clenched her legs around my foot, as if a boa constricting the life out of me. I loved her lack of facial response, only I knew what was happening. I continued nonstop oblivious to the waiter approaching the table. My heart rate rose as did my penis during this act of semi-public sexual abandon.

I continued rubbing her legs as the waiter whispered, "Have you two lovers decided what you want?"

I smiled, looked in her eyes, then turned my head in waiter's direction and replied, "Sorry young man, not yet, could you please give us a few more minutes."

The waiter left in silence as my foot got back to business.

I had had my time with *shiksas*, as well as, as my time with Jewesses. Biblical permission for my activities was found right there in the Good Book, Ecclesiastes 3:1: There is a time for everything, and a season for every activity under heaven.

I remembered being in the audience at a Pete Seeger concert, held in the auditorium of a worn-out Fallsburgh Central High School. I added some lyrics to the biblical verse.

I listened to the Byrds' version of song in my Mustang as Cousin Brucie, on AM 770 WABC discussed its history. While driving, I composed new lines and belted them out the opened window.

A time for lust and a time for love.
A time to hold on and a time to let go.
A time to take risks and a time for silence.
A time for obsession and a time for confession.
A time for faith and a time for disbelief.
A time for fear and a time for bravery.

A time for experimentation and a time for tradition.
A time for unconditional love and a time for love with conditions.
To Everything (Turn, Turn, Turn)
There is a season (Turn, Turn, Turn)
And a time for every purpose, under Heaven

Many seasons had come and gone, but I now hit my "memories rewind" button and push down on play to relive those activities under heaven and in small dark cafes.

The second reason I loved Middletown was that in this quaint town, I observed my first totally naked female. My dad wanted to show me where he worked, so he gave me a tour of the hospital. As we walked through the second floor of the main wing of mental hospital, I froze in front of a room with a large barred observation window.

There she was in all her glory. I saw all of her. For some reason only known to this Botero-sized nude, she hated wearing clothes and seemed to love exposing herself.

I observed her in a room that looked and smelled more like a jail cell. She clutched the cell's metal bars extending and contracting her arms as if she was Mighty Joe Young trying to bend them in her attempt to escape confinement. Her glorious one-hundred-and-fifty-pound body bounced against the cold steel as her long raven-black hair swung from side to side. Her ample breasts shook as if creating seismic waves on the magnitude of 7.0 on the Richter. Howls flew from her mouth and penetrated my ears. I did not try to decipher them, for I concentrated on her triangular patch.

My erection rose to full attention. I wanted to get closer to her, to take a whiff and touch her treasure. As I held my dad's hand, I wondered if he knew in advance that this nude would make this grand appearance in front of his five-year-old son. But I never asked.

Like a Polaroid, my blinking eyes continued to take in all of her, focus, click and develop. Her large tender breasts, with half-dollar sized nipples and a magnificent black muff dug deep into my psyche. Then out of nowhere, she extended her arm, pointed her index finger straight at me and screamed. "Young man, what are you looking at?"

I drew back a step and tried to find my father's hand.

That same index finger now pointed at her hairy black triangle. Then in an animalistic guttural tone she shouted, "You really want a taste of this, don't you sweetie? You really want a whiff of this, don't you honey?"

I froze in terror as if a stone statue in an Parisian park.

Now she extended both of her arms in my direction. With her thumbs pointing toward the ceiling, her index fingers aiming at me and her three lower digits curled in a ball, as if she held two six shooters pointed. She leered and screamed, "You will always be a slave of women!"

To this day, this unforgettable moment, lays imprisoned in my brain. A crazy witch had put a curse on me. Was she possessed with a *dybbuk?* Had the evil spirit of a dead person entered her body, or was it the devil himself speaking those words?

I found and jerked my father's hand in the direction of the hallway. "Dad, I'm afraid. Let's get away from that crazy lady. She's really scary."

He let out and audible laugh and said, "Son, don't worry about her. Not all women are that crazy."

The first reason I loved the town of Woodridge occurred three years after the naked mentally-ill witch's curse. My jungle gym mate, Nancy, now an eight-year-old, came to my house to play. After Twinkies (or was it Devil Dogs) and cold milk, we entered the living room. My living room was large rectangular-shaped room filled with couches, chairs, a fireplace, china cabinets and light oak book shelves. These were the couches where my father told his friends his gas chamber story.

In these cabinets and on those shelves sat an array of fancy liquor bottles bought in Italy, hand-crafted figurines of geese, ducks, horses, peasants and European nobility, a two hundred year old Meissen clock adorned with cherubs, a collection of books about World War Two and a set of the World Book Encyclopedia. I ignored these items, concentrating on Nancy's movements.

"Let's sit behind this couch. It's a good place for a game of hide-and-seek." She whispered. I followed her and we sat on the floor behind a beige couch. She then popped the question. "Have you ever played doctor?"

With all the naiveté of an eight-year-old I replied. "No, but my dad is a doctor. Do you want me to get his medical bag?

"The medical bag is not necessary. We won't need it to play."

"Well then, how do you play?" I asked.

She smiled upon seeing the excitement in my eyes. "Well, we take off all of our clothes and we examine each other's bodies, just like doctors do."

She was cute and I was curious. "Sure let's do it."

In the corner of my living room, behind a sofa, on a plush white carpet, I quickly removed all of my clothes and watched with fascination as she slowly unbuttoned her blouse. Here I stood naked in front of her with my hands covering my privates watching as each item of her outfit hit the floor. There were the yellow cotton panties I had seen so often in the playground. I now realized why I selected yellow to be my favorite color. My lucky eyes viewed this prepubescent cutie in all her glory. Silently, I thanked the Almighty for answering my prayers.

"May I touch?" I asked as my hands fell to the sides of my body.

Slowly removing her eyes from my erect penis, she looked into my eyes and whispered, "No. Not today, maybe some other time."

I sat silent, not wanting a confrontation as the words, "maybe some other time," chimed in my head like the bells.

A minute later, my mouth was awash with the bitter flavor of slavery, more bitter than the *maror* that rested on my the Seder plate. That mentally-ill naked lady's curse had landed squarely on my shoulders. An eight-year-old girl had just made me her slave.

Returning to our chosen childhood profession, we continued performing our visual examinations. We studied each other's genitalia as if we were preparing for an anatomy class. Hearing a door creak, we jumped back into our clothes – no kisses, no touches just an everlasting memory.

The next day, when I saw Nancy at the Woodridge school bus stop, neither one of us spoke a word to each other. We did not mention our medical exploration. In fact we acted like it never happened. I wonder today if she has any memory of the event.

Eight years later, I caught my next eyeful. It came from a middle-aged redhead stripper. She was no looker but I was thrilled to be in her presence. While the sexually-charged music set to the beat of then highly popular Muriel Cigar commercial, which originally came from the musical *Sweet Charity,* rang in my ears, I sang out loud "The minute you walked in the joint… Hey big spender spend a little time with me."

The stripper jiggled out of one item of clothing at a time, from arm-length white gloves, to her sequined red dress, to her red brassiere and finally to her hot pink nylon panties. They all hit the dilapidated stage floor, like a fishing lure cast into a Catskill pond.

A cloud of cigarette smoke filled the room. I watched a patron blow smoke rings in the direction of the redhead as if he wanted the rings to lasso her pasty-covered nipples. My eyes and throat burned as I strained my vision to get a better look. I knew that men who went to see strippers had to smoke and drink in their presence. With reddened eyes I watched as her body gyrated as if high on drugs and alcohol. While her breasts bounced in tune to the music, I licked my lips and focused in on the pasties that covered her nipples. The men in the crowd catcalled "Take it all off honey. We want to see all of you."

Standing on the edge of the stage, the stripper pointed and curled her index finger at the men in the audience. She cooed and taunted, "Come on up here and let me show you a good time."

In the back of my head I heard, "You really want a taste of this, don't you sweetie? You really want a whiff of this, don't you honey?"

The male audience roared, while in the pit, a three-piece band – trumpet, trombone and piano – played David Rose's, *The Stripper.* My eyes strained as she covered and uncovered her reddish-brown patch with two large yellow ostrich feathers.

That night I got glimpses of the Promised Land but I still remained a slave.

Thirteen

Our Town

My hometown of Woodridge was Anatevka, transported 70 years in to the future. A town created in the mind of *Sholem Aleichem.* A town lifted from the Russian Pale, like Dorothy's Kansas home, only to land in Northeast America. A folksy village filled with the ancestors of Eastern European Jewry. A slice of the old country found in the new. And, to a few it was considered a utopia – the Jerusalem of the West.

In Woodridge the older women still wore brightly colored *babushkas* tied below their chins. My grandmother proudly walked down the town's commercial district, Broadway or Main Street, with her headscarf protecting her hairdo. While the town's younger men broke their grandfather's traditions and religious codes by shaving off most of their facial hair, they wanted to become Americanized while living in small-town America.

We lived in a Chagall mural filled with chickens, horses, goats, dairy cows, farmers, *dybbuks,* peasants and newlyweds. In my town you could buy a goat, lay your hands on its head, and transfer your sins into the body of the ruminant . Of course to make the magic atonement-exercise work you then had to take the goat to the woods and set it free. Many a time I saw a goat foraging in the woods behind Dead Man's Canyon and wondered whose sins it carried.

Our town possessed the inhabitants of a *Sholem Aleichem* village. It mirrored the *shtetls* of Eastern Europe, filled with professionals, semi-professionals, and beggars – a fully incorporated village with a Rabbi, a village idiot, three doctors, two lawyers, two accountants, one mattress maker, two butchers, two bakers, three grocers, two house painters, two druggists, one red-headed carpenter, and at least one family of gangsters.

Our town also possessed culture. Starting in the thirties, the *Grine Felder* (Green Fields) bungalow colony became the summer home to major Yiddish playwrights and authors, like Isaac Bashvevis Singer. According to Dr. Fernhoff's daughter, Rosina, she absorbed music, poetry and drama while watching *Grine Felder's* young residents perform. As her father's chauffeur, she drove her father on house calls (as I did for my Dad years later) to the colony. Even the colony's bungalows were named after famous Yiddish writers like *Sholem Aleichem.*

It was often said that if you drove fast enough through the village – breaking the town's speed limit of 15 miles per hour – it took on the appearance of Anatevka with one major exception, life was not nearly as precarious as a fiddler performing on a roof.

The locals knew Woodridge was filled with *dybbuks,* sinners, and miracle workers. These folks' indiscretions were our town secrets, not to be discussed with outsiders. Woodridge possessed a number of married men and women with sexual urges that could only be quenched by cheating on their spouses with members of different faiths. The town's orchids were laden with low hanging forbidden fruit, arms extended skyward struggling to grab it.

Many older Yiddish-speaking locals had read the short stories of Isaac Bashevis Singer in *The Forward.* His stories taught them the price of fulfilling their temptations. The sinners knew their actions opened the doors for *dybbuks* to creep into their bodies. They were willing to pay the price for forbidden pleasures.

Singer had visited the Catskills as a summer tourist. He understood the types of people that congregated in Woodridge. He had lived with their relatives in pre-war Poland. He knew all towns had their share of gamblers, kleptomaniacs, petty hoods and petty thieves, whore mongers, arsonists, and future murderers. Woodridge had them all.

In Woodridge the line between the sane and the insane was often impressionistically blurred. Those who talked aloud to themselves were not that unusual. An observer who possessed a keen eye could spot the deranged as they strolled Broadway or Main with slight hunches as if *dybbuks* cleaved, clanged, and stuck their claws into their backs. Jewish folklore and Freud understood the power of their sexual urges, desires so strong that only an exorcist could purge them. Those that crossed way over the line found themselves confined to the Middletown State Hospital.

Woodridge was an Old Testament town surrounded by a New Testament nation, a town possessed by ghosts that had studied the *Kabbalah* as well as Washington Irving's *The Legend of Sleepy Hollow,* a small-minded town located 90 miles from the greatest city on Earth. A small town filled with wisdom , wit and gossip.

In the fifties, Woodridge had a winter population of close to a thousand people; Jews and gossipers composed eighty percent of it. The town's census had hardly changed in the last 60 years. When I lived there in its heyday, the fifties and the sixties, a resident could name most of the families that lived there.

From Memorial Day up to Labor Day, the number of Jewish families in the town tripled due to their influx of tourists from New York City.

To get out of the City's smog-filled cement canyons, they rented every hotel room and bungalow in the area. As they drove north through the mountains and green pastures, many spotted their first dairy cow or deer. Their children roared with laughter as a cow lifted its tail in the air and released a load. This was nature at its best.

These tourists guzzled the cold mountain-cleansed water and inhaled lungfuls of Catskill Mountain air. For two months their bodies and souls were cleansed.

During the day, they swam and sunbathed in their hotel pools, fished in the ponds, and played games of badminton, soft ball and *mah jong*. Over campfires, they roasted hot dogs and marshmallows on fresh sticks of maple remembering that their ancestors cooked lamb in this manner for thousands of years. For these vacationers, these three months were their most cherished time of the year.

The two commercial streets in the town were named Broadway and Main Street. This was a self-sufficient town, a town which provided every commodity and service. Broadway consisted of: an opened-in-the-summer-only movie theater; a church for the village's few Black families; Leff's Shoe and Sporting Goods Store, famous for the dust that obscured the brands of the sneakers lining the storefront window; Ritner's Grocery, where I made my daily trip for my chocolate fix of Ring Dings, Devil Dogs or Yankee Doodles; Themes Law Office; a liquor store with porcelain horse-shaped-Kentucky-Derby-winners liquor bottles in the window; Slater's Garage and Gas Station; Sol's, Charley's and Chonin's Luncheonettes; an Associated Cooperative Insurance Company; and my father's and his competitors' medical offices.

Charley's claim to fame was the proprietor's ability to fry a hamburger while a two inch long ash hung off of his cigarette. Spectators marveled at his skill in flicking the ash right before it would have landed on the burger. During the summer Charley hung rolls of fly paper from the restaurant's ceiling. You could not help noticing the thousands of flies stuck to these oily-yellowish strips of paper. Between the ashes and the flies, eating at Charley's often killed my appetite.

Main Street's stores started on top of a hill and continued downward toward the train station and Silver Lake. The street consisted of approximately thirteen stores. There were: two drug stores, Levine's and Rashkin's – Rashkin's eight-seat soda fountain was the town's popular meeting place ; Proyect's Fruit and Fish Market; two butcher shops; Kessler's and Kagan's – both bearing the word "Kosher" in Hebrew letters on their store front windows. When I strolled downtown I often wondered how Woodridge would have looked if *Kristallnacht* had occurred in the Catskills.

Abe's Candy Store had an obligatory pinball machine, a large newspaper rack and lots of girlie magazines. The magazines were pre-Playboy editions, with women dressed in tight swimsuits and posed in provocative positions without a nipple showing. Abe's was my hang out, where I went after school to take out my frustrations.

I cursed, banged and pounded the pinball as if it was a Nazi. I listened to the machine's pings and pangs as my scores rose in my attempt to win a free game. I prayed the machine would not tilt, while glancing at the scantily-clad babes on magazine covers. Abe was a law abiding citizen. He would not let me or any other juvenile handle those "girlie" magazines. To feed my chocolate addiction, I bought nickel egg creams and Chunky bars. I usually left Abe's in a relaxed and happy state of mind.

On the top of the hill rested Hechtman's Hardware Store. In this hardware store I purchased my masculinity: my BB gun, my hatchet, my tri-pronged fishing spears, my boxes filled with .22 caliber ammo containing either 50 short or long shells, my Bowie hunting knife housed in its leather sheath, my razor-sharp hunting arrows, and my bone-handled pocket knives. With these weapons I fantasized my encounters with Nazi soldiers.

At nighttime I'd walk by the yellow and blue neon flickering sign of the Kentucky Club, a dark, beer-smelling saloon made famous because gangster, Legs Diamond, frequented the establishment. I pictured Legs standing next to the Kentucky Club's long ornate bar holding a whiskey, surrounded by admiring locals, telling tales about his exploits in the underworld.

Legs, born Jack Moran, was the one and only celebrity in Woodridge. Diamond was a prohibition era Irish-American murderous hood. Legs became a close associate of Arnold Rothstein, the infamous gambler who fixed the 1919 Black Sox World Series. Assassins shot and hit Legs with gunfire on three separate occasions. He survived and recovered but on the hit men's fourth attempt, Legs' luck ran out. I wondered if Legs ever had any encounters with the members of the Catskills Mountain Ku Klux Klan Chapter.

Those were the town's grand old days when Woodridge had its own gangsters and a thriving train station on the New York, Ontario, and the Western Railroad Line.

Years later, a highlight of my country day was watching the arrival and the departure of those trains. On the station's platform, which opened on to Main Street, New York City passengers grasped their children and their valises as if a Nazi guard stood next to them. My nose inhaled the sweet odors of the locomotive's diesel engines. My lungs burned from the smoke as if I had just smoked a cigarette. My small hands covered my ears to deaden the sound of the train's screeching brakes, that awful sound of steel wheels scraping against steel rails. The train moaned, clanged and belched steamed into the air. To my five-year-old mind the locomotive appeared as a large iron monster.

I studied each car on the train from the locomotive to the caboose. I counted all the box and cattle cars. These were the same type cattle cars I saw on television, the ones that transported my father and millions of Jews to the camps. I pictured each cattle car crammed with a hundred suffocating Jews.

As you are now aware, the village had been previously known as Centerville. I asked the locals why the name had changed. The Jewish version of the story went something like this. Some Sullivan County Gentiles had a problem with the growing number of Jews moving into Centerville. This, I find hard to believe. So these Gentiles started calling the village, "Jewville" or "Yidville." The town's Hebrew population met to think up a solution. Using their Yiddish *kups* they decided to change the name of the town to Woodridge. They realized that the Gentiles with their *Goyishe kups* would never figure out to call the town "Jewridge."

These same Jewish folks had another story about the discriminatory days in the 1920s and 30s. The Ku Klux Klan had a chapter nestled in the heart of Sullivan County. The Klan made life miserable for their new, unwelcome arrivals. When the harassment became intolerable the Yids called in some favors and asked an organization from New York City to address the problem.

Members of "Murder Incorporated" or the "Brownsville Boys" drove up to the mountains with their violin cases in hand. Their ninety-mile drive featured rolling mountains covered with maples and evergreens. They learned who the culprits were and bullet-ridden bodies appeared floating in the crystal waters of Kiamesha Lake.

The coroner announced in the local paper, "The victim's bodies were riddled with bullets, .45 ACP cartridges, from a Thompson sub-machine gun. These 'Tommy Guns' are favored by American criminals because they are reliable, high volume, semi-automatic weapons. They are expensive but gangsters love using them."

The constables never collared the shooters. The local police force's failure was blamed on its size. The shooters were safely ensconced in the "Big Apple" after making a two-hour drive on Route 17 back into their Brooklyn homes.

With smiles on their faces, the town gossips crowed, "Those anti-Semitic bastards got what they deserved. Let their tormented souls, filled with hundreds of bullet holes, cry at the gates of Hell."

I asked, "Do you know what happened to that Sullivan County Klan chapter?"

"It ceased to exist and it never again reared its ugly head."

I believed these stories. I assumed embellishments but I wanted them to be true – strong, machine-gun toting Jews addressing evil and hatred with streams of bullets.

I also believed that having a large Jewish plurality in the village made most of the local anti-Semites tight-lipped.

Now that I think about it, in my whole life I have only been subjected to a handful of anti-Semitic acts: one time, a drunken Notre Dame football fan in the Orange Bowl cursed the Hurricanes football team because of the number of Jewish students attending the university. Another time, an Austrian hotel keeper would not rent my fiancée and me a room because we "looked Jewish."

The game was in the final quarter. The stadium filled to capacity. The Hurricanes were beating the crap out of Notre Dame. Their mascot, a leprechaun, stood with his fists in a fighting position wearing an Irish country hat and a green suit.

I stood behind this red-faced Notre Dame cap and jersey-wearing fanatic. On his cap were embroidered the letters "N" and "D." A leprechaun covered his jacket which reeked of the beer. I watched him point his index finger in the direction of numerous Black Hurricane football players. He yelled, "You Jew Bastards! You stink worse than my grandmother's sneakers. Yids get off this football field."

I looked at my oldest child, Jason, and in a loud voice boomed , "Is that Irish prick so drunk that he thinks Hank Greenberg is on the field."

Jason laughed.

"Does this clown really represent the Fighting Irish?" I asked.

In the Orange Bowl din I knew the players on the field could not hear him. But I wondered if they would have laughed or been upset having been mistaken for Jews.

As the bum continued his anti-Semitic rant, I became more and more pissed. I glared at him and with my fists clenched, I screamed into his ear, "Notre Dame stinks worst than your grandmother's twat. Your leprechaun isn't fit to be the toilet paper our players use to wipe their asses. Based on the score neither are your football players. Drop dead you alcoholic anti-Semitic bastard!"

My rant worked. Mr. I-Hate-Jews sat down. He remained seated and quiet for the rest of the game.

To me, this type anti-Semitic rant was a rarity. But my father heard thousands of them in Poland, Russia and Germany. It made sense for him to select a town where he and his family would be free of religious intolerance and for me to select a university where a high percentage of my brethren attended.

Fourteen

Traveling Buddies

During the summer of my junior year in college, my friend, Neal Cohen and I travelled throughout Western Europe and the northern tip of West Africa. Neal was a heavy-set, risk-taking adventurer, and I was a skinny, risk-averse tourist.

He, like I, loved travel, food, and drugs. He, like I, loved history – especially American and European history. We could talk about World War II for hours. We could talk about Jews, Nazis, and Blacks for days and we did.

He adored wearing designer clothes and I owned none. He sported Louis Vuitton belts and Gianni Versace shirts long before the kids in our high school knew about fashion designers. Neal's taste in fashion also ran in the direction of Jim Morrison. He copied the leather pants and silky shirts.

Neal, due to being overweight, had visited Dr. Robert Atkins' clinic in Manhattan. He did this before Atkins wrote his world-famous revolutionary diet book. Neal and his mom drove to Manhattan for consultations. He came back with a message for his classmates, "Carbohydrates are the bad guys." I thought it interesting that Neal was on a high protein meat diet and that his father was the town's butcher.

Neal did lose some weight but he always regained it. Kicking the carb addiction would be as hard as not smoking pot or dropping acid. However these trips afforded him quality time with his mother. She would drive their black Chrysler Imperial on these shopping adventures on Fifth Avenue and to Sam Goody's.

In high school, Neal became my Catskill Mountain travelling buddy. He was an adventurer who failed to smell fear until it hit him in the head. In our Ford Mustangs – mine red and his white – we ventured to Tim Leary's Millbrook compound and to Bob Dylan's country home in Woodstock. We left both properties at their front gates, never gaining entrance or access to see our idols.

We drove to Greenwich Village to see the hippies, buy flowery shirts, yellow, blue, and green beaded necklaces, and blue bell-bottom jeans. On my return to Woodridge, my dad, upon seeing me in my new jeans said, "Those pants make you look gay."

"Dad, do you mean 'gay' as in happy or 'gay' as in homosexual?"

He ignored the question. So in true hippie style and to get his goat, I wore those striped bell-bottoms for the next seven days.

One year later when I saw my father wearing a pair of bell-bottoms, I exclaimed, "Dad, when did you become gay?" He laughed. I smiled. Payback was sweet.

In 1968, as Yippies (Youth International Party members), Neal and I traveled to Chicago for the 1968 Democratic Presidential Convention. We were risk-takers. We protested with Abbie Hoffman and Jerry Rubin. We listened to Allen Ginsberg chanting OM, the most sacred Hindu syllable.

We listened to Norman Mailer tell us he was standing right behind us in our hour of battle, but unfortunately he was on deadline for a book; his editor was nagging him so he had to leave Chicago that night. Mr. Machismo would not be a soldier in the armies of the night.

We sang dirges in the dark like "I Ain't Marching Anymore." Phil Ochs stood with us that awful night, a night when the Chicago police rioted. On orders from Mayor Richard Daly, they shot hundreds of canisters of tear gas into groups of protestors and charged the crowd with their billy clubs.

With our eyes burning and our esophagi constricting, Neal and I held our ground and continued shouting at the TV cameras, "The whole world is watching! The whole world is watching!"

We stood locked arm-in-arm with those anti-Vietnam War protestors as they were surrounded and clubbed. The police held their shields in one arm while swinging their truncheons with the other. We cried out as protestors fell to the ground. Their heads bloodied, we listened to their screams of anguish. We had seen enough brutality, blood, and anguish so we scurried to the safety found on the edges of Lincoln Park, and like Norman Mailer, we left Chicago.

The whole world did watch. Democratic nominee Hubert Humphrey lost the presidential election and Republican Richard Nixon, the winner, "eventually" got us out of the Vietnam War. Our protest had helped him get elected but what choices did we have?

During that war, President Nixon attended a University of Miami football game. The crowd cheered him waving hundreds of rebel flags. Those Confederate flags with their blue "X" and white stars in a field of bright red made my stoned eyes see visions of psychedelic sheets blowing in the wind.

As the game progressed, multitudes of Hurricane fans screamed, "Kill! Kill! Kill!" as if they were charging through the jungles of South Vietnam. The Orange Bowl's loud speakers bellowed, "We are honored to have President Richard Milhouse Nixon with us today to watch this great football rivalry. Let us give a loud-rousing southern welcome to our great president, Richard Milhouse Nixon."

His name echoed across the stadium. Nixon stood to acknowledge the crowd's applause. He waved both arms in the air raising two victory fingers in both of his hands. The crowd roared, as I sat stoned, holding a foot-long hot dog smothered in mustard and relish in my left hand. In my right hand I held a Hurricane-season schedule plastic cup of ice-cold Coke. I looked in the direction of the president and wondered if I had the balls to boo.

I didn't.

A year later, as a skinny, long-haired hippie I went for my draft physical, a day I dreaded for months. My lottery draft number was 55 which meant that if drafted I'd be sent to Nam. I wore my blue bell-bottom jeans and inside the pocket of those jeans I was armed with two medical letters.

I had vigorously protested against the war and if I passed this physical exam, I could have become part of it. In a room full of 18-21 year old males, I stood in my boxer shorts. The doctor said, "Drop them and cough." I did, and he found and touched what I had lacked at the Orange Bowl.

They took my blood-pressure, probed my ears, and stuck a tongue depressor deep down my throat. They weighed and measured me. They tested my vision as well as my brain. They requested I do some jumping jacks and squats. And the doctors read the two letters I presented to them.

The doctor said. "I read the two letters you presented me from your eye and knee doctor. Your eyes are good enough for this man's army but your knee is not. Son, your bum knee is going to keep you out of serving your duty to this nation and possibly fighting in the war. Today you may think you are blessed. But I guarantee you; one day you will question your manhood. And on that day, you will wonder if you had the balls to fight for your life and kill other men. That's the opportunity you're giving up today."

I heard his words but they fell on deaf ears.

My ears rang with joy and politely I replied, "Thank you sir, for imparting that valuable piece of information and your heart-felt wisdom. Is there a pay phone on this floor?"

The doctor ignored my question and moved on to the next examinant.

Walking out the door of the recruitment office, I thought about how I had avoided my chance to participate in that bloody war due to a football knee injury. Joe Namath and I had something in common, knees that were keeping us out of the war.

How ironic that a sport played in the Orange Bowl, where seventy thousand Dixie-flag-waving-football fans screamed "KILL, KILL, KILL!" to encourage the University of Miami's team to cream their opponents, saved me from entering the world's most aggressive death sport.

Upon learning of my "4F" status, I dressed and I ran out of the army recruitment office. Through the basement of the Monticello Courthouse, I searched for a pay phone.

Near the exit, I found one. I dropped a dime in the slot, dialed my parents' number and smiled. After just one ring, on separate phone lines my dad and mom both answered. "Hello, Hello."

"Mom, Dad, Great news!"

And then I belted out the lyrics to "I'm Free" from the Who's rock opera, *Tommy.*

"I'm free, I'm free and freedom tastes of reality."

I doubted that they had ever heard the song, but I knew my parents got the message. My dad said, "We will talk when you get home. Thanks for calling to tell us the news. Bye."

Driving my mother's maroon Mustang back to my house, I stuck my left arm out of the window, letting my hand foil through the cool air. The Catskills backdrop of greens, browns and blues all appeared brighter. A white cloud of relief floated past my eyes as I kept singing, "I'm free, I'm free, and freedom tastes of reality."

Fifteen

Tangiers

The next summer, Neal and I were fortunate enough to make a grand tour of Europe. We travelled from near the Arctic Circle in Narvik, Norway to southern Spain, Italy, and Morocco. We roamed the continent using our unlimited train-travel Eurail passes. Every day was an adventure. That day we journeyed through France on our way to Spain.

In silence I sat in my first-class seat staring out at the moving French countryside. I observed healthy dairy cows, Jerseys and Holsteins, grazing in green pastures.

"Neal, do you realize that the rails we are riding on are the same ones that transported the Jews to the camps?"

"Yup. Pretty hard to believe."

Hearing in his voice that he did not want to talk about the war against the Jews, I dropped the subject. I returned to picturing French families being herded on to rail cars on the journey toward death.

On that train to Madrid I met my first admitted Nazi soldier. He was one of the millions of German soldiers who swore their alliance to Adolph Hitler. I pictured him with his middle and index finger raised up and his right thumb jutting out reciting it:

> *"I swear by G-d this sacred oath that I shall render unconditional obedience to Adolf Hitler, the Führer of the German Reich, supreme commander of the armed forces, and that I shall at all times be prepared, as a brave soldier, to give my life for this oath."*

He sat comfortably in the plush brown corduroy first-class seat across from Neal and I. He sat with the ease of a man who had experienced life. He was a well-groomed, German proud of his ancestry.

He introduced himself with a thick German accent. "My name is Hans. I am headed to Madrid on a business trip. You two guys sound and look like American college students. Where are you from?"

His accent reminded me of my father's. Examining his receding hairline, I determined that he was in his late thirties or early forties. He wore a deep tan, a broad smile, and a well-tailored tweed double-breasted business suit. The smell of 4711 *Eau de Cologne* emanated from his body. He was still physically fit and gave a manly appearance.

"You guessed right. We are from New York State. We are college students traveling through Europe to broaden our education. Based on your accent, I 'd guess you're German." Neal responded.

"Correct. I'm from Dusseldorf," he replied.

"Where did you learn to speak such good English?" I queried.

"During the Second World War, I was a prisoner-of-war in an American camp located in South Florida."

The temperature in the rail car dropped twenty degrees. My mouth froze and

I fell silent. I was talking to a German soldier.

Did I have the guts to look this man in the eyes and tell him that my parents were products of Hitler's concentration camps or to list the names of my relatives that were murdered by the Nazis?

I fell silent.

His smile and the tone in his voice revealed his attitude toward his capture by the American army. He considered himself one of the lucky ones. He lived out most of the war in the United States of America. He did not freeze to death in Russian snow and ice. He did not die in battle protecting Berlin from the Soviet Army.

Neal kept the banter with this German alive. I wondered if he had killed or harmed any Jews before he was shipped off to that Florida POW camp.

I felt yellow for not opening my mouth, for not asking him any questions about his tenure in the army. Was he a member of the Hitler Youth? Had he beaten or killed any Jews. I wanted to observe his reactions to these questions. Would he speak of his remorse, shame, or guilt? Would he shed a tear of cumulative guilt for the acts of his people.

I would never know because I did not ask.

I wondered if he knew we were Jews. Was he studying our reactions? If he had, he would have seen all color abandon my face. He would have observed my tongue freeze like a winter corpse in the Battle of Stalingrad.

After he bid us farewell and left the rail car in Madrid, I asked Neal, "Do you think that Nazi bastard knew we were Jews?"

"I don't give a shit. That happened 25 years ago." Neal then sang out, "Hotsy totsy we met a Nazi." Neal paused for a second then said, "He seemed like a pretty decent guy."

Now Neal had pissed me off. Was he doing this to egg me on? Would he next sing the German national anthem, *Deutschland,Deutschland über alles?*

I tried to keep my mouth shut but failed. Yiddish flowed from my mouth. *"Kush mir in tokhes!* Asshole!" You're giving me *tsuris!* Well, kiss my royal Jew ass, mother-fucker! I'm not in the mood."

Neal hushed. He stopped pushing my buttons.

We stopped for a coffee and a cigarette in the station's cafeteria. As we sipped and puffed, an American hippie dressed in an Arab robe lumbered by us.

"Hey dude, you from the States?" Neal inquired.

"Yeah man, I'm from San Francisco. My name is John. Where are you guys from?"

"John, we're Neal and Mort, from upstate New York. Where did you get that awesome Arab robe?" I asked.

John, the hippie, was tall, blonde, skinny, and stoned. The odor of hashish engulfed his body – a smell our noses knew well. He dressed in a hooded multi-colored Arab robe that hung to the station's cement floor.

In one long run-on sentence, John wowed us with tales of Moroccan days and nights. "Man you've got to go, the Moroccans are really nice folks, man dope is real cheap, it's the best hash you'll ever taste, man food is real cheap, in Tangiers you'll blow your brains out, you won't ever want to leave the place, it's far fucking out."

Then from under his robe, he reached into his shorts and pulled out a cardboard match box.

"Let me show you this shit." And just like a magician holding a deck of cards, John slowly opened the box. Our eyes lit up at the sight of five grams of soft yellow hash.

Neal nodded his approval. I knew our next adventure would take place in Morocco.

Over the screeching of train brakes, the hippie continued to give his pitch. "You guys can trade those faded blue jeans you're wearing for brand new Arab robes. You won't believe it. In the Kasbah hashish sells for a dollar a gram. An Arab guide will escort you to a dealer for a tip of few American bucks."

His words netted us in, like the sucker fish we trapped in our fishing nets in Woodridge.

My brain went into high gear. Weigh the pros and cons: What could go wrong for two Jewish kids in an Arab country? When it came to getting high, weren't we major risk-takers? Didn't that hippie just say how friendly the Moroccans were? Didn't Morocco have a Jewish community dating back to the days before the destruction of the Second Temple? Didn't Moses Maimonides live in Morocco? But I also remembered reading in my Junior Jewish Encyclopedia that for hundreds of years Moroccan Jews were forced to live in ghettos as second-class citizens.

As always, dope won. We were on the next south-bound train headed for southern Spain to meet a ship that would take us to the northern tip of Western Africa.

From the ship's railing we waved good-bye to Spain's coastline and focused on the Rock of Gibraltar. As the ship approached the port of Tangier, we marveled on seeing the old city with its minarets as well as its the modern European section.

We disembarked and were immediately assaulted by a wave of young Moroccan boys begging to be our city guides. A thirteen-year-old kid approached us, grabbed my arm, and pulled me aside.

"My name is Mohammed Ali. For one low price, I'll be your guide to the city. I'll take you to a clean hotel."

As I wondered where he learned to speak English so well, he lowered his voice, "Then I'll take you to the Kasbah to buy hashish?"

I nodded my approval.

Neal having heard the "H" word said, "Sounds great. Let's go."

Ali led us into the European Quarter via the *Rue De La Kasbah.* We walked by a street named Louis Pasteur, the great French scientist who discovered pasteurization. Ali stopped at a pastel-white stuccoed fort-styled hotel. "This is a clean hotel and the rooms are reasonably priced."

"Okay let's check in," Neal replied.

"Neal, do you remember studying the French colonization of Morocco?"

"Yup"

"I loved those French Foreign Legion movies where they fight the Arab cavalry. This Beau Gest hotel brings back memories. All it needs is a doorman dressed as Gary Cooper or Ronald Colman in that legionnaire's white *kepi* with a sash wrapped around his waist."

"Yup the doorman would stand at attention and salute us as we entered the hotel." Neal said.

The Hotel Sheherazade was built in the early forties. It looked like it came off the Casablanca movie set. We walked through the hotel's horseshoe-arched portico. The lobby's walls and floors were covered with glass mosaics and marble panels. The mosaics reflected sunlight which caused my eyes to blink, as if I had fallen into a kaleidoscope. I studied the glazed tiles looking for a drawing of Rick and Ilsa. I only found sketches of nomads riding camels, no Bogart and no Bergman. I scanned the bar – no piano, no Sam and no *As Time Goes By.*

Neal broke my train of thought, "Mort, we've got to check in."

I examined the decorative arabesque-patterned rug that hung behind the hotel's reception desk. The clerk, a thin man wearing a white linen suit asked, Welcome to the Sheherazade. Please fill out the hotel registration and I will need to hold your passports while you are guests."

We handed them to him, paid for one night's stay, and were given a key to our room. We rushed up the stairs as if Ali would leave us and not guide us to the hash dealer. After throwing our knapsacks on the beds, we washed the Saharan dust off of our faces and raced back to the lobby.

Our bar mitzvah-aged guide dressed in Levis whisked us into the Kasbah. We crossed through ancient white portals framed in blue and yellow tiles. The dust on the street caused my eyes and nose to twitch. Walking through narrow shaded alleys, we bumped into Arab men dressed in white caftans. In the short distance from the hotel to the Kasbah, we time-traveled from the twentieth century into the sixteenth.

My nostrils burned with a mixture of tobacco smoke, dog shit, and Middle Eastern grilled meats. As flies landed on its dropping, one mongrel tied to a post bore its rib cage and howled with hunger.

These odors melded together under a Saharan sun. They crawled though my nostrils, irritating my nose hairs which caused me to repeatedly sneeze.

"Gesundheit." Neal said.

"Thanks," I replied, thinking, " Yiddish in an Arab capitol – not too bright."

We halted in front of a two-story building after hearing Ali say, "We're here. Follow me up these steps."

On the second story, I focused on the door post and saw a smudge of brown paint. I imagined a mezuzah had once been nailed on the spot. I thought, "Is this an omen?" We entered a hole-in-the-wall apartment. My pupils expanded upon entering the dimly-lit living room.

Under an exposed 60-watt lightbulb stood a skinny, twenty-something, dark-skinned Moroccan. Ali introduced us, "Achmed, these are two Americans from New York. Neal and Mort, and they want to buy some of your most excellent hashish."

Achmed wore a red Polo shirt, blue Levis, and a pleasant smile. "Gentleman, welcome to Tangier."

At this point Ali interrupted, "Guys I have got to go back to the port so please pay me my guide fee."

We thanked Ali, paid him his fee, and watched him fly out the door. Our dealer continued in perfect English. "It is a pleasure to meet both of you. Please have a seat on these pillows. I will be right back."

As we sat down on the large decorative pillows, I examined the three-foot high, ornate silver hookah. It rested on the floor in the middle of the room surrounded by pillows. I studied the Persian carpets mounted on each wall.

"Neal look at each of these carpets. They incorporate scenes from the Arabian Nights."

"Yeah this room is right out of *A Thousand and One Nights.*" Neal replied.

In the corner of the room rested a solid wooden table. The table held a 1950's RCA Victrola record player and the album jacket from Nashville Skyline. The past blended with the present as the Victrola played Dylan's *Lay Lady Lay.* Dylan's voice floated into my ears: *Lay lady lay, lay across my big brass bed.*

Next to the record player a small porcelain incense burner burned. Four lit incense sticks emitted a blue glow and the scent of jasmine. The smoke zigzagged and danced to Dylan's lyrics.

I whispered to Neal, "This is fucking unbelievable. Are we part of a Hollywood set or what? We're listening to Bobby Zimmerman. Last year at this time we were trying to meet the guy at his Woodstock home."

Our pupils dilated as the Achmed returned holding two large sheets of hash. Each sheet was the size if a Spanish floor tile.

"Wow, that's one hell of a site. I have never seen such a large quantity of dope. Each sheet would be worth at least a thousand dollars in the States." Neal whispered.

But before the negotiations commenced, Achmed said, "Would you guys like a taste?"

We both nodded our heads in agreement. Achmed pinched off a gram of hash and inserted it into the hookah's bowl.

As he readied the pipe, I studied the multiple-hosed hookah with its ornate brass fixtures and a blue glass vase. With a wooden match, Achmed lit the hash. The smell of sulfur hit my nostrils. The match flame sent a flash across the room.

Placing the hose in my mouth, I took a long deep drag. After a few seconds I exhaled the sweet-smelling smoke, watching it float toward the ceiling.

After a few more hits, we were all blasted. Achmed now turned to business. "How much of this shit do you want to buy?" he inquired.

Looking Achmed square in the eyes, I replied, "We'll be in Morocco for only a short time, so we only need ten dollars worth."

The room went cold. I watched his eyes and body language change from relaxed to uptight.

"Are you Jews? You look like Jews." He sneered.

As I silently moved my lips to recite the *Shama Yisrael,* Neal uttered the denial, "We're not Jews, no, not us. We're Christians."

In my inebriated state, I paused to wonder how much better off we were with Neal's denial.

As he broke off a hand-sized piece of hash, Achmed replied, "Here's the deal assholes. Either you buy this chunk of hash for fifty dollars or I am going to ask my Uncle Mohammad to have you arrested. He is the chief of the Tangier Police Department. "

My bowels constricted, as he continued, "And if you don't know it, in Moroccan jails the only food you get is from people on the outside. The jailors provide you with only dirty water."

Hearing those words forced my stomach into my throat. My abdominal acids burned through my esophagus and tears formed in my eyes. Adrenaline ran through my veins like moviegoers fleeing a burning theater.

I looked at Neal and whispered, "You grab the dope. I'll hand him the fifty dollars. We both dash out of here and run to the hotel, nonstop!"

"Let's do it," Neal replied.

I paid and we ran out the door, down the steps, into the street toward our hotel. Neal stuck the hand-size piece of hash in his pocket. My capillaries popped as I scanned for Moroccan *gendarmes.*

In our Sheherazade room, we caught our breathe. Neal blurted out his plan, "Before the cops get here, let's eat some of this stuff and dump the rest in the toilet."

"I'm with you buddy. Let's go for it." I replied.

We each broke off a few grams, swallowed hard to avoid choking and washed down the dry, clay-like substance with a glass of water. The remainder we flushed down the toilet.

"I can't believe we just flushed over 40 grams of hash down the bowl." Neal exclaimed.

Hitting the bed, I relaxed realizing that the incriminating evidence was gone. My blood pressure leveled off as the hash started to massage my brain.

Within an hour the first hallucinations appeared. The room's walls crept toward my bed, slammed into the bed's corners and then bounced off . As I watched in a state of utter fascination the effect continued for five minutes. When I stopped focusing on the walls, the grey paisley-patterned curtains swam onto the ceiling as if they were streams of sperm in search of a solitary egg.

Thrilled and terrorized by this hallucinogenic trip, my brain went into sleep mode, a deep slumber.

Around four A.M., I was awakened by the ringing of the phone. I answered, "Hello. Who is this? What do you want?"

The male voice on the other end of the line responded in French, *"A quelle heure est votre bateau au depart?"*

"A trois heures," I replied, knowing full well that we would be sailing out of Tangier at eleven o'clock in the morning and not at three in the afternoon. Finding it difficult to fall back to sleep, I tossed and turned wondering who had called.

Was it the police?

Was it Achmed or one of his conspirators?

Or, was it a hallucination caused by the ingestion of so much hashish?

I fell back to sleep for about an hour. Only to be awakened at dawn. I heard the voices of Moroccan cattle dealers bringing their livestock to market. My paranoid, drug-induced brain, translated their Arabic cries. "Kill the Jews, Kill the Jews!" Hiding and shaking under the sheets, I pictured Arabs holding nooses and knives beneath my hotel window. My fear abated when their voices faded away.

Still shivering , I wondered how many times and in how many languages my father had heard those words? Then I cringed at the thought, "Had he ever actually seen people murdered after those words were screamed?"

That morning in the hotel restaurant, over Turkish coffee and Galois cigarettes, I recounted the whole story to Neal.

"Mort, pretty scary story. That hash blew me away. I did not hear the phone ring or the cattle dealers' chants. I liked how your brain translated Arabic to English, since you don't speak a word of Arabic. But let's play it safe. I think we should take a cab to the port right now. No sense in taking any more chances."

As our ship left the shores of Tangier, I smiled at our luck and said, " Thank G-d we made it. Last night I pictured us jailed, hung ,or castrated. They were not pretty pictures ... definitely not Hollywood."

Neal listened but remained silent for a few seconds. I guessed he still felt the effects of the hash. Then he bellowed, "Hallelujah, Praise the Lord. I think I see the Spanish coastline."

"Neal, when I get off this boat I am going to kiss the soil of Spain." And I did.

Wolf Laitner as toddler in Poland circa 1916

Dr. Wolf Laitner with group of European Physicians (date and location unknown)

Portrait photo of my father circa 1947

"The mystery photo" of my father holding the doll in the labor camp

Wolf and Henia Laitner, Germany circa 1948

Clockwise from top left:
Wolf and Henia Laitner, Germany 1948
Wolf, Henia, and Mort Laitner, in Feldafing, Germany
Mort Laitner and Henia, State Hospital, Middletown, NY circa 1953
Mort & Shelley Laitner Wedding, June 27, 1971, New Haven, CT
Back: Wolf & Barbara Laitner, Mike & Renia Cukier
Front: Rose Zelinger, Shelley & Mort Laitner, Henia Laitner & Terry Cukier
Wolf, Henia, Barbara & Mort at Colonial Inn Motel, Miami Beach, FL circa 1960

Sixteen

Toy Soldiers

While my father had faced Nazi soldiers carrying loaded rifles, I played with toy soldiers holding plastic rifles. As a five-year-old in Middletown, New York my war-game therapy commenced only to end years later in the attic of my Woodridge home. I played with these war toys on a daily basis until my parents gave the collection away. From then on the battle scenes were played out in my head.

As the music from *The Guns of Navarone* resounded in my brain, I worked as a saboteur with Gregory Peck, David Niven and Anthony Quinn. My backpack held enough nitroglycerine to blow up the colossal German cannons on the mountains of Navarone.

I made the Great Escape on a motorcycle, holding on to Steve McQueen's back, as we dodged bullets shot from a Nazi prisoner-of-war camp guard tower.

I became the thirteenth commando in the Dirty Dozen during their pre-D-Day invasion of a French chateau which was filled with high ranking Nazis. I splayed bullets into the general's body as my comrades were shot down before my eyes.

When fighting the Japanese Imperial Army, I whistled the tune from *The Bridge on the River Kwai,* marching in step with William Holden and Sir Alec Guinness. As a starving, abused POW, I helped built the railroad bridge over that river and fell on the detonator to blow it into smithereens.

As any good general would do, first I developed a battle plan. I surrounded the enemy soldiers with machine-gun toting U.S. infantry and hand grenade-throwing troops. A division of Sherman tanks moved into position as Army Air Corps Mustangs pounded the Krauts from the air. The Nazi perimeter shrank as I held an American soldier, or a plane or a tank between my thumb and index finger, systemically knocking down all the German troops. I tasted the catharsis of eliminating my mortal enemy while wondering if I would ever see battle. I fantasized about killing any soldier in a Nazi uniform – aiming and shooting bullets into the swastikas they wore.

My dad bought most of the plastic and lead military figures for my collection. On a daily basis, when he returned from working on an ambulance, I would run to the door to hug and kiss him. He'd reach in his pocket and pull out a toy soldier. My eyes would light up as he handed it to me. At the dinner table gripping my new treasure, I would place it next to my plate to admire it throughout dinner.

On a cold winter day, the ambulance in which my father rode, skidded on ice and smashed into a tree. My father returned home scraped and bruised. At the front door, my worried mother hugged and kissed him. I looked at my dad, ran up to him and asked, "Daddy, do you have a toy soldier?"

He spoke no words, just looked at me, smiled, and reached into his pocket. As he handed me my new toy soldier I kissed his bruised cheek and whispered. "Daddy, I love you."

If I was alone in the house, my imagination required no plastic or lead soldiers. I'd walk back and forth across the hallway on the second floor of my home talking to myself. I cut a path in the carpet as I walked miles making arm-flexing gestures as if I were General Montgomery leading his campaign against Rommel in North Africa or General Eisenhower directing his troops to a landing on all of the beaches in Normandy: Sword, Juno, Omaha, Gold, and Utah. I waded in on those beaches watching my comrades-in-arms die by the thousands.

I drove a motorcycle through the French hedge rows as German bullets screamed passed my head. I climbed the ropes and ladders up the Point Du Hoc cliffs with the Ranger commandoes to destroy the German machine gun positions. I sat on the decks of battle ships watching our shells blow up portions of the Atlantic Wall.

I marched with my band of brothers across those landing beaches, onto Operation Market Garden, into the Battle of the Bulge, into the horrors of Dachau and finally into Hitler's Eagle's Nest. I turned the pages of *Stars and Stripes* to find my picture and name in print as a hero.

Together we marched through European cities in divisions, battalions, brigades, squadrons, and platoons.

I hit the gold-colored carpet with my imaginary carbine in my arms and slogged through the muck as if I were encased in wet, blood-soaked sands. As a man of war I ran for the protection of the cliffs. As waves crashed across the length of my body, bullets sunk into the brave and dying.

I spent at least a half-hour a day conjuring up war scenarios. I used Rambo-like techniques to free Jews from the death camps: cutting though electrified-barbed-wire fences, stabbing vicious, barking German shepherds, planting explosives, and plunging detonator boxes that blew up guard towers.

I played the role of Sasha Pechersky, the Jewish/Russian prisoner of war at Sobibor, who organized the most successful uprising and mass-escape of Jews from a Nazi concentration camp.

Pechersky met my definition of a war hero: a killer of Nazi concentration camp guards, a leader of men with limited weapons, a strategic planner, a liberator of the camp's prisoners, a man who approached death a thousand times and each time laughed in its face, a man who was fearless in the presence of Nazi death mongers. He was one in a million. He was my hero.

Using street-fighting skills, I killed the Nazi guards. Waving and slashing my machete I cut off their heads with a single blow. I struck, wrestled and grappled the bastards using Krav Maga moves.

These moves were developed by Imi Lichtenfeld. Lichtenfeld taught and structured his art of self-defense in his native land in the 1930's. His goal was for Hungarian Jews to be able to fend off attacks committed by fascist thugs. Due to his success, he was eventually kicked out of Hungary. He was labeled by the government as a trouble maker. He immigrated to Palestine and taught his craft to the Palmach, the forerunner of Israeli Army.

If I ran out of ammunition or lost my Bowie knife, I moved into hand-to-hand combat. I aimed kicks into their groins, poked out their eyeballs, and dug my nails into their throats. I struck my head into their skulls knocking them unconscious. With my bare hands I choked them to death.

As cathartic waves ran through my brain and body, I sat down on my bed to rest. I then got up and continued my pacing fantasy-walk across the hallway.

I crawled through the sewers in Warsaw holding a Molotov cocktail. I threw the explosive at a German tank and watched the tank ignite in flames. As the tank driver exited the vehicle, I shot him in the throat.

Through the windows of a bombed-out building I lead a group of Warsaw- Ghetto fighters to freedom, including a boy in knickers, the "Warsaw Ghetto Boy," whose picture I had studied over a thousand times. The boy wears shorts, almost knee high black socks, a cap and the terrified look of fear. His tiny eyes squint in the sunlight as his lips tremble. He walks with both hands raised as an SS trooper points a gun in the direction of his back. I gunned down that SS trooper and then managed to escape the ghetto with the child.

Bringing supplies of food and medicine, I marched into the concentration camps with the American and Russian armies.

These fantasies were played on such a regular basis, causing me to fear that one of my family members would observe my behavior and recommend psychiatric therapy. Luckily, they never caught me.

As part of the luckiest generation in American history I live in the land my father loved. The land of the free, the brave, and the land of minimal racism. I say, "minimal" because in our den, on our black and white Zenith TV set, burned the images of such hate mongers as Robert Shelton of the Ku Klux Klan and American's neo-Nazi George Lincoln Rockwell.

When they appeared on the glass screen, I watched my father's face tighten and his eyes glaze. I wondered what thoughts ran through his mind. Sometimes he spat a curse word in Polish or Yiddish at the screen. Had the Germanic curse followed him to America?

Decades later I listened to my dad's *Shoah* tapes. I learned that he feared what happened in Europe could take place in the States. As a precaution, he bought property in Israel. He had an escape plan, something his Dad failed to have. Who could blame him?

While I – who lived in the States for over six decades and had only five anti-Semitic experiences under my belt – felt no such paranoia.

SEVENTEEN

AMERICAN *FÜHRERS*

In the early eighties, I drove with my wife, Shelley, toward our K-Mart, when my eyes laid sight on a group of five hooded Klan members.

"Honey, look at those creeps. I've never seen these clowns in their robes before," Shelley bellowed.

"Me neither. They're dressed in their white-hooded robes but their faces are exposed. I wonder if we can recognize the bastards?"

Slowing down our Ford Aerostar minivan to get a better look, my eyes burned. Five of them stood on a busy intersection of Griffin Road and University Drive. They held placards and broad grins. The signs read: WHITE POWER and SEGREGATION FOREVER. The Kluxers positioned themselves on the median of this busy intersection, right on the border between the towns of Davie and Cooper City.

Flabbergasted, I intoned, "Honey, this is the Eighties! These assholes have some gall! What f'ing chutzpah! Who the hell do they think they are? Where the Hell do they think they are? This community has a substantial number of Jews. These five turds are an anachronism. We're living the middle of the eighties and these pricks still think it's the sixties, when Davie was the capital city of the Florida Klan."

"Let's send them a message." Shelley exclaimed.

Then it hit me; I remembered what Neal did in South Carolina to the Confederate Flag. "Honey, watch this," I said.

I stuck my left hand out the window, shot my middle finger at the creeps, while squeezing down on my horn. The noise caught their attention. A message was sent.

As we drove by the Kluxers, Shelley said, "Honey, that felt real good. Let's find some American Nazis and do it again."

George Lincoln Rockwell founded the American Nazi Party. Before this self-created neo-Nazi wore his first swastika armband, he had reached the rank of Lieutenant Commander in the U.S. Navy, serving in World War II. While in the service, Rockwell devoured such classic anti-Semitic texts including, Hitler's *Mein Kampf* and *The Protocols of the Elders of Zion.*

When I heard he read *The Protocols of the Elders of Zion,* first I remembered this Russian forgery, created by the czar's secret service, that a small cabal of international Jews sought to control the world. Then my memory jumped to Henry Ford. This so-called American genius had reprinted the *Protocols* in his newspaper – the *Dearborn Independent.* Ford reprinted the *Protocols* as fact. The newspaper's banner read "Ford's International Weekly." It sold for a nickel a copy or a dollar for a one year subscription.

Henry published a continuous series of 91 anti-Semitic articles in his paper. Ford had managed to write the American version of *Mein Kampf* years before Hitler completed his book. Their anti-Semitic theories ran parallel to each other. They followed the standard, Hate-a-Jew checklist. They both pointed out that Jews have a distaste for hard physical labor, created communism, controlled the banks, the media and cultural institutions such as the arts and music. Having read one of Ford's articles entitled, *Jewish Jazz – Moron Music – Becomes our National Music.* I thought the article was written by a Nazi.

In Germany these stories were bound together into a four volume set entitled *The International Jew* and subtitled *The World's Foremost Problem.* Ford not only spread his hatred through the *Independent* but handed out free copies in some of his car dealerships across America. When you bought a Ford, the some dealers put a copy on your front seat.

Ford, like Hitler, attributed all evil to Jews or to Jewish capitalism. Henry, like Adolf , blamed the Jews for World War I.

They both claimed a vast Jewish conspiracy was infecting America. Heinrich Himmler said Ford was "one of our most valuable, important, and witty fighters." No wonder that Ford was the only American referenced in *Mein Kampf*.

I wondered how much hatred Hitler's *Mein Kampf* stole from Ford's publication. Adolf regarded Ford as an inspiration. He hung a life-sized portrait of Henry Ford next to his desk in his Munich office. Hitler also kept a copy of *The International Jew* in his library. Hitler said of Ford, "I shall do my best to put his theories into practice in Germany."

Hitler was such a fan of Ford's anti-Semitic literature and his mass production techniques that in 1938, in honor of Ford's 75th birthday, his Nazi regime awarded Henry Ford the Grand Service Cross of the Supreme Order of the German Eagle. Twenty-two Americans received similar awards but only Ford received the highest rank. The award consists of a Maltese cross and four German eagles gripping swastikas surrounded by wreathes.

When Leni Riefenstahl, the film director of *Will of Triumph* and *Olympia*, met with Ford that same year. He told her, "When you see the Führer after your return, tell him that I admire him and I am looking forward to meeting him at the coming party rally in Nuremberg."

I studied the 1938 birthday-gift photograph which appeared in newspapers across America and the world. Two diplomats,

German Counsels from Cleveland and Detroit, awarded Henry the highest Nazi decoration given to a foreigner. Ford not only received the medal, Hitler sent him a personal note of thanks for his "humanitarian ideals" printed on a parchment scroll.

I wondered if either of the two items or photograph were on display or housed anywhere in the Ford Museum in Dearborn. When I visited the museum I know I did not see them.

In the photo, one diplomat gives Ford a congratulatory handshake as the other pins the medal on his jacket. Henry wears a white suit, a dark tie, a large sash and devilish smile. Henry stands out as he is framed by the two German consuls wearing dark suits. The picture shows that the thin-lipped, anti-Semitic bastard relished every moment of the ceremony.

A similar award was granted to aviator and anti-Semite, Charles Lindbergh. James Mooney, a senior executive for General Motors, accepted this so-called honor because it meant good business for GM. Ford and GM made significant profits in their German auto factories. Thomas Watson, chief executive of IBM, said in his acceptance, "I take pride and deep gratitude for the award." Watson's computers were invaluable to the Nazis for tracking confiscated property of Jews who were on their way to the camps.

In disgust, I pictured these four gentlemen proudly wearing the medals. Ford never relinquished the award not even after the United States entered the war against Germany.

The Nazis spent years calculating the most efficient assembly line techniques for the extermination of the Jewish race from ghettos, to the train depots, to the cattle cars, to death camps, into the gas chambers, and finally into the crematoriums. Hitler kept his word; he did his best to put Ford's theories into practice in Germany.

Ford was sued for libel by a Jewish lawyer and agricultural organizer for one million dollars. In 1927, as a settlement to the lawsuit, Ford allegedly wrote a letter of apology, recalled copies of his newspaper, acknowledged his error, and asked for forgiveness. Ford claimed that he was "mortified" to learn that the *Protocols* were a forgery. He later claimed the signature on the agreement was a forgery. Publicly it was announced that the articles on Jews would never again appear in the *Independent.*

In 1927, Ford shut down his anti-Semitic rag. A boycott by Jews and Christians was costing him money. During the Second World War in 1942, Henry Ford, for the good of the war effort, wrote another letter condemning anti-Semitism. Henry died in 1947. But before his death, on seeing photographic footage of a concentration camp, Ford suffered a heart attack. I thought, "Quite fitting since this was the same heart upon which the Maltese cross, the German eagles and the four swastikas had rested."

Eleven years after Ford's death, George Lincoln Rockwell another tall, well-spoken bigot received an 18-foot long swastika flag from an admirer. He hung it on a wall, placed Hitler's photograph on it and then completed his shrine by lighting three candles in front of the flag and photo. At this moment of religious clarity, he swore alliance to his *Führer,* his leader, by raising his arm in stiff salute to these symbols of hatred and yelled, "Heil Hitler!"

For the next nine years, Rockwell drove his swastikas-painted Volkswagen van, known as the "Hate Bus" to rallies throughout the nation.

As he drove hate across the nation, I tossed on my University of Miami dormitory bed, carefully reading every word of Alex Haley's interview of Rockwell in Playboy magazine. I was not surprised to learn he denied the existence of the Holocaust. Rockwell stated, "I don't believe for one minute that any six million Jews were exterminated by Hitler. It never happened." However, his solution for American Jews sounded eerily familiar.

In that same dorm room, in that same year, I watched the national news and learned that George Lincoln Rockwell had been assassinated. The reporter said, "Mr. Rockwell was executed by a former member of his Nazi party while he was leaving a Virginia Laundromat. Two bullets, from a German manufactured Mauser pistol passed through his car's windshield and into his body. As his Chevrolet slowly rolled backwards to a stop, Rockwell staggered out of the front passenger side door of the car, pointed toward the shopping center roof, and then collapsed face up on the pavement."

As I digested the news, the taste of hate dissipated on my tongue. I wondered when and if my dad heard the news would his taste buds have a similar chemical reaction. I should have called and asked but I didn't.

I wondered what taste ran across Robert Shelton's mouth when he heard the news. Robert Shelton and his Ku Klux Klan received more press than Rockwell and his neo-Nazis. He had a much larger organization, some 30,000 members, and seemed to be in control of the South. The civil rights movement of the early sixties sparked conflict across southern segregated communities which ignited Klan membership.

On road trips through the land of cotton, my eyes read Klan's billboards welcoming "white folks" to their territory. On television their rallies seemed well attended. I watched in horror as they lit their eighteen-foot high crosses in ceremonial glory. The Kluxers also marched carrying three-foot burning crosses. They wore their white sheets with their pointed white hoods, with two eye openings masking their identity. These hooded men of the night were just as intimidating as their torch-carrying Nazi cousins.

I recalled watching TV as a semi-hooded fat redneck spewed, "Death to the niggers and their communist-controlling Jewish masters." Then he yelled, "Send the niggers back to Africa and the Jews back to Israel!"

These images must have brought horrible flashbacks to my mom and dad.

This get-the-hell-out-of-our-country concept reminded me of Adolf Eichmann, who in 1937, landed in Haifa, then a Palestinian city under British control. He was there to arrange a final destination for German Jews to go after their forced exile from the Third *Reich*. Hitler wanted Germany *Judenfrei* (free of Jews) or *Judenrein* (clean of Jews). He wanted the *Reich* cleansed of those of Hebraic blood, even those with only one eighth of the contaminated fluid. These German compound words became popular before and during the Second World War after German and European cities or towns rid themselves of their Jewish citizens. Large banners were hung across the fronts of closed synagogues proclaiming, "This city is free of Jews!"

Eichmann failed to meet with any officials in Palestine because he was not granted a transit visa by the British. He then went to Cairo and met with a representative of the Haganah (future branch of the Israeli military) to discuss the matter. These Zionists needed Jews to create a nation. These Zionists also read *Mein Kampf* and knew the fate of their brethren in Germany. They dealt with the devil but failed to get the job done. The irony of Eichmann's Palestinian visit was that twenty-five years later, Eichmann would stand trial and be hanged in Jerusalem which is a little more than an hour's drive from Haifa. As Eichmann hung, a collective sigh of relief was heard across the Jewish world. I rejoiced.

I wished Eichmann's fate on Kluxer Robert M. Shelton. He was a car-tire salesman who climbed to be the leader of the United Klan's of America. In 1961, he became their Grand Wizard. His 30,000 member organization was responsible for numerous lynchings and the notorious Birmingham, Alabama firebombing of the 16th Street Baptist Church in which four young Black girls were murdered.

In 1964, Klan members shot and killed one Black and two Jewish civil-rights workers. This was the first time the Klan targeted Jewish civil rights workers with death. I recalled their names: Chaney, Schwerner, and Goodman. It was the summer of the freedom project, where young college students, mainly from the North, tried to get Blacks registered to vote in Mississippi.

I read that the victims had not been beaten before their deaths, but I doubted it. A twenty-six-year-old dishonorably discharged ex-Marine, Roberts was the trigger man. He first shot Schwerner, then Goodman, then Chaney, all at point blank range. Their bodies were driven to a dam site on the Old Jolly Farm. The dam site was owned by a Philadelphia, Mississippi businessman. The businessman announced at a Klan meeting, before the arrival of hundreds of civil rights workers to Mississippi, "Hell, I've got a dam that'll hold a hundred of them." The three bodies were thrown together in a hollow at the dam site and then covered with tons of dirt by a bulldozer.

The story caused two flashbacks to cross my mind. The first showed Nazis ordering Jews to dig their own graves. Once dug, the Jews received a bullet in the head, the momentum of the shot caused them to fall forward into the pit. The second photo showed bulldozers pushing dirt over the skeletal bodies after the camps were liberated.

Eighteen

South of the Border

The Klan thought their heinous acts would intimidate "Yankees" from coming to Meridian, Mississippi or Miami Beach, Florida. They were dead wrong about Miami Beach. But in 1969, on my trek down to the University of Miami, I still feared redneck towns, redneck cops and their speed traps, and the Klan.

I needed, or at least wanted, my mom's Ford Mustang to drive around campus to impress the coeds. So my mom with some gentle persuasion – I threatened not to go back to school – allowed me to take her car.

On this 1500-mile road trip from Woodridge to Coral Gables, my friend Neal accompanied me in my mother's red 1967 Ford Mustang with its black vinyl roof. Before setting off at daybreak, I strolled past the rear of car, slapping the backside metal panel, as if it was the rump of a stallion. I opened the door and smelled the aroma of leather bucket seats. In the fresh morning mountain air, the off-white leather seats were cold to the touch. I wanted to get on the road.

Neal looked at me and asked, "You still have a thing for horses don't you? I bet you still want to be a cowboy?"

"Yup and yup," I replied in cowboy fashion. Then I jumped onto the bucket seat and yelled, " Hi Yo, Silver! Away!"

"Ke-mo sah-bee, drive stallion in safe manner. We have long journey ahead of us." Neal replied.

We each took three-hour driving shifts and only stopped for gas, bathroom breaks or fast food. Through New York, New Jersey, Pennsylvania and Maryland, the radio blared out the Stones, the Doors, Dylan, Hendrix, and Joplin. We knew the lyrics and sang along to the anthems of our youth. We were young, innocent, and happy.

As we entered Virginia, I saw our first "South of the Border" sign. I pointed and exclaimed, "Neal, that sign means we have officially entered the Confederacy – the land of cotton, tobacco, moon pies, and grits. Dude, be ready for cultural shock to set in your bones. In one day we'll have gone from the Borscht Belt to the Bible Belt, from the Jewish Alps to the Blue Ridge Mountains. Pretty scary."

"Mort, you forgot the land of ribs, barbecue, okra, and black-eye peas. Hey all this Southern talk is making me hungry. Let's stop at the next Stuckeys. I have a hankering for a pecan log and a praline."

"Neal, you're pushing it, remember you're just a Yid from the Catskills. I doubt you can handle Southern cuisine."

He laughed and pulled into the next Stuckeys.

Seated in the restaurant we both longed for a Jewish deli.

"Neal, you know I'd give my right pinky for a hot pastrami on seeded rye."

In his best Yiddish accent Neal countered, "Oh vey! I vish we were eating in a Monticello or Liberty deli. I'd be ordering a handmade egg cream, a knish and three slices stuffed *derma – kishke* smothered in gravy. Oy vey! I can now smell the aromas of my Yiddisha grandma's *flanken* and a slice of rye bread smothered with schmaltz.

"Kvetch, kvetch, kvetch, you're in the South my *l'shana madela.* There ain't no Jewish delis down here. There ain't no Reubens or Rachels either." I chuckled.

"Mort, you have some *chutzpah* to remind me of that fact as I am fantasying about *kasha varnishka*, noodle kugel, a *latke* and a cheese blintz."

Sipping my coffee, I glared at Neal, "Mazel tov! You have succeeded. I no longer want to eat this pecan log. I'm taking it to the car."

Back on the road, we took turns reading each of the South of the Border signs out loud. Each sign told us how many more miles to the tourist trap. We yelped in amazement upon seeing a sign which read, *Shalom! South of the Border.* Neal sighed,

"A great miracle has happened here! At least somebody in Dillon, South Carolina has a Jewish sense of humor. We have got to take a break with Pedro, the South of the Border mascot. That Mexican *bandito* is one tough dude, with his *sombrero, serape* and his *huarache* sandals."

G-d must have heard Neal and laughed. The next song on the radio was *Tzenda, Tzenda, Tzenda* by the Weavers. We could not believe our ears. Hebrew school had paid off. We knew the words. We sang in unison as if Pete Seeger rode with us. We had learned *Tzenda,* a Hebrew song from the early Fifties, which told young Israeli women not to hide themselves away but to go out and see the soldiers in the *moshava* (farming community).

To show off his superior knowledge of music, Neal commented, "The DJ screwed up. He must have wanted to play Goodnight Irene which is on the flip side of the record. We are lucky dogs."

"Not as lucky as those girls who followed the songs advice and spent time and gave up their virtue to those soldiers," I replied.

Neal laughed and for once remained silent.

One hundred SOTB signs later, we finally arrived. On entering the restaurant we were greeted by a poncho-wearing waiter. He tipped his *sombrero* and said, "Y'all just follow me. I'll take you to your table."

My breakfast consisted of grits, bacon and runny eggs which activated my intestinal tract. Holding my gut, I jumped out of my seat and yelled.

"Neal, I have to hit the head. I'll see you in the gift shop."

I ran toward the bathroom. With great relief , dashed through its door, made it into a stall, locked the door and lowered my pants just in time. As I sat, counting my blessings and my timing, the graffiti carved into the stall's door hit me. The usual uncreative crap accosted my eyes:

All Niggers and Kikes must die!

The only good Nigger is a dead one!

Hitler was right!

Three swastikas of different sizes found the corners of the door.

The KKK will rise again!

If we don't send the Kikes back to Israel, we are going to end up with a Nigger president.

I laughed out loud and mumbled, "That will be the day."

Next I focused squarely in the middle of this collection of drivel, finding a message of hope. A magic-marker message proved that love does conquer hatred: For a good time call Eva 555-8911. I smiled, picturing Eva entering the stall with her pen in hand to inscribe the message.

These hatemongering scribblers impressed me with their knowledge of exclamation points and capitalization. My Yankee prejudice took hold of my brain as I asked, "Were these scribblers really educated in the South?"

These pen-knife writers found their private space to post their messages. One reader at a time became their captive audience. I had seen similar writings up North but down South the authors seemed to write in a larger font. They attempted to cover every inch of the painted door. I wondered, "Should I carry a paint brush and a bucket of white paint into every public restroom in the South." But I did not. Whitewashing these messages would be a temporary fix. These pen-knife hate mongers would strike this stall within a day or two. I wondered, "Had my dad read similar graffiti in Polish and German stalls. Had the German and Polish pen-knife wheedling author's fervor matched that of their American racist brethren?" I speculated that they did.

Leaving the restroom, I entered the gift shop. A bombardment of every possible redneck *tchotchke* (knickknack) rained down on me. Most of these souvenirs bore Confederate flags. Here is a short list: shot glasses, porcelain dinner bells, mugs, license plates, hanging car deodorizers, aprons, cloth patches, cuff links, watches, lighters, charms and lapel pins.

I found Neal studying the Dixie cuff links.

"Dude, you gotta take a trip to the crapper there is a collection of graffiti on one of the stall doors that will knock your socks off."

"Bro, I'll take a look before we leave. Do you see all this Confederate crap? I guess some outdated Jim Crow law required this ancient form of propaganda be sold to Yankee travelers making the trip to Miami Beach."

I laughed out loud, "You got it right brother."

Neal, in a loud obnoxious tone exclaimed, "I'm tempted to buy some of this Southern crap to decorate my mansion. You never see this shit sold up North. Look at this statue of a funny looking little Confederate general yelling, 'Hell no, the war ain't over yet!' A hundred years after losing the war, these Southerners fail to understand the outcome."

Some of the employees and patrons of this establishment started to glare.

I whispered, "Idiot, lower your f'ing voice! You're going to get us tarred, feathered, and castrated!"

I stepped away from Neal and wandered over to the far less humorous shelves containing the porcelain figurines of bandana-wearing mammies.

"*Oy gevalt!* These figurines remind me of Aunt Jemima pancakes."

I turned around looking for Neal but I could not find him.

Handling the mug, I recalled that Aunt Jemima represented the "Happy Slave" or for more polite Southerners, the "Happy Negress." She wore a broad smile filled with pearly whites. The joys of antebellum servitude were plastered on all these "colored" folk's faces. A framed print advertisement, which sold for a buck pictured Aunt Jemima, the national pancake-flipping Black maid exclaiming, "I's in Town Honey!" and "I's offering a free collection of my Aunt Jemima's family rag dolls."

I recoiled thinking, "White Southerners enjoy making fun of Blacks, just as Margaret Mitchell did in Gone with the Wind. The degradation of a race based on the mistaken belief of their own superiority sounds familiar."

Next to these mammies stood bald-headed Uncle Toms wearing black bow ties, white shirts, black suits and polite smiles. I knew that the term "uncle" was used in the South to refer to old Black men. Southerners did not have to refer to elderly African-Americans by their name; the term uncle would do. These happy Southern domestic servants reminded me of the box of Uncle Ben's Converted Rice. But I was wrong, the Uncle Ben pictured on the box was a *maitre d'* of a Chicago hotel. The Uncle Ben name came from a Black farmer known to grow the best rice in the South.

My mother always stored a box of Uncle Ben's rice in the cupboard. Rice was one of her culinary specialties. The sweet, soft taste of rice topped with a slice of melted butter or smothered with goulash gravy.

Now that I think about it, a trio of Blacks resided in our Jewish house – Rastus, the Cream of Wheat chef, Aunt Jemima, and Uncle Ben. We were an integrated family.

On a shelf below the uncles and aunts sat "colored" boys devouring watermelons. These bulging eyed, red-lipped, little Black boys represented happiness and laziness. Rednecks knew the pleasure of not working, and eating watermelon. The Sons of the Confederacy branded all Blacks as lazy just as Germans branded all Jews in the same manner.

Neal approached me from behind, looked at the watermelon eaters and in his best redneck-imitating-Blacks accent intoned, "Did you know that G-d and Jesus eats waty melon in Heaven? I think I just read that message on the stall's door."

"Hallelujah, Praise the Lord." I bellowed and laughed picturing the two deities devouring large wedges, their faces covered in sticky red juices as they looked into each other's eyes as only a father and son can do. I decided my vision needed to be painted on the ceiling of the Sistine Chapel or at least on the panels of a watermelon-carrying truck.

But I knew my redneck accent could beat Neal's any day of the week. "Lawdy, I sho do loves fried chicken an' dat der watymelon."

Holding his gut, Neal almost fell on the floor. He then rose to acknowledge my victory with an oriental bow and nod of his head.

I continued examining these racist *tchotchkes* and asked, "Neal were these objects really made for white folks to feel superior or were they created just to make Blacks feel inferior?"

"I think it is a little of both." Neal replied.

I did not fully understand how hurtful these items were to Blacks until years later when I visited *Yad Vashem,* Israel's Holocaust museum. For the first time, I saw a display of German and Austrian porcelain tooth-pick holders and mugs made in the 1930's. Bigoted artisans crafted these porcelain souvenirs into greedy, fat, hooked-nosed Jews and unkempt black-bearded orthodox rabbis wearing caftans. These figurines reminded me of the propaganda posters plastered on walls throughout the *Reich.* These posters preached that Germans not deal with, buy from or associate with Jews. Why? Because they were filthy vermin. I now tasted African-American pain.

"Neal, Jews and Blacks have got a lot in common. Did you know that Jews in Germany had to walk on separate paths and not on Aryan sidewalks?

"Well in the South, Blacks had to cross the street if a white woman was on the same sidewalk as them." He continued, "Both groups were prohibited from furthering their education and working in many trades."

I countered, "Blacks had designated bathrooms and water fountains. 'For Colored Only' faded signs can still be seen throughout the South. Right here at South of the Border we could have seen two sets of bathrooms or a 'for whites only' swimming pool."

"German municipal swimming pools had signs reading: *'Fur Juden Verboten'* and I know what you're going to say next, Blacks were not allowed to swim in white designated pools or beaches."

I added, "They had their racial laws and we had Jim Crow."

Neal countered, "On April Fool's Day in 1933, the Germans boycotted businesses owned by Jews. Yellow stars of David were painted on store fronts. The message was clear: Jews get the hell out of our Aryan nation. The signs read, 'The Jews Are Our Misfortune' and 'Go To Palestine!'

The Nazis made Jewish shopkeepers display the words: JEWISH BUSINESS in their storefront windows. They did that so that 'good Germans' would boycott. To intimidate any shopper, uniformed SA, *Sturmabteilung,* stormtroopers, also known as the 'brownshirts,' stood at attention in front of the stores."

I interrupted, "Five years later, in 1938 on November 9th and 10th , was the infamous *Kristallnacht,* or the Night of Broken Glass where those storm troopers and civilians smashed those window panes and covered German city streets with a carpet of glass. A carpet woven of six million shards and slivers."

"Can you imagine the sound of all that glass crashing on the ground. A thousand synagogue stained-glass window panes being smashed by stones thrown by storm troopers, then splintering into pieces as they disintegrate on the road. I wonder if Goebbels quoted Ecclesiastes, and told the storm troopers, today is our time to gather and throw stones. Today is our season to harvest Jewish glass?" Neal asked.

"That noise would have scared the hell out of me," I replied. "Can you imagine being a little Jewish kid hearing that continual din for two consecutive nights. Can you imagine a million tears running down and burning the cheeks of Jewish children on *Kristallnacht.* Their parents had to realize it was the time get the hell out of Germany. "

"Mort, we once broke some window panes. Do you remember those old abandoned Woodridge bungalows? The ones hidden in the woods."

"Yup. We were real bad asses in our teens. We enjoyed hearing that.

"Neal, here are the *Kristallnacht* numbers to this 'spontaneous violence': around 90 murdered, thousands injured, and 30,000 arrested and sent to concentration camps. The Nazis had the balls to call these arrests 'placing people in protective custody.' Of the imprisoned, 2,000 Jews died in their 'protective custody', seven thousand Jewish businesses were looted, Most of the synagogues in Germany and Austria were looted and burned, and, there were untold numbers of rapes and suicides. All of this mayhem occurred under the watchful eyes of the German police and fire brigades. They stood by and didn't lift a finger to stop anything."

"Mort, you know that *Kristallnacht* was Hitler's reaction to a 17-year-old Polish Jewish kid's assassination of a German diplomat attached to their embassy in Paris. I think his name was Herschel Grynszpan. He was a fighter and his friends nicknamed him Maccabee."

Neal continued, "He was a handsome kid with a macho, rebel, Hollywood gangster look. I saw a photo taken after his arrest. He looked like a combination of Paul Muni and Marlon Brando, strands of hair hanging across his forehead. He wore a tie, white shirt and Bogart overcoat. His eyes said three words: anger, grief, and vengeance. He understood the Biblical message of: A time to keep silent and a time to speak. He spoke the language of bullets, the only language the Nazis truly understood."

"I saw that photograph...very film noir. The photographer was an artist. He used light and shadows to capture Herschel's angst – for his parents living in limbo on the Polish border, for

Herschel facing murder charges, and for all the European Jews facing the Nazi onslaught."

"Mort, I wonder if Robert Capa took that shot?"

"I don't think he was based in Paris in 1938, but it does look like his stuff," I answered.

Neal continued, "He was living in Paris when he received a postcard from his sister begging for money. His parents were Poles who had moved to Germany. They and 12,000 other similarly situated Jews were ordered out of the country by the Nazis. However Poland refused to grant them reentry. Instead of sending money, Herschel sent a message of bullets into the body of a German representative – a message to all Nazis that there would be a price for their actions. He was a top-level risk-taker, willing to risk his life for his parents and 12,000 European Jews trapped between two countries. Before he shot Ernest von Rath, Herschel wrote a postcard to his family. His quote went something like this:

'My heart bleeds when I think of our tragedy and that of the 12,000 Jews. I have to protest in a way that the whole world hears my protest and this I intend to do.'"

Neal added, "He begged for forgiveness from the Almighty and his family."

"Neal, this kid had heart. He was a believer and respected his family. "

"Mort, he never mailed the postcard. I wondered why."

Neal kept on telling the story. "He took five shots at the Nazi, two of which entered von Rath's body. He sat in the embassy chair and awaited arrest. On arrest he said, "I did it to avenge my parents who are miserable in Germany."

"Sounds like he was seeking martyrdom, a Jewish John Brown. He wanted to put Hitler's policies on trial as Brown did on the subject of slavery. But I don't think Herschel thought the Jews of Paris would follow his lead in armed revolt as John Brown thought the slaves living near Harper's Ferry would join him in rebellion," I commented.

"Good analogy. You're absolutely correct. In a French court he told a judge a line that sounded a lot like Shylock in The Merchant of Venice. 'It is not, after all, a crime to be Jewish, I am not a dog. I have a right to live. My people have a right to exist on this earth, And yet everywhere they are hunted down like animals.'"

"Neal, I bet the teenage avenger really learned a lesson about the law of unintended consequences, when he read the papers, after the death of diplomat Ernst vom Rath and the Night of the Broken Glass. I bet this defender of the Jewish people had no idea that Nazis had the Night of Broken Glass all planned out before the assassination. The Brownshirts and the Gestapo only had to wait to get orders for the posting of *Kristallnacht* preapproved graffiti, REVENGE FOR THE MURDER OF VON RATH. Hitler needed a match to light the Holocaust's flame. Herschel provided that spark. Hitler's henchman and thugs then torched the temples and snuffed out 90 lives as collective punishment – their act of revenge for Herschel's act of revenge. The Nazis mastered the subject of collective punishment. Partisans throughout Europe knew for every German, they killed, at least a hundred innocent villagers who lived near the site of the act of resistance would be murdered. If you lifted a finger against the Nazis they cut off your hands, your family's hands, and an entire village if they thought it just. As a final act of absurdity, the Nazis decreed that Germany's Jews pay a fine of one billion *reichsmarks* to atone for the sins of the *Kristallnacht* murderers, rapists, arsonist, thugs and looters." I took a deep breath and continued.

"I bet Herschel thought that Jews from every nation would call him a hero, when in fact many French and German Jewish groups condemned his act as homicide. They labeled it a catastrophe. Only Leon Trotsky asked, "What is so astonishing is that so far there has been only one Grynszpan."

Neal jumped in, "He's a hero in my eyes, like those armed Jewish resisters, like those who rose up in the Warsaw Ghetto, or the Bielski partisans. He fired the first shot in the Jewish war against Hitler. He taught us well. But few bothered to listen. There were not nearly enough bullets fired on the Krauts. Europe needed more Jews, like Herschel, with guns and the desire to snuff out Nazis at any cost."

Neal lit a cigarette, blew out the match, and dropped it on the store's floor. Blowing out a ring of smoke he continued, "He killed a Nazi bastard. This seventeen-year-old outraged Jew had his revenge. Herschel reminds me of those *Murder Incorporated* gangsters who came up to the Catskills and murdered Klansmen. The only big difference being that Herschel sat there waiting to be arrested and the New York City thugs headed home to Brooklyn. They both knew how to send a message. Those New York City thugs saved the Hebes in the mountains a lot of grief. These Jewish gangster families broke up German American Bund rallies in the Thirties. They used baseball bats and lead pipes to get their message across loud and clear. Nazis were not welcome in America.

"Neal, did you know after *Kristallnacht* the Germans passed a law requiring all Jews to hand in their pistols and rifles?"

Neal puckered his lips and blew out another perfect smoke ring. "Nope. But I bet many of those law-abiding, docile German Jews were dumb enough to hand them over. They couldn't even figure out that one day those pistols would be their only source of protection. I recently read a book called *The War Against the Jews 1933-1945* by Lucy Dawidowicz. She blames the rabbis for

Jewish submissiveness. Once the nation of the Hebrews was lost, the rabbis 'elevated powerlessness into a positive Jewish virtue.' What a virtue – POWERLESSNESS!

"I memorized what the rabbis preached to their congregations. 'The Holy Spirit says, I adjure you that if the earthly kingdom decrees persecutions, you shall not rebel in all that it decrees against you, but you shall keep the king's command.' "

"Wow; what a pile of shit. I didn't know that. The rabbis indoctrinated their congregants to take the pain. Those rabbis created the infamous thirteenth tribe of Israelites, a group not officially listed with the sons and daughters of the patriarch Jacob. They are called the Do-As-You-Are-Told-And-Everything-Will-Turn-Out-Alright Tribe, also known as, the This-Too -Will-Pass-Tribe. This clan of risk-averse, prayer-driven Jews still exists today but they are hard to find in the state of Israel," I said.

Neal chuckled at my comment and then added "Those rabbis must have read the New Testament and accepted all that 'turn the other cheek crap.' What the rabbis should be teaching is the post-Holocaust holy trinity: Never forgive, never forget, and never again."

I thought, "Those three nevers would make a great motto for the state of Israel."

Neal continued his history lesson, "Ironically, *Kristallnacht* saved a lot more Jewish lives than the 90 or so who were murdered."

"How's that?" I inquired.

"Many Austrian and German Jews realized their lives in the *Reich* were in serious peril. They fled to Palestine or other countries. You could say Herschel's gunfire saved their lives; 118,000 fled Germany. It also allowed Hitler to accomplish one of his primary goals, to make greater Germany Jew free."

As Neal talked, I thought about my mother and father reading the *Kristallnacht* headlines in a Yiddish or Polish newspaper, how they must have slowly digested every word in the article. Had they memorized the *Kristallnacht* numbers to repeat them to their friends? Hitler was their next door neighbor and he wanted Poland as living space for the master race. My father said the Poles often copied the anti-Semitic actions of the Nazis. Did they fear a similar anti-Semitic program in Poland?

A fountain of "I wonders" flowed through my brain, "Had they discussed *Kristallnacht* with their parents? Did they act like ostriches and stick their heads in the sand? Did they hope that if the matter was not discussed it would *gey avek* (go away)? Did they create contingency escape plans, or just pray to G-d for his protection? Had they cursed Hershel Grynszpan for his act of revenge or did they consider him a hero? I wondered, "Would I have had the guts to murder a German diplomat to avenge Hitler's treatment of my parents? From 1933 to 1945, how many Nazis were killed by European Jews, excluding the half million Russian Jews who fought in the Soviet army? What was the kill ratio of dead Nazis murdered by European Jews to the six million? Finally, what did the French justice system do to Hershel and what did the Germans do to his parents?

Years later, I learned more about his fate. After France surrendered to Germany, the Vichy government handed Herschel over to the Nazis. The Germans shipped him to a Berlin prison. He was going to be the subject of a show trial. But the show trial never happened. Hitler personally cancelled it. From the Adolf Eichmann trial transcript, which was held in Jerusalem in the 1961, I learned that Eichmann, a self-proclaimed expert on Judaism, personally interrogated Herschel. For the show trial the Nazis needed to pin Herschel's actions on international Jewry. Eichmann failed. No Nazi records exist as to how and when Hershel was murdered. Experts speculate that Herschel was most likely executed by the Nazis as the Allies closed in on Germany. Herschel's dad survived the war, having escaped the Nazi invasion of Poland, and made it into Soviet territory. He was the first witness to testify for the prosecution in the Adolf Eichmann trial held in Jerusalem in 1961.

The "who-had-it-worse?" pissing match continued as we walked to the South of the Border restaurant.

"Can you imagine being a kid growing up in Germany in the middle 30s, having to wear the star, not being able to go to a movie or a circus and, as a teenager not being allowed to drive a car?"

"Well, I guess in the 30s, American Blacks were allowed to go shows and sit in segregated seats in the balcony. and drive cars if they had enough money to own one."

"Mort have you ever worn a Star of David around your neck?"

"Neal, you know I'm not into jewelry. All I wear are these hippie beads. I'm not into that religious stuff. No *chais, hamsas* or *Mogen Davids* worn around my neck. G-d knows I'm a Jew, but I'm not a believer in these pendants and medallions. They are not going to protect me from harm or the evil eye. They did not work well for the six million. If you want to see the symbol that David had on his shield when he killed Goliath go to my gravestone. It will be there – carved deep into the granite so it will last for hundreds of years. That will be my identification marker. Now let's get back to our Jew-versus-Black debate.

"Can you imagine how those Jewish kids suffered when they learned that the Nazis passed a law requiring only Jews to surrender their household pets – their dogs and cats were put to sleep. These children could not even give their pets away to a friend or neighbor. It was as if the dog had been infected by Jewish blood. They had to bring the dog or cat to a veterinarian to be euthanized."

"Well slaves were treated like pets in the South. They had no civil rights." Neal countered.

"Well the Jews had yellow-painted benches in parks designated for them to sit on," I added.

"Why always the color yellow? Didn't the Jews have to wear yellow Stars of David in the ghettos as well as in the camps?" Neal inquired.

"That color thing goes way back before the Nazis. A yellow badge of shame was around as far back as 1434 when in Germany, Jewish men were ordered to wear yellow pointed veils. In the 1500s yellow badges and collars were required to be worn by German Jews. To answer your question, I have no idea why those emperors chose yellow. But even today if you call somebody yellow you're branding them a chicken or a coward."

Neal pondered my words in silence and then I added.

"The Star of David patches on the striped pajama uniforms are an interesting topic. I saw a concentration camp poster with multiple different designations. The Nazis were so anally compulsive; I think it is inbred in them. They had color-coded markings for: political prisoners (red), criminals (green), immigrants (blue), Bible Students–Jehovah Witnesses (purple), homosexuals (pink), and Germans who did not work hard enough (black). So a gay Jew would have a Star of David made up of yellow triangle and a pink triangle."

Neal asked, "Do you think there was ever a lazy German, Gay, political prisoner who was Jewish? He would have had to wear two Jewish stars."

"I doubt it, but stranger things have happened."

"The Germans were obsessed with labeling Jews, from the large "J" on their passports, to adding 'Israel' or 'Sarah' to their legal names, to yellow cloth stars, to paint on store windows, and finally to tattoos on their arms."

Neal seemed to find the point interesting as he pondered it silently for a few seconds. He returned to our comparative discussion.

"I read that the first generation of slaves found their experiences so painful that they rarely discussed them with their children. Just like many Holocaust survivors, your dad and mom, hardly talked about their experiences with you."

I had had enough of this debate, this greasy restaurant, and its red-neck gift shop." Neal you're right about my parents and I can't handle looking at this junk anymore. Let's get the hell out of here but let's do it with style."

We left South of the Border whistling Dixie. Having had our fill of Southern culture, we headed to the car.

It was my turn to drive the unairconditioned Mustang. The steering wheel and the window handle knobs burnt my fingers. We left *South of the Border* with the windows down and our eyes wide open. We had opened a door filled with graffiti and entered a racist *Twilight Zone* episode.

Ten miles down the road, I slowed down and pointed at an 18-foot Confederate flag, flapping and snapping in the wind.

"Neal, look at that red, white, and blue flag with its stars and bars. What a disgrace to Old Glory. The Klan Flag. Real warm Southern hospitality. A slap across our Jewish faces. That's the flag my father and I saw waved at those Klan cross-burning rallies on TV."

Neal put on his best General Patton face and muttered, "In that case, let's burn down the motherfucker."

Pressing down hard on the gas pedal, I heard the powerful 289 horsepower cubic inch V-8 engine roar like a lion. The Mustang passed the flag pole at 75 miles per hour. Neal stuck both of his arms out the window and shot two birds at the flag. He aimed his two middle fingers as if he was shooting a Colt revolver. We both let out an uneasy laugh.

"Neal, I should have brought my .22 rifle with the mounted scope or at least my 410 shotgun on this trip. I had two fresh boxes of ammo in my dresser."

"Yeah, a lot of good those guns and ammunition are doing us resting in your bedroom instead of the trunk of this pony," Neal replied.

"Neal, did I ever tell you that my dad never fired a pistol or a rifle in his whole life. He never even shot my .22, but during the Second World War that fact saved his life."

"Bro, you got to tell me that story."

"Well, you know that on September 1, 1939, the Germans invaded Poland."

"Yeah."

"Well my dad and his family tried to evade the Nazi onslaught. I guess their escape plan entailed driving into the Soviet-Occupied territory. They packed up their car and a horse-drawn wagon heading east toward The Soviet Union. But their attempt to escape failed when they were overtaken by the invading German army. The *Wermacht* confiscated their automobile and their wagon. The Laitners were forced to head home on foot.

As my father and his family headed home, a Pole saw the expensive watch on my father's wrist. He yelled. "Jew, give me your watch!"

My father replied, "Why the hell should I hand it over to the likes of you?"

"The Nazis are going to murder all of you... so you might as well hand it over to me."

My dad stared into his eyes and said, "Go to Hell!"

The Pole smirked and cackled, "You kike son-of-a-bitch, you will be dead by tomorrow. Your family will be real sorry you didn't hand over that damned watch."

Within an hour, the Pole reported my dad to a German soldier. They arrested my dad. The accuser pointed his index finger into my dad's face and said, "This Jew is a partisan. Yesterday I saw him shooting at German soldiers from those woods."

My father thought he was going to be shot on the spot. Then the German officer questioned him. "Is this true?"

He replied in perfect German, "I have never held or shot a pistol or a rifle in my whole life."

Unbelievably, the officer accepted my father's statement .The Germans shot the lying son-of-a-bitch Pole."

"Wow, your dad was a lucky son-of-a-gun. What are the odds that a German would believe a Jew over a Pole?

"Now turn on that radio I want to hear some rock and roll."

Twisting the radio knob, I found none. To protest this lack of music, I flicked off the radio and belted out some of Dylan's Blowing in the Wind: *Yes, how many deaths will it take till he knowsthat too many people have died? The answer my friend is blowin' in the wind,the answer is blowin' in the wind.*

Stuck in the heart of Dixie, without an eight-track tape player forced us to suffer in radio silence.

Neal broke the quiet, "You know, Southern radio stations suck. They consider rock and roll the devil's music. Just as Hitler labeled jazz as "*Schwarze musik* or nigger-Jew jazz." Hitler prohibited jazz on the radio. He considered it a contaminant of the Aryan race. He had Germans arrested for even owning jazz records."

"Yeah anything Jews touched was considered degenerative – degenerative art, degenerative music and degenerative books. They all had to be burned along with the artists that created them," I said.

Twisting through the whole dial for the third time, I still only found country music artists, Baptist preachers, local news and weather reports. For a few minutes, we'd listen to preachers interpret the "Good Book." They always found ways to get out G-d's message while seeking donations. The country-western tunes with their high pitched fiddles made my ears bleed. I turned the radio on and off in an attempt to avoid yodelers and singers with unintelligible twangy voices.

When the news came on, we heard a reporter read the verdicts rendered in a Klan murder case.

"Judge Cox imposed sentences on Mr. Roberts and Mr. Bowers of ten years. Mr. Posey and Mr. Price each received six year terms, and the other three defendants received four."

Judge Cox said, "The sentences were fair, since they killed one nigger, one Jew, and a white man. I gave them all what I thought they deserved."

"Neal, Judge Cox got it wrong on two counts: Those convicted murderers deserved much longer sentences, and there was no 'white man killed,' only two Jews."

"Yeah, down here, that's what they call Southern justice?" Neal mocked.

Thirty years later, I read, Klan leader Shelton's unrepentant words of failure, "The Klan is my belief, my religion. But it won't work anymore. The Klan is gone ... forever."

I knew his prophetic words were merely symbolic, like the Confederate flags I saw plastered on Ford pickup trucks. Hate groups never seemed to die. They always hung onto bare threads, hoping the Confederacy and the Klan would rise again.

Nineteen

Tobacco

On the border between South Carolina and Georgia, Neal slept as I drove past the green tobacco plants rising from the ground. I observed faded brown curing barns and thought about my father. In bare feet he stood on the tile floor wearing white boxers and a sleeveless cotton undershirt. He coughed his lungs out. Seven days a week, my father, the doctor, acted out his morning ritual and I listened. He hacked, coughed, and wheezed while stooping over the toilet bowl until a globule of phlegm appeared floating on the water's surface. I thought, "What a way to start your day. Why does he keep smoking?"

How I prayed, "G-d give him the strength to wrestle those cancer sticks out of his hands. Help me flush those cigarettes down that toilet." My prayers went unanswered. I wanted to grab his pack, tear up the cigarettes and flush them out of his life. But I did not.

I did not loudly or softly protest his insanity. I do not remember ever telling him to quit. He was a physician, a survivor who must have prayed for tobacco in the camps, and a man who needed a nicotine fix for moments of relaxation.

Who was I to tell him how to live his life?

Neal awoke, stared at the tobacco fields, and interrupted my daydream. "Did you know Hitler abstained from tobacco, meat, and alcohol?

"I knew about the tobacco but not the other two." I replied.

Neal then launched into a dissertation on Hitler and smoking. "I read a book by Robert Proctor entitled *The Nazi War on Cancer.* Proctor thought Hitler smoked as a youth but when he became aware of its dangers, he quit. Hitler's conversion, like that of many smokers who quit, led to his total detestation of smokers. Once in power, most people who hung around him never smoked in his presence. He called smoking, 'the wrath of the Red Man against the White Man, vengeance for having been given hard liquor.'"

"Hitler must have been a big fan of American Westerns to know all those facts about Indians. Based on his hatred of Jews, I bet he didn't believe in that old Indian parable about walking a mile in another man's moccasins before you judge him," I replied.

"I have no idea what movies Hitler liked but I bet he thought Indians were another inferior race," Neal responded.

"Hitler's antismoking campaign stressed the virtues of hygiene and purity. He discouraged drinking booze and encouraged his followers eat a nutritious diet."

"Neal, we would have made lousy Nazis, the way we smoke, eat and drink."

Neal continued talking, ignoring my comment.

"Did you know Hitler was such a control freak that he held every German responsible to the entire nation for all his deeds? No German had the right to damage their body with drugs."

Now I neglected to answer Neal's question, but followed it with one of my own.

"Buddy, do you know why Hitler never told his father to quit smoking?

"No. why?" Neal queried.

"Because as a kid, his father almost beat him to death. His hospital recovery lasted more than a month. He had one hell of a Dad; he definitely drove his kid nuts."

I cleared my voice and said. "I wish that beating had been a deadly success."

Neal continued, "In one of my cinematography courses, I saw a film in which German scientists taught about the connection between tobacco and cancer. They even held up a poster that depicted fat Jews and skinny Blacks puffing away on cigars and cigarettes. Their message was clear:only inferiors needed to smoke, for to do so made them feel superior."

I gripped the steering wheel and returned my thoughts to my dad coughing over the toilet. I remembered swearing, "I will never smoke those cancer sticks." But during the year of my Bar Mitzvah, I pilfered one cigarette a day from my mother's pack of Newports. It was easy to get away with the theft since she smoked a pack a day.

I smoked because it was cool. The ads on my black and white TV displayed hot, young women staring at virile men holding a cigarette to their lips. These ads were not subliminal. Smoking led to sex. I wanted sex, *ergo* I had to smoke.

Woodridge had the perfect spot for teenagers to light up. Dead Man's Canyon provided privacy for us to do what are parents did publicly.

I smoked because I wanted to be that Marlboro man, riding my mustang through red-stone canyons with a cigarette hanging off my lower lip. I'd be headed to a saloon to get a taste of manhood, to fondle and suckle breasts that popped out of the top of barroom dresses – to smell their whore perfumes as I mounted their bodies. Still wearing my boots, I'd climax in their pink canyons. After our session, we'd both light up and make idle chatter.

I smoked because the teenage girls I shared cigarettes with allowed me to touch their breasts. Their round developing expressions of womanhood were covered by the white brassieres.

These bras easily snapped off, freeing their tightly wrapped melons. My eyes gloried in their exposure. My hands caressed them as if I touched the flesh of a deity. My fingers focused in on their dark nipples flicking each tip, in an effort to get them to stand at attention. I reveled in their hardness, while trying to build the courage to lower my head and suckle each of them.

Through the bulge in my jeans, these girls saw their success in arousing my erection, but they too lacked the daring to uncover its mysteries.

Between breast groping and cigarettes, we French kissed. We tried to perfect our kissing style. Our tongues darted into each other's mouths in an attempt to taste tonsils. Instead we tasted mentholated nicotine mixed with Juicy Fruit and saliva.

After a make-out session, the girls naughtily put on their bras and buttoned their white cotton blouses. I proudly left Dead Man's Canyon having safely reached first base. I'd steal more of my mother's cigarettes in hope of reaching second on our next smoking encounter.

As Neal smoked and drove, I caught glimpses of the farmers stooping next to rows of five-foot high tobacco plants, selectively picking the leaves and softly laying them down in a pile as if they handled a newborn.

These farmers grew and handled the plant, that my dad smoked, that burnt his lungs, which hardened his arteries and that eventually killed him. These were the folks that harvested the tobacco plant, that I purchased, that created the smoke, that I inhaled, that made me cough until I realized I did not want to die like my father.

TWENTY

EIN VOLK, EIN REICH, EIN FÜHRER

Years before I smoked my first cigarette or made out with teenage goddesses, I learned about the Holocaust by reading my father's collection of Time-Life Books on World War II or his copy of Leon Uris's novel, *Mila 18,* or by repeatedly watching *The World at War.*

My studies took place decades before *Schindler's List* and *The Pianist,* mandatory high school Holocaust study classes and the litany of self-published survivors' memoirs. These were still the days of shame, the how-did-we-let-this- happen-to-us days. These were the days when survivors, as well as the media, hardly ever discussed the *Shoah.* These were the days before Jewish television networks and the plethora of Holocaust doctoral research. These were the days when no one said, "Stop telling those Holocaust stories. They have been told over and over. Move on to anything else."

In those days the topic was too fresh, too raw and too unbelievable. The camp photographs spoke for themselves. No one needed to see them on TV or in movie theaters. The movies arrived in the Sixties with films like, *The Diary of Anne Frank, The Pawnbroker* and *Judgment at Nuremberg.* It took an additional 30 to 40 years for before Spielberg and Polanski fully opened the sore, allowing the healing process to commence.

I opened my sores by squeezing and popping the pimples buried deep in my back, as I studied my *World Book Encyclopedia* and *The Junior Jewish Encyclopedia* searching for the few pages dedicated to the Holocaust.

Giving my eyes and fingers a break, I speculated, "Are those oily, puss-filled pimples that are burrowing into my back related to my fear of Hitler, or anti-Semites, or a second Holocaust."

Then for a short period of time in 1960, the Holocaust-informational floodgates opened with the Israeli capture of Adolf Eichmann. In 1961, as a twelve year old, I sat glued to my chair with my eyes straining at our black and white TV. The trial of Adolph Eichmann played out nightly on the three national networks.

In our den, sitting next to three survivors, my grandmother, my father, and my Mother, I saw the man responsible for the administration of the whole process, from the trains that transported millions, first into the ghettos and then into the extermination camps. This man was responsible for the death of many of my relatives and the imprisonment of the immediate family that sat beside me.

Eichmann attended and participated in the Wannsee Conference. A conference where the participants decided how to implement the Final Solution of the Jewish question – immediate death to the young, the old, and those incapable of forced labor and the rest to be worked to death.

For fourteen weeks of testimony, Eichmann wore his black suit, his black framed, plastic eye glasses, his narrow dark tie and a tight-lipped contorted smile. A sneer-like smile that said, "I am not sorry for anything I did. I would do it all over again if I had the chance." This soldier was just following orders.

In an Israeli court, in the capital of the Jewish state, Mr. Final Solution sat behind bullet-proof glass in a booth with an Israeli police officer seated on each side of him. Justice demanded this banality of evil not cheat the hangman's noose. The glass and the policemen were there to make sure of that.

I studied Eichmann's receding hairline, wondering if his loss of hair was caused by old age or his fear of capture. A procession of fears ran across my brain. Did he fear hanging? Did he fear death? Did he fear Hell? Did he fear seeing the souls of the persons he murdered? I didn't have a clue. But I would soon learn the answers to my questions.

Hidden behind those thick-lensed, black-framed plastic glasses was a puzzled man, who questioned the legitimacy of this Israeli tribunal. What authority did this nation of Jews have over this former *SS-Obersturmbannführer?*

When alone, I cursed his electronic image on the glass screen, "Fucking murderer!"

"You and your kind killed my grandparents, my uncles, and many more of my relatives!"

"You fucked up my parents' lives!"

"You fucked up my life!"

"You bastard! I hope your hanging is real slow!"

Fifteen days after my twelfth birthday, Eichmann hung. Here was my belated birthday present from the gods.

At his request, he donned no black hood. His last words were, "Long live Germany. Long live Argentina. Long live Austria. These are the three countries with which I have been most connected and which I will not forget. I greet my wife, my family, and my friends. I am ready. We'll meet again soon, as is the fate of all men. I die believing in God."

I thought, "What a prick; not one word of remorse. How dare this motherfucker believe in G-d. May his family and friends meet him in purgatory, a hell in which they are the prisoners housed in Auschwitz for eternity."

Testimony at the Israeli trial showed the type of man Eichmann was. In 1945 he said, "I will leap into my grave laughing because the feeling that I have killed five million human beings on my conscience is, for me, a source of extraordinary satisfaction."

As I pictured Eichmann leaping, laughing, and sneering as the rope constricted around his air pipes, a burden leaped off my shoulders. My mouth tasted sweet revenge. But I wanted more.

I wanted to be the executioner, to be able to select the shortest rope to guarantee slow strangulation. I wanted to wrap the noose around his neck, spit in his face, and then pull the lever that released the trap door. I wanted to see the brown stains on the outside of his pants. I wanted keep the noose as a souvenir so I could donate it to *Yad Vashem.* I wanted to see the noose displayed at *Yad Vashem* in an opened case to allow visitors to touch it. I wanted to urinate on his body as it lay on the ground. I wanted to kick his body into a ditch and watch buzzards pull off strips of flesh. I wanted to say the last words Eichmann would hear, "Die motherfucker! Hell awaits you!"

On the day Eichmann hung, I wondered what my dad's thoughts were. Did he have similar thoughts? But I did not ask.

By my sixteenth birthday, a full-blown Holocaust obsession infected my body. Just like the bacteria growing deep into my back, I was obsessed but not obsessed enough to draw cat, mice, and pig cartoons representing Nazis, Jews, and Poles as did Art Spiegelman in his graphic novel, *Maus: A Survivor's Tale.* Nor was I obsessed enough to cover my refrigerator with magnets that named the death camps. Nor was I obsessed enough to collect actual relics or reproductions of the camp paraphernalia. Nor was I obsessed to buy one of the seven sets of artist, Zbigniew Libra's, rendition of a concentration camp made of LEGO bricks. His art project consists of barracks, guard towers, electrified fences, hanging posts, crematoria, and black guards beating white skeletal prisoners. Today two of these sets reside in the Museum of Modern Art in Warsaw and the Jewish Museum of New York.

Mine was a mental obsession that caused my eyes to burn every time I saw photos of the piles of naked corpses being readied for cremation or tears to flow as I examined the photo of a ten-year old boy, with his hands raised in the air as Nazi soldiers led him out of the Warsaw Ghetto.

And, in a small way, like that child with his hands raised high, I became a victim of one people, one German nation, and one *Führer.*

Twenty-One

Law School

At twenty-one, I was a newlywed, who attended law school, and stopped putting on *tefillin.* I attended Stetson Law School in Gulfport, Florida. Stetson was Florida's first law school. It had Spanish courtyard's and towers, architectural style meant to mimic Seville's thirteenth century Torre del Oro. As I studied the buildings I recalled the Spanish Inquisition. Staring at the top of the tower into the sky, I prayed, "G-d may my fate in this law school be better than that of the Spanish Jews in the fifteenth century."

These Spanish structures were first opened in the 1920's as the Rolyat Hotel. In 1954 the hotel was converted into the law school. A law school named after John B. Stetson a cowboy-hat manufacturer. This fact seemed like a good omen, since my first chosen profession was to be a cowboy.

In my first semester at Stetson, I laid on *tefillin* every morning as I had done in junior and senior high and at the University of

Miami. This religious ritual had its roots in a biblical commandment found in Deuteronomy: "And thou shall bind them for a sign upon thy hand, and they shall be as frontlets between thine eyes." Inside the two black leather boxes, which I wore on my forehead and arm were parchments proclaiming the existence and unity of G-d. They served as a reminder to the wearer of our escape from Egyptian slavery.

I had a verbal contract with the Creator concerning his existence. My putting tefillin on was my sign of dedication to him. We had a binding agreement in which I made an offer: "Let me pass my Bar Mitzvah day without humiliation and I will be a believer and a follower."

G-d accepted my offer and as consideration, I received my blessed day in the sun. There were only two witnesses present at this contract's creation. But now all bets were being pulled off the table.

I was a dismal law student. Competing against older and smarter students stacked the deck against me. My sloppy handwriting further compounded my professors' ability to grade my tests. I had not discovered the value of putting all the key legal terms and cases into a simple chart. I had not yet developed my mnemonic memorization techniques that allowed me to master the essence of the course on one sheet of paper. Without correcting these weaknesses, failure at Stetson was assured.

At Stetson, no matter how hard I studied, I failed or barely passed. My frustration led me to believe that the Almighty no longer gave a shit about my future. My G-d had forsaken me.

I still had the common sense to draw up an emergency escape plan. I'd leave Stetson before I was asked to leave. This maneuver would allow me to transfer to another accredited law school.

On my last day at my St. Petersburg apartment, with the *tefillin's* black leather straps wrapped tightly around my left arm and its other box resting heavily on my forehead, I prayed, "G-d of my fathers, you have broken our deal. It is now a nullity. Therefore I am no longer bound to fulfill my promise to be a follower and lay *tefillin.* I am still a believer in your existence, but this daily morning, prayer ritual is over."

On that day my Israeli-made, blue-cloth tefillin bag, containing my tefillin, with its embroidered yellow Star of David found a new home on the back shelf of my bedroom closet. From then on the bag was only taken out for trips to new homes. Upon arrival into each new house, They were relegated into rear closet space.

One year before I stopped putting on *tefillin,* I had one of the two religious experiences of my life. This miracle occurred on my first pilgrimage to the Holy Land. Walking through dark alleys of the Arab sectors of Jerusalem, toward the foot of the western side of the Temple Mount, I fixated on shopkeepers hawking: rugs, shawls, jewelry, kippahs, hookahs, mezuzahs and olive-wood-carved camels.

Just as in Tangiers, time-traveled from the twentieth century to sixteenth. Just as in the Kasbah, pungent odors invaded my nostrils. My nose hairs twitched at the smell of burning tobacco. I craved tasting the Turkish coffee being brewed on every street corner. The sounds of children's voices echoed off the cavernous walls.

At the end of an alley, I walked into a clearing. Before my eyes appeared the Wailing Wall and gold-colored Dome of the Rock. The Dome reflected the Sun's rays into my eyes. Placing my hand over my eyes, I observed hundreds of plants growing out of the wall.

I had made it to my people's most sacred structure, our Western Wall, our *Kotel.* Here was the only surviving retaining wall of the Temple Mount. Here was one of the four walls Herod the Great built to support the plaza on which the Temple stood. Here stood hundreds of devotees praying to the Lord. Here was the place where my ancestors craved to pray for close to two thousand years.

Approaching the Wall, an Orthodox Jew asked me in English, "Are you Jewish?"

I replied with a clear, "Yes," and two nods of my head. Even though I needed no help, he assisted me in putting on the *tefillin.*

Then he handed me a piece of paper with Hebrew and English prayers on it. With the phylacteries secured to my arm and head, I moved to within six inches of the large lime stones. I swayed, stood, prayed and squeezed a small piece of paper into a crevices of the wall. On that snippet of paper I had written in English, " G-d keep my family in good health." I prayed the *Shema Yisrael:*

שְׁמַע יִשְׂרָאֵל יהוה אֱלֹהֵינוּ יהוה אֶחָד

While reciting the *Shema,* I was engulfed with a Divine presence. An electrically-charged field haloed my body. I had been touched. I had felt the presence of G-d.

G-d gave me one more present before I left Stetson. While perusing the library stacks, to my amazement, I discovered that law library had been selected as a repository of Robert H. Jackson's collection of judicial papers. Here I was, a struggling freshman, with little time to spare, with a treasure trove of Holocaust materials. Here was Robert H. Jackson's complete set of beautifully-bound leather-covered books on the Nuremberg trials. While holding each volume in my hands, I touched history.

I remembered seeing *Judgment at Nuremburg* in the Woodridge theater. It was the summer of 1961. The movie had an all-star cast: Spencer Tracy, Burt Lancaster, Richard Widmark,

Marlene Dietrich, Werner Klemperer, Judy Garland, William Shatner, Montgomery Clift, and Maximilian Schell. Those were the days of casting. In my twelfth year, Hollywood decided it was time to make a Holocaust film. It took them sixteen years from the end of the war to do it. The movie had been nominated for 11 Academy Awards. The night I went to the movie, I watched CBS coverage of the Adolf Eichmann trial.

Judgment at Nuremburg was a military tribunal film dealing with the subject of Nazi culpability. As I watched, I wondered had my Dad ever testified in a military tribunal? Had my Dad met Justice Jackson?

Robert Jackson was a former U.S. Attorney General and then an Associate Justice of the U.S. Supreme Court. In 1945 he took a leave of absence from the Court because President Truman appointed him the U.S. Chief Legal Counsel for the prosecution of Nazi war criminals in Nuremberg.

In one eight-hour session, I read the volume entitled, *The Holocaust.* Names like Albert Speer, Herman Goering, Reinhard Heydrich ... Hitler's parasitic henchman appeared across each page. Some were defendants, while others had already died.

That day I concentrated on the pages that referenced Reinhard Heydrich. I owned a stamp with his face on it. He was a key architect of the Holocaust. He died in June of 1942, in a Prague suburb. On a hairpin turn on May 27,1942, a Czech assassin heaved a bomb into Heydrich's Mercedes Benz convertible mortally wounding him. Heydrich did not have his boss's luck. But Adolf honored him with a postage stamp.

In the German World War II section of my stamp album, rested a Reinhard Heydrich death mask stamp. Printed on the stamp were: his dates of birth and death, the names of the Protectorates of Bohemia and Moravia, where he was the Deputy *Reich* Protector, and the SS thunder and lightning bolts because he had reached the rank of general in the SS.

Since Reinhard was the chairman of the Wannsee Conference, what should have been printed on the stamp were the electrified barb-wire fences and crematorium.

I studied the dimensions of Reinhard's death-mask nose. To my surprise, the Nazis had not shaved it down. It looked Jewish. That nose was why as a child, Reinhard was bullied by his classmates based on rumors of his Jewish ancestry.

As a party member, he was investigated and cleared of the Jewish blood libel and then rose rapidly through the Nazi ranks. By 1934, Himmler appointed him the head of the Gestapo. Hitler called him "the man with the iron heart." He also had many other nicknames: The Hangman, The Butcher of Prague, The Blond Beast, The Young Evil God of Death.

Heydrich was a key organizer of *Kristallnacht,* where SA storm troopers and civilians burned temples and businesses, murdered Jews and sent many Jews to concentration camps. I saw a copy of the telegram signed by Heydrich printed in German. Reading the translation, I learned his telegram was sent to Gestapo offices throughout Germany and Austria. The telegram coordinated Nazi activities for the "Night of the Broken Glass." It read in part that "as many Jews – particularly affluent Jews – are to be arrested in all districts as can be accommodated in existing detention facilities ... Immediately after the arrests have been carried out, the appropriate concentration camps should be contacted to place the Jews in the camps as quickly as possible."

Four months before his death, Heydrich attended a meeting in Wannsee, Germany. Wannsee is a suburb of Berlin. Heydrich chaired the conference and presented a plan which was approved by the attendees to deport and transport 11 million Jews from every country in Europe to death camps. All the German officials in the room consented to the plan. The Jews were to be worked to death or killed outright.

In his speech Heydrich said:

> "Under suitable direction, the Jews should be brought to the East in the course of the Final Solution, for use as labour. In large labour gangs, with the sexes separated, the Jews capable of work will be transported to those areas and set to road-building, in the course of which, without doubt, a large part of them will fall away through natural losses. The

> surviving remnant, surely those with the greatest powers of resistance, will be given special treatment, since, if freed, they would constitute the germinal cell for the re-creation of Jewry."

Exhausted from reading euphemisms like "special treatment," I stopped reading. I had devoted another day of my life to the Holocaust.

Because of my grades, my studies at Stetson were coming to an end. I had become a surviving remnant, non-*tefillin*-wearing Jew on his way to Southern University Law School in search of a doctorate in law.

Twenty-Two

The Doctoral Dissertation

As I reached the sixth decade of my life, my eyebrows started turning grey. I sat in my office thinking whether to pluck out those signs of aging. I thought about my father's bushy grey eyebrows and his life in retirement. I remembered how much he loved playing with his grandsons after he gave up practicing medicine. The phone rang, I picked up the receiver and heard my sister, Barbara's voice.

"Hi, Mort, how you doing?" Not pausing to let me respond she continued. "I have some exciting news. Dad's been referenced in a scholarly Israeli article about his imprisonment in the camps. The author received her Ph.D. for that paper. I'll email you the website. He is only referenced in a footnote or two. Let's discuss the article after you read it."

"Sis, thanks for calling. We're doing well. How are you, Jeff ,and the boys?" Following her lead, I jumped into my next sentence without letting her respond. "It's quite ironic that you called at the exact time when I have been thinking about Dad. What a coincidence. I can't wait to read the paper. I'll call you the minute I finish reading it."

As I hung up the phone, I thought about how much I missed my dad, his relaxed demeanor, his full laugh, and the way his dark eyes penetrated my heart.

A week passed and no email, article, or website arrived, so I called my sister.

"Barbara, how are you, Jeff and the boys doing?"

"All is well. What's up with you Mort?"

"Everything is great but it has been a week and I haven't received that website you promised me about the article concerning Dad."

"Sorry, Mort; I've been real busy and I am having problems with my computer," she replied. "Hopefully I will get it fixed this week. Why don't you call or visit Uncle Mike? He has a copy of the article."

"Thanks, Sis. Sorry your computer is not functioning. I'll make that visit to Uncle Mike's. Bye. Love you."

Placing the receiver in the cradle, I thought this story must not have much information on Dad. Barbara said it only referenced him in a footnote or two. Barbara now acted like this Ph.D. paper was no big deal. Had she even read the article?

The next day, as I drove to my Uncle Mike's condo in Lauderhill, I recalled the first time I read my story "The Stairs" to a large audience. I walked to the podium, positioned myself in front of a microphone and stared out into the crowd. Two hundred adults sat in this Miami Beach bookstore located on Lincoln Road. There was not an empty chair in the house.

My life had gone full circle. Lincoln Road was same street where my dad, mom, sister, and I had proudly walked as winter tourists 42 years earlier. Now I stood in front of a crowd of 200 talking about him.

I started reading. My voice tightened with tension. My ears picked up restless body movements, coughs and sneezes.

A minute passed before I paused to catch my breath. Now I only heard the sounds of silence. The transfixed audience did not flex a muscle. They ate the tale out of the palms of my hands. My captivated audience was under my spell. I felt the power of the story. I felt the clout of the storyteller.

At the next traffic light, my thoughts shifted to the stories that I told my family and friends every Passover. Every *seder* my family learned something about slave laborers and the meaning of freedom.

Twenty-Three

The *Seder*

I sat at the head of the Passover table like a king in his dining hall, resting on a black-lacquered chair covered with two satin-embroidered pillows, my head covered with a crocheted blue yarmulke emblazoned with a bright yellow Star of David, the same symbol the Nazis forced my family to wear throughout the war. The *Talmud* taught us that we wore *kippahs* so that the fear of heaven rested upon our heads. But rubbing its coarse wool, I felt no fear, only the warmth of family.

I examined the soft, white linen tablecloth on which it rested: Wedgewood plates, bowls, crystal glassware, polished Gotham sterling flatware, white cloth napkins and a blue and white floral bouquet in a cut-lead vase. This table setting reminded me of a Gourmet magazine cover photograph – a representation of the perfect *seder* table.

Next to each plate setting rested a 62 page – distributed free by Publix – *Haggadah* booklet that was printed by the Manischewitz Company. This company was made famous for their mass production of *matzo* and cheap sweet Kosher wine. They were and are the largest producer of Kosher products. Manischewitz understood the meaning of marketing. In its honor I raised my body and my wine glass and toasted, "Man-o-Manischewitz, what a wine!"

Those around the table responded with a resounding "Amen!"

While I stood toasting, the aroma of chicken soup permeated my nostrils. This smell brought back memories of my father's Woodridge home and my grandmother's chicken soup.

In the background, on the stereo, Zero Mostel sang, *Tradition.* My family sang along understanding the value of this holiday meal.

My wife lit the *seder* candles. Their flames reflected love on the crystal glasses.

Uncle Mike, Aunt Renia and two neighbors joined us at the *seder* table. Uncle Mike or Motek, his Polish name, stands five feet, nine inches tall with a husky build and square jaw. This handsome man survived of Auschwitz and has the tattoo on his arm to prove it. On arrival to the death camp, in the ensuing chaos, Mike and his father were pushed apart. His dad was selected for slave labor; Mike for the gas chambers. In their search for each other, they blindly crossed paths. Mike's father was gassed and Mike survived.

After the war, Uncle Mike went to Palestine where he joined the Israeli Army and fought in the 1948 War of Independence. One night during that war, Uncle Mike found himself stationed in a field covered in blood. He thought he was mortally wounded, but wondered why he felt no pain. At daybreak he learned the pack mule that rested beside him had taken a bullet; he was covered in mule's blood.

Aunt Renia, my mom's sole sibling, also bears a tattoo on her arm. She, my Mom, and my grandmother spent most of war together in slave labor. At the close of the war, they survived a forced Winter death march. Many of the other marchers were not so lucky. During the march, my mother convinced their female Nazi guard to seek shelter for the night by having a nervous breakdown.

We marched through the *Haggadah* reading the story aloud. The Manischewitz booklet gave us the order of the *seder* and the story of the Exodus.

When we read the portion of the text on Moses asking Pharaoh for his people's freedom, we belted out the words to "Let My People Go" as if we were cotton-picking slaves in pre-Civil War Georgia.

We tasted the *matzo* covered with *maror*. The *maror* – chopped horseradish – burnt our tongues, ran up our nasal passages and caused our eyes to tear. In those few seconds of bitterness, we had a taste of slavery.

I discussed the symbolic nature of the other items resting on the *seder* plate. Pointing to the *charoset,* I said, "This mixture of chopped nuts, grated apples, and sweet red wine represents the mortar our ancestors used to build the pyramids." Holding a piece of *karpas* in the air I said, "We dip this parsley into this bowl of salt water to represent the tears our ancestors shed as Pharaoh's slaves."

I touched the shankbone. "This bone symbolizes the offerings our ancestors made to G-d in the Temple in Jerusalem." Holding a hard-boiled egg in the palm of my hand, I said. "This egg also symbolizes sacrificial offering in the Temple in Jerusalem."

Then I pointed to the yellow Star of David baked into the center of the porcelain *seder* plate. "Here is the *Mogen David,* a six-cornered star made by combining two triangles, our ancient symbol found in temples built in the third or fourth century. But in the twentieth century this star reminds all of us at this table of how it was worn with dread on the streets of Europe from the thirties until 1945, and how today it is the proud symbol of the state of Israel."

I toasted the land of Israel and the IDF. I chanted the Kiddush, the blessing over the wine. My family responded with a hearty, "Amen."

Blake, my youngest, asked the four questions in Hebrew. Jason, my oldest, read the answers in English. We all discussed the tale of slavery and our escape from the land of the Nile.

I placed my *Haggadah* on the end table which held empty and half-full bottles of Concord Manischewitz wine. Picking up my Passover speech, I paused to look into the eyes of my three sons. They were the miracles my wife and I had created.

Coughing to get everyone's attention, I started my speech.

"Tonight, I transport all of you to the Sobibor death camp. I am going to tell you about a tale of slavery, bondage, plagues, and freedom. Here is a story I found in Wikipedia, which I read twice, which I read slowly, and from which I took copious notes. Here is a story told by survivors and our protagonist, Sasha Pechersky. He told his version of the story in his autobiography. To make sure you are paying attention, after I finish the story, I am going to ask all of you two questions.

"Our setting is German-occupied Poland in September of 1943. This story's main character is a modern-day Moses named Alexander (Sasha) Pechersky.

"He was a handsome man, who arrived in the Sobibor in the usual manner, crammed in a cattle car. In the train's cattle cars, he and his fellow Russian POWs were housed like African slaves on a Portuguese slave-running ship. There were over 2000 POWs in those cattle cars.

"Alexander was one of 80 prisoners selected to work in the camp. The remaining 1,920 Soviet soldiers were fed to the gas chambers. These chambers were not the usual Zyklon B crystal gas chambers. The Nazis generated carbon monoxide gas by turning on a 200-horsepower tractor or tank engine. This method, being slower, was a more torturous way of murdering the chamber's inhabitants. During the war, Sobibor's gas chambers devoured more than 250,000 Jews.

"Before his capture and imprisonment, Sasha obtained the rank of lieutenant quartermaster in the Soviet Army. However in October of 1941, his unit was captured by the Nazis in the Battle of Moscow. For the next twenty-three months, Sasha suffered through four slave-labor camps. In one of those camps a Nazi doctor examined him. Seeing his circumcised penis the doctor inquired, 'Are you a Jew?'

"'Yes,' Sasha replied.

"For that admission, he was thrown into the 'The Jewish Grave.' For ten days, he survived in a dark cellar. He received 3.5 ounces of wheat and a cup of water every other day. I ask all of you to imagine if you could last for ten days in the dark cellar on that small amount bread and water?

"I now take you back to Sobibor. On his first night there, Sasha asked a fellow inmate, 'What are those fires burning behind those trees in the woods? And what is causing this horrible odor inside the camp?'

"The inmate replied, 'Do not even look in the direction of the flames, for to do so will get you a whipping.' The inmate added, 'They are burning the corpses of your murdered comrades who arrived with you today. Almost every day a train arrives with 2000 Jewish men, women, and children who are murdered. This has been going on for over a year. We are the so-called 'lucky ones.' There are about 550 Jewish prisoners who work in Sobibor.'

"In his third day in the camp Sasha earned the respect of his fellow inmates by standing up to a senior SS officer.

"When the Nazi officer whipped a Jew who was too weak to chop a stump. Pechersky watched the beating while resting on his ax. The SS officer asked Sasha, 'You don't like what you see?'

"'Yes, *Oberscharführer,*' Pechersky replied.

"'Then I will give you five minutes to split this tree stump in two. If you fail, you get 25 lashes and if you succeed you get a pack of cigarettes.' He looked at his timepiece and yelled, 'Begin.'

"Sasha split the stump in four and a half minutes. Then the Nazi handed a pack of cigarettes to Sasha. '*Oberscharführer,* I do not smoke,' he replied as he recommenced chopping up the tree stump.

"The SS officer returned in 20 minutes with an offering of bread and butter.

"Pechersky advised the officer, '*Oberscharführer,* the rations in this camp are adequate and I am not hungry.' These actions of

Sasha made him a hero and a possible leader in the eyes of the other prisoners.

"They needed a plan on how to escape the camp and join the partisans who lived in the woods. Pechersky drew up a plan. The urgency of their actions became clear when they found notes in the clothing of dead Jewish prisoners from the Belzec Concentration Camp. One of the notes read:

> 'We worked for a year in Belzec. I don't know where they are taking us now. They say to Germany. In the freight cars there are dining tables. We received bread for three days, and tins and liquor. If all this is a lie, then know that death awaits you too. Don't trust the Germans. Avenge our blood!'

"Sasha's plan commenced with SS guards being lured into workshops. There, they were stabbed to death with axes, awls, and chisels. The prisoners collected the dead guards' weapons: grenades, pistols, rifles, and a submachine gun. When they proceeded through the gates of the camp, an all-out battle occurred. The battle resulted in the deaths of eleven SS soldiers and an unknown number of Ukrainian guards. Of the approximate 550 Jewish prisoners who worked in the camp, 130 did not participate in the revolt, 80 prisoners were killed during the revolt either by machine-gun fire from the watchtowers or from mines that surrounded the camp, 223 prisoners escaped, and of that number 170 were recaptured, Sasha and 52 other prisoners made it to the woods and survived the war.

"SS Chief Heinrich Himmler, within days after the revolt, ordered Sobibor shut down. He not only closed the camp but he had it dismantled. Pine trees were planted on the camp's grounds to conceal its past. At its closure, the camp's remaining 300 prisoners were executed."

I paused, sipped the wine, and asked, "What are my two questions?"

Jason piped in, "Why did that group of 130 prisoners not participate in the break out?"

"You're absolutely correct. Those 130 knew their fate. But weren't able to join the revolt. They possibly put their faith in G-d to keep them alive."

Travis jumped in, "Jason, some people are not risk-takers. They are indecisive folks. Decision-making wears them out. No matter how bleak things appear, they are going to leave their fate in the hands of the Almighty."

Blake piped in with the second question, "Dad, I got the second question: Why were the other 170 prisoners recaptured when Sasha and 51 others made it to safety?"

"Well son, you got the second question right. However the answer given by our hero Sasha is not all that satisfactory. He turned out not to be a Moses. He came to the conclusion that as a Russian soldier, it was his duty was to make it back to his army's lines. He didn't feel he had a chance to move so many people, so he left the 170 behind."

A cloud of silence fell at the table as we all thought about Sasha's decision. The silence broke as Shelley entered the room with Maxwell House Coffee and dark chocolate-dipped macaroons.

Twenty-Four

The Computer

The next morning I was still full from our seder meal as I drove north on University Drive. I was headed up to my Uncle Mike's condo to get that article about my dad. Here I was on same street where 20 years earlier I saw my first and only group of hooded Klansman.

I drove into the city of Lauderhill. Signaling left onto Oakland Boulevard, I saw the city's landmark water tower. I turned left and entered Inverrary.

A security guard in his air-conditioned booth opened his door and greeted me. "Hello. Who are you here to see?"

"Hi sir. I'm here to visit my Uncle Mike in Apartment 12." I replied.

The guard wrote down my license plate number. Then handed me a parking pass. The guard continued, "Please park in the spots designated for guests, and post this parking pass on your dashboard."

I laid the yellow permit on my dashboard and proceeded to pull into the parking lot.

Walking from the guest parking spots to the condo, my sneakers stuck to the asphalt as if I had stepped on a gob of chewing gum. Approaching the condominium's electronic door opener, I wondered if I was going to get a copy of the Ph.D. paper. While pressing their apartment number and awaiting entry, the suspense of being able to finally read the article caused my stomach to turn. This tension continued as the elevator climbed to the eighth floor. My heartbeat raced as I approached my aunt and uncle's front door. With open arms they greeted me. I hugged and kissed both of them.

"Mort, come sit down in the kitchen. Would you like something to eat and drink?" My Aunt Renia asked. " I just brewed some coffee and I bought a Publix New York-style cheese cake," she added.

"I'd love it. I missed my morning cup."

My father had taught me manners. The dissertation would have to wait another hour as we chit-chatted about family, Israel, and American politics.

After our coffee break, I asked, "Uncle Mike, Barbara said you sent her an article about my dad in the camps and I'd love to get a copy of it. Barbara's computer is not functioning."

Uncle Mike moved slowly from the kitchen to his computer room. Seated in front of his desktop, he scrolled down a list of ten emails before opening the one he had sent my sister.

"There it is," he said as he clicked on the attachment.

For some unknown reason the attachment failed to open. For the next ten minutes Uncle Mike kept trying. My frustration level simmered. Am I ever going to get to read this article? "Uncle Mike, just email it to me. I'll open it when I get home."

"Sure, Mort. I just forwarded it to you. Sorry for the inconvenience."

"Uncle Mike, I'll call you after I read the article. I want to discuss it with you. Love you. See you in a few weeks. Bye Bye."

As the elevator descended, I thought, "My luck. I drive up to Lauderhill for an article and I leave with *bubkes*."

Twenty-Five

Barbarossa

That night after reading the Ph.D. paper, I lay in a fetal position tossing, turning and trying to doze off. Sleep escaped me. I moved to the family-room couch where my video-sleeping pill awaited my arrival. Tivoed on my digital recorder was a series called *The World at War.* The episode was named Barbarossa. I had viewed it at least fifty times. I needed only ten minutes to numb my brain to sleep.

The program narrator's voice massaged my cortex. After so many viewings, I had memorized the dialogue. "This was bloodiest land battle in history, the battle that was to eventually decide the outcome of the Second World War." Word-for-word I repeated Sir Laurence Olivier's quote. Here was the battle to end all battles, best described in Professor Thomas Childers' words as "the largest military undertaking in human history."

Moving my index finger onto the fast forward button on my clicker, I tapped away commercials. I focused on the footage of Nazis being routed, captured, killed, or frozen to death.

Right before sleep set in, I tapped on my remote's power button. Simultaneously the television and I fell into sleep mode.

Each time I watched, I had no idea that my father had played a role in this epic battle. On June 22, 1941, over three million Axis soldiers, 600,000 motor vehicles and 750,000 horses invaded the Soviet Union. Hitler gave the code name "Barbarossa" (Red Beard) to the operation. He took the name from a German leader, Frederick Barbarossa, a medieval Holy Roman Emperor.

Barbarossa started off as a phenomenal success for the Nazis, with the German Army capturing large swathes of Soviet territory. However by 1942, the tide had turned against the Nazis. The Germans were so desperate for manual labor they even sent three hundred and fifty, young Jewish men to the front to fix railroad tracks and keep them free of snow. A German labor organization known as Organization *Todt* was created. It was responsible for these three hundred and fifty. My father was selected for this group as their medical officer.

My father, on his tape said, "We were outfitted with black uniforms and shipped by train to the Russian front."

Twenty-Six

Organization *Todt*

After my son, Blake, graduated from college, we headed south from Plymouth, New Hampshire in his fully packed, air-conditioned Ford Escort. He and I took turns driving from Plymouth State University to our Cooper City home.

While he drove through the White Mountains, I examined Blake's full smile, penetrating eyes, and dark curly hair. His hair reminded me of my father's crop, as well as my own, thick dark brown locks closing in on black.

Blake, like most of his friends, wore their Plymouth State hoodies. It was his badge of honor. He attended a state college and received a degree. While being quite thoughtful, Blake acquired the Laitner sense of humor, always willing to crack a joke. If one bothered to look, he appeared in the poster for the laid-back generation, the "where-is-the-party-crowd?"

His group of friends were throwbacks to the hippie generation. They copied the hair style, the clothing, the pot, and the music. Thumbtacked to their walls were the same posters that had adorned my 1969 college dormitory room. There were the faces of: Hendrix, Dylan, Joplin, the Jefferson Airplane, the Grateful Dead, the Beatles, the Doors and more. There were my favorite blacklight posters: the one with the *Kama Sutra* positions, R. Crumb's, "Keep on Trucking," the tie-dye peace sign, the marijuana leaf, and the acid-laced Bill Graham's Fillmore Auditorium signs.

Blake found a party almost every night on and off the Plymouth campus. He was a known entity. When he walked across campus, students yelled out his name.

He summed up his two-part philosophy as: when life becomes tough, roll with the punches and apply for the part of as a cast member. Even if you have the looks and the talent, don't take on any leading roles.

Blake's looks led to a short-lived modeling career. When he was five or six, his mom, Shelley, went to a photographer to create a professional modeling portfolio. Once a week they would travel to Miami Beach to casting studios in an attempt to land jobs on TV commercials or in the print media. To my astonishment, Blake was featured in a few commercials and photo ad campaigns. To my surprise, Blake took his modeling career seriously, listening and obeying the requests of the photographers. Later, I wished he would have been as conscientious with his school studies.

The summer Blake was six, he was featured in a Liberty Clothing photo advertisement. The picture found a home in every Wal-Mart Store across the nation. That summer our family traveled by car from Florida to California and back. We invented a game called, "Spot the Wal-Mart" When anyone in the car saw the store, they would yell out, "Wal-Mart." Then, I'd pull into the parking lot so the kids could take a bathroom or snack break. While the kids ran through the store, Shelley and I scoured the store for Blake's Liberty Clothes advertisement. When we found the photo the first one to yell, "There it is!" won the game. We must have seen that ad in ten different stores, in ten different states and each time we found it, a yelp of parental pride jumped out of our mouths.

As I drove through New Jersey, I remembered examining that photo and becoming disturbed. There was a hidden message within its visual frame. My eyes focused on the two cute, blond six year olds – a boy and a girl – the boy smiling as he examined his cute playmate wearing her new outfit. A dark brown, curly-haired Jewish looking kid stood segregated off to the side. He watched the two kids play. Blake looked like he wanted to join them but made no move in their direction. He was an observer, watching but not joining in their games. I wondered if the photographer or the ad people caught their hidden message. I wondered if Liberty sold a lot of the outfits these kids wore. I wondered if I was paranoid.

Then I looked at another one of Blake's print advertisements. There stands five-year-old Blake, his head full of black curls and his mouth slightly ajar, looking up at a seven-year-old blonde whose right arm rests on his shoulder. His eyes ask, "Why does this cute blonde have her arm around my shoulder?" The blonde smiles directly into the camera. They are both dressed in bright camp shorts and pastel tank tops. Blake's right hand rests on top of a large Freudian, Crayola plastic crayon which almost reaches the top of his head. In their left hands both children hold colored markers. My eyes ask, "Does Blake have my obsession for tall blondes?"

With my hands gripping the wheel as we entered Virginia, southern radio stations still seemed to give too much air time to the likes of Hank Williams or Patsy Kline. I knew Blake hated the sound as much as Neal and I did on our journey south in the Sixties. But now in my fifties, I had grown accustomed to the twang and the syrupy voices of the country-western singers just as my father had. Their message of lost love, drowned in a pool of alcohol resonated truth. Life is sad.

And the truth was as I aged into my father's genetic mold, his musical and fashion tastes blossomed within me. Just as my dad did twenty years earlier, I bought pearl-buttoned cowboy shirts in Davie at Griff's Western Wear. I learned the country western song book and memorized the names of the country stars and the history of the genre. I went a step past dad's couture when I bought my cowboy boots. He had never acquired the black-leather cowboy boots I wore, the ones with points so narrow that I killed roaches in the corners of my hippie apartments.

My thoughts returned to our road trip and I asked, "Blake, how would you like to spend a day on the Washington, DC Mall and visit the Holocaust Museum?"

"Sure Dad, let's spend the morning in the Smithsonian and the afternoon in the Holocaust Museum."

Then I turned off the radio and said. "Blake, I have now listened to Grandpa's Holocaust tapes for the fifth time. Each time I hear his voice, it is hard to believe he has been gone for such a long time. I picture him smiling at you and your brothers and cracking jokes. Those tapes bring us back together again. Each time I listen to them, I always pick up a few new facts, some new nuisances that I had never focused on before."

"Like what Dad?" Blake inquired.

"I heard Grandpa say that he was selected by the Nazis to join a paramilitary group known as Organisation *Todt.* I had never heard of it. He said he was selected due to his youth, his relative good health, and the fact that the Germans needed a doctor to take care of the other selected slave laborers. He was part of a contingent of around three hundred-fifty Jews. They were chosen to work on changing the gauge of the railroad tracks – Germany and the Russia had different-size tracks – and keeping the railroads in the occupied portion of Soviet Union free of snow and in good repair."

"Gramps must have had one hell of a hard time fighting winter in mother Russia."

"Well the *Wehrmacht,* the German armed forces, needed fresh troops to replace the fallen. The troops needed supplies to keep fighting in Russia. The road system was terrible. Therefore the rail lines were critical. Grandpa said that he and the group were given black uniforms but he neglected to mention what insignias were sown on those black uniforms."

Blake scratched his scalp and queried, "I wonder why?"

"Me too," I replied.

"Son, so the next thing I did was some computer research on Organisation *Todt.* I learned it was a civil and military engineering group founded by Fritz Todt. Before the war, Todt's labor force constructed the *autobahn,* Germany's high-speed highway. Due to his success, Hitler named Todt the Inspector General of German Roadways. The *autobahn* became a showpiece for Hitler to display Aryan engineering abilities to the world."

"I heard that there is no speed limit on the *autobahn.*"

"You're right," I replied.

"Did you know that Jewish-slave labor built and maintained the *autobahn* during the war?"

"I had no idea, Dad. The last time I listened to Grandpa's tapes was years ago. I've forgotten most of what Grandpa said but I have a bunch of questions I wanted to ask you about Grandpa's experiences and the Holocaust."

"Blakester, we're stuck in this car for at least ten more hours, shoot away."

"What are the five most horrific symbols of the Holocaust?"

"Tough question but I'll take a stab at it. But I am not going to try putting them in any order of importance.

"First, the yellow Star of David patch with the word *Jude* housed in its center. You see it sewn on the jackets and worn on armbands. The faces of the people wearing the stars display a mixture of fear and agony."

I glanced at my forearm remembering how I tried not to stare or even focus in on my parents' tattoos.

"Second, the tattooed arms of survivors, especially if it is a child's arm. As you know most of the kids were sent right to the gas chambers, so pictures of tattooed children were pretty rare. However at the liberation of the camps, Allied photographers got children, five or six-year-old kids, to roll up their sleeves and show their identification numbers. I cannot get that image out of my brain."

I paused, "Blake, do you remember seeing the tattoos on your grandparents' arms?"

"Yeah, Dad. That would be kind of hard to forget."

"Did Grandpa or Grandma ever talk to you about their numbers?"

"I can remember Grandma telling me that she went to the race track and bet on her tattoo numbers one race at a time in chronological order. She said she won a bunch of money. I know Grandpa and Grandma wore their tattoos as badges of honor. They weren't ashamed of them. They wore them proudly."

"Son, I just read an article in Wiki about the Nazi tattooing of Jews and others."

"Pops, do you really trust the info on Wikipedia? Anybody can mess with it."

"I do, but I read other sources to confirm their facts. The Nazi bastards knew tattooing dehumanized the victim. Their goal was to make their slave laborers feel like branded cattle. If a Jew managed to escape the camp, the inked number would be another means of identification. They tattooed 400,000 prisoners. The victims that were sent straight to the gas chambers were not tattooed." Pausing to take a breath I continued.

"I learned in the article that the only camp that systemically tattooed prisoners was Auschwitz."

"Pop, I thought all concentration camps did it."

"I thought the same thing.

Here's the history. First they identified prisoners by sewing numbers on their striped-pajama uniforms.

In 1941, Soviet prisoners of war were tattooed on their chests with the letters "AU" for Auschwitz. In 1942, the Jewish prisoners were tattooed in numerical order. Some Jews had an engraved triangle which identified them as Jews. I guess half of a Jewish star. Then in 1944, the "A" and "B" series tattoos were first issued to Jews.

"Do you remember your parents' tattoo numbers?"

"Not a one. I don't think I wanted to memorize their numbers. Blake, did you know Grandpa had the job of tattooing prisoners toward the end of the war?

"He told me, that he whispered to some prisoners, 'I'm putting on this tattoo in such a way that in a few weeks, it will disappear. Don't touch it, and leave the scab alone. Dad, I remember a number that will never disappear, the partial number carved into that large sculpture that visitors call 'the arm.' It's part of the Miami Beach Holocaust Memorial. It was 'A-13."

"Blake, you've got a great memory. How did you recall that?"

"The 'A' was for adult and the 13 was for the year of my Bar Mitzvah when I became one."

Dad, why the sculptor selected the number 13?

"That monument is located on 1939-1945 Meridian Avenue. It consists of over a hundred naked skeletal figures climbing the arm toward the hand, aiming toward the heavens. Some say it is a *muselmann* arm, representing camp prisoners on the verge of death. I think there are 130 figures on that arm."

As I spoke, the first two figures froze in my brain. Again thirteen, the year a child reaches manhood; the year I cut my deal with G-d. I remembered the letter "A" stood for Auschwitz.

I pictured the bronze arm rising out of the earth as if a scene from an American horror film.

"Blake, some critics say the sculpture represents a dying person's last grasp for life. Others see the arm and hand as a gesture aimed at G-d, asking the Almighty the ultimate question: Why?"

"Dad, that is the eternal question summed up in one word."

"I'm amazed at my long-term memory. I can even remember the title the sculptor gave the statue, "A Sculpture of Love and Anguish."

"Dad, anguish is displayed all over the faces of the 130 climbing bodies. But I fail to see love anywhere on that statue."

"Some of the 130 are true believers who are sure that death will bring them closer to the Almighty; their love of G-d cannot be taken from them. The sculptor, Kenneth Treister, was tasked with coming up with a piece of art that would honor the dead, comfort the survivors, and inform the viewers about the horrors of the Holocaust. I'm not sure he succeeded in comforting the survivors but two out of three isn't bad.

"Here is a religious interpretation: Those 130 climbers are on one of G-d's arms, struggling to get into his palm to be lifted into Heaven."

I wondered, *Is he buying any of this or was he just being politely silent?*

I broke the silence by continuing my list. "Number three: the photos of the piles of children's shoes found in the camp. In a way those photos are more horrifying than seeing the *muselmann* standing in front of the barbed wire fence or housed in the camp's barracks or even the naked piles of bodies being readied for the crematorium. You realize that every pair of shoes had a child attached to it. You realize that cruelty to children is always twice as bad as cruelty to adults.

"The fourth is the Warsaw Ghetto Boy, the one with his hands raised high over his head. His fear-covered face says it all. He knows his life is over.

"The fifth is the rounded, black-iron-furnace doors of the ovens with the metal stretchers which were used to place the bodies in the crematoriums. I picture the Jewish inmates forced to look for gold in the teeth of the dead, then lifting the corpses onto the stretchers and shoving them into the oven."

"Dad, do you have a list of any iconic photos from that period in which Jews were presented in a positive light?"

"I can only think of one – a 1933 photo of Max Baer. He was an American Jewish boxer who beat a German named Max Schmeling. The German boxer had been a former heavyweight champion. Hitler dined with Schmeling before he left for the fight which was held New York City. The fight took place in

Yankee Stadium in front of a standing-room-only crowd. Baer had a large Jewish star sewn on his boxing trunks. In the photograph, Baer stands victorious with his boxing-gloved right hand raised in the air. Next to him stands the vanquished Schmeling. Before the fight, Baer told the press, 'Every punch in the eye I give Schmeling is one for Adolf Hitler.' And in the ring, as Baer landed the winning punch he said, 'That one's for Hitler.'"

"Dad, I didn't know that story. Baer's fist in the air reminds me of the Miami Beach Holocaust statue with the arm and hand raised toward the sky. It's a symbol of victory. The Jews weren't wiped off the face of the earth."

I nodded in agreement.

Blake continued, "Dad, you create lists as quickly as Max Baer threw punches. You seem to have a knack for creating lists."

"Well here is a short list for you. How many miracles have I experienced in my life?"

Twenty-Seven

You Led a Good Life

Blake, I previously mentioned that I had two religious experiences or miracles in my life. The first occurred as I prayed at the Western Wall. The second one occurred in the seat of my spanking-brand new, blue Mazda Miata. I do not know if G-d or my dad in heaven intervened on my behalf but a finger pushed the play button on my life's VCR allowing me to tell you the following story.

"It was one of those days where my life's real troubles were apt to be things that never crossed my worried mind, the kind of day where I was literally blindsided at 9:00 a.m. on an idle Tuesday morning.

"At 8:00 a.m., I voted in the Bush-Clinton presidential election.

"At 8:30 a.m., I cruised, top down, in my spanking-brand-new blue Miata. As the cool November breeze parted my hair, the sun baked the top of my head. I smiled the smile of a trouble-free man driving his mid-life toy. No need for the radio to be on, this picture needed no background music.

"Damn it!

"I heard the mood-breaking, troubling beeps emanating from my pants pocket. The digital number displayed on my beeper was a co-worker, followed by our emergency code. As I pulled off I-95, I worried about finding a pay-phone in this dangerous neighborhood. I found one and, of course, it was broken. The next phone I located worked, but my co-worker failed to pick up.

"Machine: This is the Department of Health and Rehabilitative Services, please clearly enunciate your name, phone number, and message after the beep.

As my mood shifted into negative mode, I responded in a firm tone, 'If you beep someone with an emergency, please try to be near your phone so you can respond.'

"At 8:39 a.m., catharsis, the scream worked. I felt much better as I turned off the freeway. I was two blocks away from my office.

"At 9:00 a.m., I drove under the overpass. Shadows in dark shades of grey reflected on the cement pillars as I waited for the light to change. Green appeared. I inched forward as I glanced at my watch.

"At 8:45 a.m. – fifteen minutes wasted. I jumped back in my car, clicking on my seat belt, as I started driving toward the 401 building. I remembered the promise I made to that state trooper three months earlier who was about to write me a ticket for failure to wear the belt. 'Officer, as a fellow state employee, I promise you from this day on, I will always wear my seat belt when behind the wheel of my automobile (The promise worked, I didn't get the ticket).'

"At 8:58 a.m., I felt the beeper in my shirt pocket. I screamed, 'I HATE PEOPLE WHO YELL EMERGENCY WITHOUT WAITING FOR A RESPONSE!' (You can scream in a convertible on I-95 because and no one but G-d hears you).

"I fixated on a ten-ton dumptruck running the red light right into me. I entered a slow motion world. I heard a deafening screech of brakes. Then, the loudest crash I had ever heard.

"I blacked out as my brain shifted into pause.

"In total darkness, an inner voice said, You're dead.

"The voice then said the five most important words I ever heard, You led a good life.

"Now the viewing screen in my mind imagined a large VCR and a heavenly finger pushing down on the play button. The VCR and the hand disappeared, only to be replaced by black and white twirling clouds. These clouds formed a tornado. This speeding funnel disappeared as my eyes began to focus on the exploded air-bag. The smell of burning rubber and noxious gasses burned my nostrils as my body rattled from the blow of the air-bag.

"I had to get out of the car.

"I was alive!

"Next thought: *am I a quadriplegic?*

"Moving my left hand pinkie finger on the door handle, I appreciated that I had control of one of my hands.

"*Am I a paraplegic?*

"Slowly I popped the lock and the Miata door opened. Breathing in toxic fumes, I said a silent prayer, Please G-d let me get out of this car.

"I scanned my body for injuries. As I looked for blood, I only saw a small scratch on my ring finger from which one tear-shaped droplet of blood flowed.

"With all the energy I could muster, I pushed my body out of the wreck.

"I screamed and jumped for joy, I'm the luckiest man! I'm alive! I'm not paralyzed!

"Standing next to me was the lady whose car the truck had slammed my car into. In amazement she asked, 'Are you okay?'

"'Am I okay? I am the luckiest person in Miami,' I bellowed.

"She eyeballed my destroyed vehicle not appreciating my love of life and health.

"The police arrived and issued the truck driver a ticket.

"Then the ambulance arrived. The paramedics examined me. As I lay on their stretcher with a blood pressure cuff strapped to my arm, I studied my ring finger. I couldn't believe what I observed. Miraculously, the scratch and the blood had vanished. The paramedics recommended I go to the hospital for further tests. I declined their offer, still mystified over what happened to the cut. As I walked the two remaining blocks to my office, I reflected on how the air bag and the seat belt had saved my life. I marveled at the sun's rays piercing though the clouds. I wondered out loud, 'Had I really led a good life?' For the third time that day, I stared at my ring finger which triggered the memory of that heavenly finger pushing down on the VCR play button. On that cool November day, I no longer worried about my life's troubles because I knew the answer."

"Yeah, Dad. I remember that day, I was so glad to hear you were okay."

Twenty-Eight

Risk-Taking

As Blake drove through Northern Georgia, I felt a rant coming on. I wanted to teach him about risk-taking. He had taken some serious risks. He would be able to relate to some of the stuff I had learned over a lifetime. So I started.

"Blake, in the year I found beauty in a woman's crow's feet, I started asking myself three questions:

"Am I a risk-taker?

"What is a risk-taker?

"Was your grandfather a risk-taker?

"Your grandpa took enormous risks during the war. I, in contrast, have led a pretty risk-free existence."

"Okay, Dad, I'm in a listening mood. I'll keep quiet while you play professor and give me your risk-taking lecture. But I won't promise not to interrupt every once and awhile."

"Well I spent months defining the term. I asked my students at Barry University for their thoughts. From their answers, I deduced that risk-taking was a relative term.

"'Dead soldiers are unlucky risk-takers, while living war heroes knew how to handle risk,' my students said.

"'One man's risk is another man's folly.' I retorted.

"'Was risk-taking, like beauty, in the eye of the beholder?' I asked them.

"I came to the conclusion that, just as with *shiksas* and happiness, degrees of risk-taking can be placed on the rungs of a ladder, into the boxes of a matrix ... categorized, weighed, and examined – not just examined, but scrutinized.

"I, like your grandfather, am obsessed with numbers. Therefore, I categorized risk-takers from a high first-degree to a low fifth-degree. Here are some definitions and examples in each degree.

"The first degree is the highest level of risk-taking. A person, intentionally or unintentionally, places his or her life on the line and sometimes his family's life on the line.

"Here is an example: My friend Joel and I had decided to swim to a raft situated in the middle of a lake. Our eyes had played a trick on us by miscalculating the distance to the raft. Somewhere between the raft and the shore, Joel said, 'Mort, I don't think I'm going to make it to the raft. Can you help me?'

"'Keep swimming, I don't think I can get there either. But I know I don't have the strength to save you! Keep going; we'll make it!'

"When we both climbed onto the raft, Joel screamed, 'I can't believe we made it. We're alive.'

"As we waited for a boater to rescue us and take us back to shore, I thought, *Close call. You dumb fuck, you almost died.*"

"Your grandfather almost died an untold number of times during the war. He risked his life when in the Soviet Union. He tried to cover up a typhus epidemic among Jewish prisoners from Nazi doctors. He risked his life when he dared to demand of the German soldiers that they honor their promises made to the Jewish slave labors. He risked his life when he entrusted his friends with confidential information about the timing of camp inspections. He risked his life when he stole food from the Nazis, knowing if he did not, that death was on his doorstep."

Blake seemed interested, so I continued.

"Now I am moving on to the second degree, which is risking the loss of your freedom. Your grandfather knowingly put his life and freedom at risk when he volunteered to go into a slave labor camp so his brother could stay at home with his parents.

"I risked my freedom when I possessed a large quantity of hashish in Morocco or small amounts of grass in the States; when I first fought with Iraqi students on the U. M. campus in protest of their government hanging Jews in Baghdad; and, when I faced arrest as a anti-Vietnam War protester in 1968 on the bloody streets of Chicago.

"Third degree is the placement of your health or your family's health in serious jeopardy, like your grandfather's two-pack-a-day addiction to tobacco – a habit that lasted for 30 years.

"He and I both had periods of excessive eating in our middle years. We will never know, if he had not smoked or put on those 20 extra pounds, how many years or days of additional life G-d would have granted him.

"I, like your grandpa, needed cigarettes to calm my nerves or to act cool with members of the opposite sex. Unlike my dad, my habit lasted for ten years and maxed out at one pack a day. But I gained more weight than my dad, I'm 40 pounds overweight. Who knows what the grim reaper is going to fine me for that excess baggage.

"Your grandfather and I both enjoyed speeding in our cars. While speeding might seem a small risk, I, as a teenager, risked jail time and serious injury by drag racing my Mustang.

"The fourth degree of risk endangers the loss of your career, wealth, or marriage. By smoking grass, I not only faced the possible loss of my freedom, but probably risked being fired from my government job. When your grandpa and I stole statutes from abandoned hotels, we could have gone to jail and he could have lost his medical license."

My lips stopped flapping, as I thought about my failing to reach fourth degree after counting the number of Eva's pubic hairs, the 18 strands that escaped from her bikini bottom. I recalled how these exposed hairs glistened in the sunlight, how I left her swimming pool with only a kiss on her lips. A risk-taker would have risked his marriage or a beating from a distraught ex-German husband in exchange for an hour of sexual bliss. A risk-taker would have torn into her and not kept silent as he did it.

"In last place, Blake is the fifth degree. Here you risk loss of happiness, the joys of life. Your grandfather failed to reach this rung when it came to telling Aunt Barbara and me, *tête a tête,* about his Holocaust experience. I believe he did this not only for the sake of keeping his sanity but to avoid a barrage of ethical questions as to his actions, a barrage of questions from children who had never entered the gates of Hell. For your grandpa to have painted for his two children his whole slave labor and concentration camp picture would have risked family happiness. That is something he would never have done."

Blake broke his silence. "Do most people during their lifetime step on each of these five rungs?

"Yes, I think they do. But your question leads to three additional questions: How many times do people face these five degrees of risks?, for how long a period of time do they endure these dangers?, and what affect, if any, do these risks have on their lives?

"Blake, in our brains we all have our own internal risk-benefit analysis gauge – a gauge electronically powered by our subconscious, fueled by our love of excitement, or throttled by fear. We all claim to want to live life to the fullest. That gauge in your brain has a red line which reads: Dare to Live Fully."

"Dad, do you have a list of gauges that are found in our bodies?"

"Sorry, son; no list right now. But I'll work on it."

Twenty-Nine

Lists

Son, as you get older you'll develop a knack for list creation. The more experiences you have in life the more lists you'll generate. Lists create structure. That's why religion is so chock full of lists. Lists help you compartmentalize. I have often said, 'A life without lists is not a well-ordered life.' At work, my to-do list ran my office and at home the 'honey-do' list was just as important."

"Dad, so you think G-d is a list maker because of the Ten Commandments."

"Yup."

"Are Jews obsessed with lists?"

"Obviously! The Jewish holidays are filled with checklists, lists of the order things must be done and lists of names to be memorized. There are the lists of death camps and the lists of the murdered, lists of survivors and Schindler's list. There are the list of the richest Jews in the USA and the world. There is even a list of the sexiest Jewish men alive – a short list but a list. For Jewish shoppers there is Craig's List. For Jewish parents with children in high school, there is the list of the best Hebraic colleges in the South. Had enough?"

"Very funny Dad. But you know another group obsessed with lists?

"I'll bite. Who?"

"The Nazis kept lists of every Jew they killed and tattooed. IBM computer cards list all Jewish property stolen by them and list identifying designs of camp prisoners."

"Those Nazis wanted to get credit for all of their actions," I replied.

"Dad, did you know that on the Internet there is even a list of the best 100 lists of all time; Schindler's made the top 100."

"Son, all of America is obsessed with lists. There is a top-10 list for almost any imaginable subject and as a kid I loved Casey Kasem's American Top-40 list.

"Blake, I remember your first list; it referenced all the toys you wanted from Santa."

"Dad, I think Power Rangers was on that list but let's talk about a subject dear to my heart. Do you have any lists concerning sex?"

"Yup. Here are some sexual lists for you to mull over. You may have already commenced the process of fashioning some of these lists.

"You will produce a list of all of the members of the opposite sex that you slept with. As you age some of their names fade but you will never forget the wild ones. You will classify the best of them. You may call it, 'the ultimate-top-ten list.'

"You'll create a list of the girls who you wanted to screw but didn't. That list can be bifurcated into females you still have contact with and still have a chance for redemptive sex with, and ladies you most likely will never see again.

"You'll make a list of women that you could have had sex with, but for some unknown reason it just didn't happen. Then you will create a list of reasons you failed to secure the love of those women.

"You will keep another record of reasons other women succumbed to your charms.

"You may construct lists of the women with the largest, the smallest, the softest, and the hardest breasts. You'll make a list of nipples sizes, on which you suckled, from dimes to quarters to half dollars."

"Dad, you obviously have a list obsession. Did Grandpa have one too?

"I don't know. He never told me if he did and I never asked."

I paused to think of any examples of list creation that came out of my dad's mouth but failed to recall a single one. So I continued.

"You may even create a list of the textures of women's pubic hairs ranging from the coarsest to the silkiest. That grouping will correspond with the International Waxing List."

I stopped talking for three seconds because I knew I had him. He was hooked. He'd ask the next question.

"You mean there is such a thing as the International Waxing List?" Blake asked.

"Yup. How a women waxes the hair around her pubis bone takes much thought. Once she decides *au naturel* is not for her, she can decide to go American, French, or Brazilian."

"Dad, now you have touched upon an area that I have not read about. Please go on ."

"Well, an American wax job creates a triangle. It was designed to protect women wearing bikinis from exposing 'unsightly' pubic hairs."

"Dad, I guess the creator of the moniker felt that American women being somewhat sexually inhibited deserved the title."

"I think you're right," I replied.

"A French waxing is far the more sexually adventurous, just like French women. It's commonly called the 'landing strip.' It is also known as Hitler's moustache, because of its design. The wax technician clears the labia of hair and then creates the 'air strip.' Fetishists say it makes the muff an artistic vision like a feather resting on top of an orchid."

"Pop, That's poetic. How do I get a job as a wax technician?"

I laughed and without skipping a beat jumped in. "Try courses in a beauty school or in a barber college. Why don't you Google it. I did, having guessed you would ask a whole bunch of questions on the subject. I learned about a program called the Esthetic Institute – great name. They say waxing the human body is an art.

"Chagall would have gotten a kick out of that statement." Blake interrupted. "Well it's not all electrolysis. There are many methods of hair removal. You'll have to master techniques, theories and even intuitive skills to get your certificate."

Blake chimed in, "I wonder if that certificate is made out of wax and how much money a waxer makes?"

"I read up to about 40 grand a year."

"That's not bad for doing something that gives you untold pleasure. I'll look into it. Now please finish your dissertation," Blake requested.

"Okay, finally, there's the full Brazilian, aka the bald beaver or the bald eagle, a waxing that creates the hairless crotch. No perfumes of musk emanate from these Brazilian treasures."

"Wow! Beavers and eagles oh my!" Blake said in his best Dorothy voice.

I laughed again.

"Blakester, thanks for making this torturous drive so much fun."

"Dad, You're a walking, talking Wikipedia machine but what about a list of women with yeast infections?"

"Son, I thought I piqued your curiosity with this topic and you still manage to keep me in stitches with your one liners. But I'm not stopping my rant."

"Roll on, Dad."

"You will create a list of women who taught you how to make love. That list will be paired with the list of women you taught the ways of the world.

"Remember that book I bought you, *Oh, The Places We Will Go.* Dr.Seuss was a big proponent of the art of list creation. Remember his *One Fish, Two Fish, Red Fish, Blue Fish?* That's an example of the work of a great listologist. If Suess wrote books for adults, he would have titled them, *The Places Where We Did It* or *One Girl, Two Girls, Black Girl, White Girl.*"

Now it was Blake's turn to laugh.

"You will always remember the wildest, craziest places you ever did it, and of course, you'll create a list of every wild place."

"Dad, At Plymouth, I read a psychological study that discussed the subject of sexual-risk-takers. It said that risk-takers love the thrill of doing it in places where they think they will be caught doing it. They used the example of Bill and Monica in the Oval Office. That means risk-takers create a Most-Adventurous-Venues list."

"I wonder how many venues are on President Clinton's list?"

"Pretty funny and creative, Dad. So you're saying that people create lists of *ménage a trois* experiences and making it with different races, religions. and nationalities or in your nomenclature, the 'I-got-to-try-it-at-least-once-in-my-life' list."

"You got it son. Folks are always trying new stuff. They've got to keep it interesting. I named that the 'Spice-or-Variety' List. The grouping comes from a quote by poet, William Cooper. He said, 'Variety's the very spice of life that gives it all its flavours.' "

"How appropriate to mention spices, flavors, and sex in one thought process. Here's another list to add to your collection. The 'honey-what-should-I-cover-it-with?' list; whipped cream or pop rocks?"

I laughed out loud. Happy not to be behind the wheel so I could let it all out.

"Son, I'm really glad Mom and I bought you all those Dr. Seuss books. It really paid off. You're creativity is spellbinding."

Blake glanced off the road and into my eyes as I paused to do some self-reflective calculations on all of these new lists.

Then he pulled me out of my daydream, "Dad, I bet there are a few men on this planet who have an 'I-made-it-with-women-who-look-like-Seuss'-characters' list.

"Now that I think about it, I dated a Horton and a Lorax. I even had a crush on a Plymouth State girl who wore that silly-looking red and white striped hat all over campus."

I smiled. "I bought that floppy hat for one of your brothers. We may still have it in the house. When Jason was three or so, we even themed his room based on that mischievous trouble-making cat. He was everywhere: plastered on the wallpaper, hanging from a mobile and sewn onto a quilt that lay across the crib railing. I remember that year, we had Publix bake Jason's birthday cake with that striped red and white hat centered in it."

"I'm glad you didn't do that to my room."

Knowing he was on a roll, Blake continued. "I could even create two lists of foods I had eaten before and after Seuss sex. I'd start the list off with green eggs and ham."

I laughed again.

He continued in rhyme:

I'm ready to tape some lists on my wall.
And if I run out of space I move to the hall.
I know this will be quite a interesting caper,
So I will write the lists on yellow, blue and green paper.

Blake broke up, causing the car to slow down as tears of laughter streamed down our cheeks.

"Dad, I need a break. You have got to take over driving."

Blake pulled over and we switched seats. I drove a mile in silence and then continued, "You will keep an account of the women who screamed the loudest as they reached orgasm. You will remember and list the Jewish girls who intoned, 'Jesus F'ing Christ' as they achieved *le petit mort.*"

"Dad, since the big "O" is so indescribable, yelling 'Oh My G-d I'm cumming!' is just complimenting the creator for his handiwork."

"Hallelujah, praise the Lord! My son is a true believer. He understands the power of prayer. He appreciates that the Lord acts in mysterious ways. He recognizes that G-d knew how to finish off our reproductive process."

I laughed realizing I had just complimented G-d again for his humorous handiwork.

"Pop, what is the funniest line you have ever heard a women scream in her state of rapture?"

Without a pause, I bellowed, "Oh, Aunt Jemimah!"

He doubled up for a good fifteen seconds, before a teary-eyed Blake asked, "You're kidding right?"

I remained silent to make him wonder. He would never know.

Blake pulled together his composure before he asked the next question. "Dad, how about a list of things women say in bed to piss men off?"

"That's not a list; that's a text book," I replied.

"Remember they are testing your concentration skills. Let me paraphrase Rudyard Kipling. If you can learn to ignore their untimely words in the heat of passion and manage to still reach climax, 'Yours is the earth and everything that's in it, And, which is more – you'll be a man, my son!"

"I remember that poem. You bought me a fancy printed copy with a tassel hanging off of it. I hung it on the wall in my bedroom. Talking about poetry, a friend of mine created a list of foreign cities that he substitutes for his girlfriend's private body parts."

"Okay, I'll bite, give me some examples."

"I love fingering your Mogadishu or, look at the size of that Benghazi."

"Great idea. He is learning the cities in the news by sexual association. I'll incorporate that idea in my book of lists," I joked.

"That same college buddy says he rates all women on a scale from one to ten, from the masturbatory nun who he rates as a one to the prostitute who pleasures 12 men in one day who gets a ten."

"What's the value of his rating system?"

"He says it is important to understand that they, as we, are all sexual animals, with needs and desires that must be met. It is an equalizer on the playing field."

Now I rested my mouth and kick-started my brain, rating women from my past. For the next 60 seconds of silence my hands gripped the steering wheel in the ten and two o'clock position as images of ladies and Arabic numbers dashed across my mental screen.

I broke the silence by returning to the topic of sexual list-making.

"Well here's a list you can tell your friend about. It is entitled, the 'Super Orgasmic Women or the Good-to-Great-in-the-Sack-List.' That's the list of the ladies that make your toes curl. First you segregate members of the opposite sex into four groups: the multiples, the solos, the fakers, and those unable to cum.

"Wow! Dad, do you break down those groups based on the number of minutes of clitoral stimulation required to make them spasm and see an endorphin light show?"

"Of course," I replied.

I continued, "You will produce a list of sexual positions you would have liked to have tried on your failures and a corollary list on your conquests."

"Dad, it is times like this that I wished I had a pen and paper to take notes."

A hint of sarcasm flowed between his words but I played along. I pointed to the glove box, "You'll find both in there."

Observing his lack of movement, I realized he was just playing with me and continued.

"Some folks, and I'm assuming females create these same lists in their heads as men do, write down their names, while other folks just replay their names, faces, and bodies in their heads as they try to fall asleep."

"Dad, do anal retentive folks write their lists down rather than keeping them in their heads?"

"Good Freudian analysis. Sure, just like writers, they're addicted to the touch and smell of ink on paper. They must hold it in. Like photographers, they fear the loss of memory; they must keep diaries, logging in their personal record of their life's events all the while adding their commentaries. On a daily basis, their thoughts and observations attach to the page like barnacles on the sides of a ship. In these books of empty pages, they record lists of their hopes and fears. Obviously, an organized diarist is a far better list creator than the dysfunctional scribbler."

"Dad, I remember reading Anne Frank's *The Diary of a Young Girl.* She did a great job of listing her hopes and fears."

"Sad to say, she was one of the best. A sad girl without much time to find happiness in life."

"Some folks create lists of the happiest and saddest days of their lives."

"Dad, I wonder if Grandpa Wolf and Grandma Henia ever created those lists. How did the Grandpa and Grandma keep-their sanity?"

"Son, I have no idea. If it happened to me, I would have ended up in an asylum. Somehow they were capable of compartmentalizing that period of their lives. Other survivors found purpose in building a new state, or in seeking retribution, and some just wanted another shot at experiencing happiness."

I paused, scratched my nose and continued. "Son, remember that happiness is ephemeral, fleeting, like a migrating bird. It comes and it goes. The only way you can capture it, is with the happiness formula."

"Dad, now you have my total attention with your transition from lists to formulas."

"The formula groups and grades your daily joyous activities on a numeric grading system. It can be summed up as A+B=C.

"'A' equals the event or activity. 'B' equals the number of points for that activity. And 'C' equals the total number of points for the day. You have to figure out what things brings joy into your life. Then you apportion points to those events. Here are some examples."

"Pops, slow down, let me get in a word or two. I love the title, *The Happiness Formula;* sounds like a great name for a movie."

"Son, then you assign points starting from ten and going up to one hundred points for each happiness-creating activity. Each activity never gets less than ten points and no more than a one hundred points. This allows you to add up all the numbers in your head. Any questions so far?"

"Nope, Dad."

"Here's a list of some key point-assigning sectors to remember: sex, family time, food, nature, flora, fauna, celestial bodies, entertainment, culture, architecture, design and humor. Blake, can you think of any other sectors to add to the list?"

"How about video games, music, and lectures from your father? Songs like Dylan's *The Times They Are A-Changin'* and *I Gotta Feeling That Tonight Is Gonna Be A Good Night* by the Black-Eyed Peas."

"Mazel Tov, You're right, good additions and two good examples." I laughed. "Twenty points if both of those songs were on the radio right now."

"Please continue; I'm listening." Blake said.

"Let's start with the food sector. Take caviar for example; your taste buds are a critical component for point evaluation. Caviar's appearance and smell are significant. Your sense of taste must come to life, signaling your brain: sweet, salty, bitter, or sour. I love the taste of caviar, its texture on my tongue, its color – ten points."

"Dad, how about comfort foods like mac and cheese?"

"Sure; mac and cheese meets the criteria. The sharp-cheddar taste, the soft noodles covered in gooey cheese – ten points."

"What about the ambiance of the restaurant or the dining room table? Does that get you an additional ten points."

"Of course it does. Ambiance is a key factor. If the meal is presented with *panache,* for example when a chef decorates the plate with sauces as if it is an artist's canvas. That would add ten points to the meal."

"Does the proper pairing of the wine with each course of your meal add points?" Blake asked.

"You bet," I replied. "If the meal captures your brain and transports it to another place and time, that's worth 50 points. If the meal's aromas rise through your nostrils and go straight to your heart and you say 'Wow, life is good,' that's 100 points.

"Here are some examples of a food-point listing: A toasted poppy seed bagel smeared with Philadelphia Cream Cheese and covered with nova, capers, a slice of onion, and tomato with a freshly brewed cup of coffee – ten points."

"Dad, I can almost taste that bagel."

"A *café au lait* with a right-out-of-the-oven blueberry scone at Panera Bread – ten points.

"Now you are getting me hungry. I got a twenty-pointer: the Dutch Baby at the Original Pancake House with Canadian Bacon and a cup of java."

"Son, you got the point. Let's move on to the 'family-time' sector. You and I together in this car for a day – a 100 points, versus speaking to you on the phone – ten points."

"Pops, in the 'observing flora and fauna sector,' I got some ten pointers: Seeing robins, butterflies, squirrels, rabbits, orchids, dandelions and African violets."

"Let me add to your list on nature: waves crashing in the Atlantic, a kite soaring in an azure sky, a full moon, red sunsets, a constellation, sunrises and an eclipse."

"Dad, how many points make a great day?"

"If you hit 1,000 when you put your head on the pillow, you hit a home run. But, before we get bored with this exercise, let's move on to one of your favorite subjects, sex. Starting with the ten-pointers: loving encounters such as a warm, moist kiss on the lips or playing footsies under a restaurant table. For the baseball purist, you get to first base – 20 points, second base – 30 points, and you slide into third base – 50 points. 100 points for a home run. Each different sexual position you performed, from missionary to doggy style, gets you a whopping 100 points."

"Pop, you can climb to that 1000 point level pretty quickly if you run through a good number of sexual positions."

"Blake, you're right, but remember, everybody can create their own grading-point system. When you tabulate the numbers in your head or on your fingers, work in multiples of ten. Once you're totaled your numbers, you have measured the quality of your day. The more points garnered, the happier you are."

"Can you go over a thousand points?"

"Sure, those days are hard to forget. In bed, right before you fall asleep, with your head resting on your pillow, you give thanks, 'G-d that was one-hell-of-a- great day! Thank you."

"Dad, a 'happiness formula' is highly subjective but I think it might be a worthwhile experiment. Thanks for the insight."

"Give it a try for a few days. I think you'll like it."

"Pop, do you know the name of the most important list for old folks?"

Thinking I knew the answer, I still asked, "What is the name of that list?"

Blake snickered, "Your bucket list, Dad."

We laughed and fell into silence.

Thirty

The Photograph

Gripping the steering wheel, I paused to take a deep breath. We had entered northern Florida. I glanced out the window to study a slow-moving muddy river that ran parallel to I-95. Then I handed Blake a book that rested in the crack between the seat and the automatic stick shift. "Son, this afternoon, I'm going back to discuss Grandpa's wartime activities with you."

I pointed between the seats, "Please pick up that book . It's called *Sala's Gift*. In the photograph section, there is a photo of your grandfather. I'd like you to study it for a minute. Then give me your thoughts; it poses some mysteries."

"Dad, I'm game."

Blake opened the book and found the picture. For over a minute, he scanned the photo in silence, acting as if he was Sherlock Holmes. "Dad I now think I'm ready for your questions."

"First let me tell you what I know about the photo. Your grandfather signed his name and wrote, 'Laurahutte, 1942' on the back of the picture. That indicates that he owned the photograph. Gramps was then a prisoner in the Laurahutte forced labor camp.

"The camp got its name from the Prussian village in the Province of Silesia in which it was located. This forced labor camp housed about a thousand prisoners. From April of 1944 until January 23, 1945, the camp manufactured anti-aircraft artillery. On the last day of its existence, the remaining camp prisoners were evacuated to Mauthausen Concentration Camp.

"Mauthausen was an extermination-through-labor camp but it also gassed prisoners."

"Dad, I know what extermination-through-labor means, the Nazi's worked the prisoners to death while starving and abusing them."

"You're right. Now, let's get back to the photograph. In the picture, Grandpa wears a white medical coat and grim facial expression. He holds an infant doll in his right arm while his left hand is stuck his pocket. No doctor would hold a child so carelessly. So why did your grandfather?

"There are seventeen prisoners in the photograph, four men and thirteen women. The men are dressed in their work clothes.

Two of the women jut out their breasts as if they are proud of their physiques. Two other women interlock their arms with the men, including women who appear happy to be holding on to your grandfather."

"Dad, do you think that is his girlfriend? The one who saved him from the gas chambers."

"Sorry, I don't know. But let's focus on the photograph.

"They stand in front of a building. The weather is dreary. They wear clothing that indicates it's fall. Many of their faces say they do not want to be in the picture.

"The doll Grandpa is holding belonged to the granddaughter of one of the camp's Nazi guards. That guard commissioned Sala Garncarz, who was a seamstress in the camp, to sew clothing for the doll. Well Son, any thoughts or questions?"

"Yeah Dad, I scribbled down a list of eight questions."

Why was the photo taken?

What was the purpose of the photo?

Was it used for Nazi propaganda?

Who took the photo?

Why was Grandpa holding the plastic baby doll?

Was Grandpa sending a message in the way he held the doll?

Why is there a black marker glued to the photo right above Grandpa's head?

Was Grandpa sending a message with the smirk on his face?

Pausing for a minute to digest the questions, we sat in silence.

"Great questions. Here's what I know: According to Anne Kirschner, the author of the book you're holding," Dr. Wolf Leitner(sic) also managed to commission a group photograph of his friends and colleagues, and autographed one for Sala who stood in the upper row."

"Why would my Grandpa commission a photo in which he smirks and holds a doll? It doesn't make sense. Why would a doctor have such a photo taken? Was my grandpa so 'elite' that he could commission photographs?"

"Maybe he believed that the picture would act as an insurance policy, proving to other Germans that he was a physician?" I replied.

"Here is what I do know: Jewish slave laborers were not allowed to own cameras or possess photos of camp life. There was an article 19 in the Nazi concentration camp rule book which mandated the death penalty to prisoners for collecting information, any information, about concentration camps. It would have been nuts for the Germans to allow the prisoners to photograph the brutality in the camp. I'm surprised that they even allowed your grandfather to possess the photo. Kirschner made a big deal of how dangerous it was for her mother, Sala, to possess any photographs in the barracks. After Dad died, I never saw any photos of the camps in his possessions.

"The photo might have been a privilege the Germans granted him for being the camp physician. Maybe he wanted to send it to his family to show them that he was still alive?"

"Why the smirk? Why the attitude?" Blake asked. " It is almost a leer. I don't remember ever seeing Grandpa leering. I would have recalled something that scary."

"You're right, son; I never saw your grandpa leer like that.

"So, my guess is that a Nazi guard shot the photo, maybe the one whose granddaughter owned the doll. That might also explain the dour looks on most of the faces in the group. Why should they voluntarily smile for a German?

"The guard developed extra photos and gave them to my dad, who gave one to Sala."

Blake added, "If a German took the photo it could have been used for propaganda to entice other Jews to agree to go to forced labor camps. That's the only reason I can think of why Grandpa would hold that doll like that."

"Son, I agree but the group's demeanor may have had the opposite effect on those who studied the picture closely."

"But to Jews starving in ghettos, the group looks pretty well fed and dressed in clean clothing."

"I think your grandfather held the doll in that lackadaisical manner to send a message. A signal to anyone who saw the photograph. That smirk on his face can be interpreted as saying, 'life in this hellhole sucks.'"

"Dad, why the black marker over Grandpa's head?"

"I don't have a clue – but whoever put it there wanted to identify your grandfather.

"I have one last question for you about that photograph. Where is G-d in that picture?"

"Dad, G-d is not in the photo. In 1942, he could not be found anywhere near a Jew in Europe."

Thirty-One

The Arrival

After an interminable wait, the article arrived via email. I moved my mouse to the print icon and gave it a shaky tap. I watched, listened, and waited as all 36 pages came to life. I placed the pages in order, neatly stacking them together, before slamming down on the stapler.

I picked it up with both of my hands and started to read: *Jews in the Service of Organization Todt in the Occupied Soviet Territories, October 1941 – March 1942* by Bella Gutermann.

I scanned the bottom of the page: 1/36 *Shoah* Resource Center, The International School for Holocaust Studies. This 36 page paper was extensively footnoted.

I knew *Yad Vashem* had a resource center, having visited the museum on each of my trips to Israel. I knew *Yad Vashem* was conceived in Palestine during the Second World War.

I had visited the museum on three occasions but still did not have the intestinal fortitude to visit Auschwitz.

I recalled my revulsion at seeing the 1920's anti-Semitic German manufactured, porcelain figurines of large hook-nosed bearded rabbis housed in a glass case in the museum. I reflected on the multitude of porcelain Uncle Toms and Aunt Jemimas quarried on shelves in the South of the Border gift shop.

I flashed back to walking through the different branches of the museum: the Children's Memorial, the Hall of Remembrance, the Memorial to the Deportees, the domed Hall of Names, covered in pictures of the deceased, the Eternal Flame, and the Garden of the Righteous Among Nations. This garden recognizes those Christians who risked their lives to save Jews.

I remembered viewing a slide show about *Kristallnacht* with a snapshot of one of my heroes, Herschel Grynszpan, a lone gunman with a rare Hebraic obsession to seek justice against brutality through the barrel of a pistol.

Outside the museum walls stood two ten-meter long European cattle cars which made up the Memorial to the Deportees. Who knows how many hundreds, or even thousands of Jews rode to their deaths in that one car.

The Nazi's Hebraic obsession was so strong that an SS manual recommended that 50 people be placed in every freight or cattle car and that each train have 50 cars. The Nazi goal was to ship 2,500 Jews to the death camps at one time.

Some cars were stuffed with up to 150 standing occupants. After days in the cattle car, many of the prisoners died in transit. The Nazis provided no water, no food, and no space. The only amenities in the car were a small barred window and a bucket latrine. I tried to imagine the putrid odor, the thirst, the claustrophobia, the screams of those going crazy, the wails of babies and the fear.

I wondered what type of railcar my dad rode in on his way to Auschwitz. Did my father ride in the museum's "Auschwitz Wagon." How could my Father survive such a train ride.

I wondered how much more chilling the effect would be on the visitors if *Yad Vashem* had purchased or asked Poland for a whole train – a locomotive pulling 50 cattle cars.

At *Yad Vashem,* in a wooded area, two cattle or railway cars appear at tree-top level. The rail cars rest between two hills, on a portion of a wooden trestle which sits on steel beams. These two railway cars were given to Israel by the Polish Government. They are placed too far away for the visitors to touch or smell. I question their placement.

The rear car hangs precariously close to the edge of the incomplete trestle. It appears that a bomb has blown apart half of this bridge. The metaphor of that car's potential destruction does not escape me. Nor does the symbolism of a blown railroad bridge belie the fact that the Allies could have saved thousands of lives by bombing the rails leading to the death camps.

I recall the first time I looked up at the hill, spotted the cars and shivered, as a chill ran through my body. I studied the cars: bleached-out wooden planks, the words *"Deutsche Reichsbahn"* painted on its side, its sliding wooden doors, its rusted wheels, its two metal mesh-covered windows and the exterior door latches. I pictured the faces of the transported as they heard the clanging metal on metal sound of the latch being shut. I pictured myself locked in the sardine-packed cattle car, with my claustrophobia, going crazy within minutes of hearing that latch lock.

Turning away from the rail cars, I headed toward the Children's Memorial. Through the narrowing cement corridors, I headed to a hollowed-out domed cavern. The dome was covered by photographs of hundreds of children. The photos disappeared as the lights dimmed. A somber prayerful moan filled the chamber. I was left standing in a room lit by one and a half million stars – one star for each murdered child. Repeatedly, a voice intoned, in Hebrew, or Yiddish or English, a child's name, age and nationality: "Jacob, five, Poland." Each child's name cut deep. As tears formed in my eyes, I wanted out. I had heard enough names. But I was a prisoner of the darkness. Until the room lit up, my feet remained frozen to the floor.

Carefully exiting the domed cavern, my eyes were blinded as they hit the sunlight. Simultaneously, my brain was hit with two new names for this museum building: "The Where Was He Hiding? Memorial" or "Had He Forgotten His Obsession With His People? Memorial."

In the next memorial building, I walked toward the Eternal Flame, while remembering the names of many of the death camps. There they were on the floor, surrounding the Eternal Flame, carved into stone, in English and Hebrew. This continually burning flame served as a remembrance of the Six Million.

My thoughts now left the museum and returned to the Ph.D. paper. I had never heard of The International School for Holocaust Studies. If I had, I would have considered studying there, or at least my sister or I could have asked about our dad when we were at *Yad Vashem.*

Now I remembered my sister saying on the phone, "Dad is only mentioned in a footnote or two." I knew that my Uncle Mike had read the article. He did not seem to be overly excited about it.

I scanned the 36-page dissertation for that one footnote. But there in the text Dad's name appeared over and over again. Barbara had only scanned and not carefully read the story. I decided not to jump to the portions of the article written about my father but to take my time reading every word in the document. I highlighted the article in yellow and wrote comments in the margins.

Again I studied the top of each page where the name of Bella Gutermann's employer appeared: *Yad Vashem's SHOAH* Resource Center with their logo and e-mail address. I studied the logo. I recalled first seeing the logo in the museum near the Eternal Flame. It appeared to be a zigzagging road or a crooked line of smoke headed to six impressionistic, triangular human figures or possibly a six-candled menorah. I thought, How artistically appropriate this logo is for the murdered Six Million, on the road to heaven or going up in smoke in the crematoria.

I then recounted my father's words, on how he looked for magical numbers or signs that showed he deserved to live another day in the camps. He believed in numerology. Here was an example. The number 6, for the six million, multiplied by the length of the war, six years, equals 36. The exact number of pages in Bella's dissertation.

On page one of those 36 pages, Bella stressed the importance of German trains heading east during Operation Barbarossa and the difficulties these trains faced.

I had read books and watched movies about Operation Barbarossa. I wonder, Did my dad play a role in the greatest land battle in history?

There it was in print on page one, "And much to their misfortune, a small group of young Jews became involved in attempts to alleviate this problem." Bella said this mysterious event had never been studied. "The conscription of young Jews from Eastern Silesia – prisoners in forced-labor camps under the auspices of Organisation *Schmelt,* disguised as employees of Organisation *Todt* (OT) – for the task of rehabilitating the Soviet railroad system is extremely puzzling."

Was my dad conscripted? I didn't remember him using that word on his tapes.

Was my dad, "disguised or camouflaged" not to look like a Jewish laborer? I do not recall him ever using either of these words on tape.

Bella had me hooked. I read, underlined and wrote notes at a turtle's pace trying to capture the essence of every word she had written as if each word was a diamond.

I flashed back to listening to my father talking on tape about being issued a black uniform by the Germans. I remembered his lack of detail about the uniform. I recalled Blake asking questions about the insignias on the black uniform on our drive from Plymouth to Fort Lauderdale. Would I now learn those details in this article?

On page two Bella called this program "a bold experiment … which became a tragic event in the lives of 350 young people." Here were Organisation *Schmelt's* Jews handed over to Organsation *Todt.* Here in the winter of 1941/42, Jewish workers participated in Operation Barbarossa. They went by train deep into occupied Soviet Union, near Leningrad, and my dad acted as the physician for this group of three hundred and forty-nine men.

I had watched documentaries of Russian partisans blowing up tracks and trains, and shooting at the passengers. In my head, I cheered the partisans as they killed German railroad personnel or soldiers. These partisans were slowing Hitler's march into mother Russia. They cut supplies of food and weaponry meant for his *Wehrmacht.* They, in partnership with mother winter, halted the progress of the Hun invasion. Little did I know that my dad could have been blown to pieces by the bombs the partisans had placed on those tracks or by the bullets they aimed at those trying to repair or shovel the snow off of those tracks.

As a member of this "select" group, my father and the young Jews were taken to a camp near Breslau and moved into barracks that were segregated from the other prisoners.

Here for the first time in months they were fed a healthy ration of food and given time to rest. Gutermann said, "During this time the men were isolated from the other prisoners and pampered in a way that piqued their curiosity. These young Jews were forced to parade, to line up in groups of five, and made to perform military-order drills." A survivor in the article said, "They even practiced leaping off moving trains. Some of the drills were carried out at night, "as if we'd been drafted into the army: marching drills, cap on, cap off, and it had to be done in one smack so they'd hear it when we placed the caps on our legs and in the main we walked back and forth."

I pictured my dad jumping off of a moving train, marching on a parade ground with hundreds of other men dressed in uniform, and slapping his cap on his legs to create a loud sound. In my wildest dreams I could never have imagined my father doing these activities. But the story got even more bizarre.

"The next day they were given new clothing … including a black overcoat without a lining, an armband on the right sleeve bearing the inscription *Arbeitseinslaz der Reichsbahn* – OT with an embossed swastika underneath. They were given dark berets. One survivor, Yosef Anzel testified, 'We didn't know what was going on. Suddenly we were Jews with armbands with a swastika and the *Reichsbahn.* We didn't know what was happening here. Those who returned from work looked from afar, unable to believe their eyes when they saw us, as if it were Purim. And some of us were even proud.'"

Could my dad have been one of those men who were proud? I doubted it. But here was the answer to Blake's question. Grandpa's uniform did have a swastika on it. My father had conveniently neglected to mention that fact on his Holocaust tape. I understood why. To have mentioned the swastika insignia would have opened him up to a hundred other questions not only into his trip into Russia but to every aspect of his imprisonment.

The Germans told the 350 young men that, "They were about to leave for security work that would enable Germany to advance on the eastern front." I paused to wonder how my dad must have felt knowing he was assisting the Nazis advance into the Soviet Union, home to millions of Jews.

Gutermann added on page 19 a survivor's memory (Avraham Hornung). He said the 350 were repeatedly told, "You're no longer Jews, but a German labor Unit." Although the official who said this, sensing that he was getting carried away, hurriedly corrected himself, " You're Jews, but not like those Jews in the camps. "He even noted, "Today you're getting supplies just like those in the *Wehrmacht.*" On innumerable occasions, the men were told emphatically that they were about to take part in defeating the Russians and/or were threatened with death if they dared to reveal their nationality and identity to anyone."

I learned that this contingent of Jews, in the autumn of 1941, spent the next two weeks drilling at this facility. Then in November, a representative of Organisation *Schmelt* advised them that they were to march "*von Westen nach Osten, von*

Moskau nach London," that if they did their work for Germany well, the Jews would be given Palestine at the end of the war, and that those who failed to perform well would be punished with death.

Those words brought back the memory of: *ARBEIT MACHT FREI* (work sets you free) written in iron on the gates and in paint on the signs at Dachau, Auschwitz, Sachsenhausen, Theresienstat and Gross-Rosen Concentration Camps. The prisoners made these signs which were placed at the entrances of the camps. The manipulative bastards wanted the Jews to work themselves to death in hope of freedom. Here was another example: "you help us win the war and your reward will be freedom in Palestine. You don't help us and you're dead." I wondered if my dad ever believed anything the Nazis said.

I glanced at the bottom of page 20. I had passed the halfway mark. My eyes burned and bladder begged for relief.

Standing over the bowl, I shut my eyes and tried to imagine living in a state of perpetual fear. I failed. As much as my mind tried to imagine perpetual fear it was an inconceivable concept to grasp. After washing my hands, I thought only those exposed to the constant threat of death had a shot at it.

I darted back to my office chair, to my printed copy of *Jews in the Service of Todt.* I lined up my writing instruments and dove back into the story.

Julius Siegel, an Austrian Jewish army officer in World War One, was chosen by the Organisation *Schmelt* leaders to assist in assembling the group of 350 before they headed east to Russia. Siegel played the role of Prussian officer to the tee. He wore a monocle, a green uniform, highly polished boots, and riding breeches. To maximize his authority, he carried a whip in his hand. Siegel made a request of the *Schmelt* representative on behalf of the contingent. He requested the Germans to take care of the departing men's families. This statement may have caused my father to hope that this request would be honored.

Gutermann continued, "At the end of roll call, with the German's consent, Siegel ordered the prisoners to sing *Hatikvah*."

My mind's eye pictured a totally unbelievable sight: 350 young Jewish men at a paramilitary roll call, wearing uniforms with swastikas arm bands singing *Hatikvah* (The Hope) in the presence of saluting *Wehrmacht* soldiers. Bella called the scene "surreal." Here was the ultimate example of truth being stranger than fiction.

The 350 sang a Hebrew song about hope, when they possessed almost none of it. This was a song written by a subject of the Austrian-Hungarian Empire, a Jewish poet, named Naphtali Herz Imber; a ballad, which became the Zionist anthem of 1897, and which years later would become the Israeli national anthem; a song about a people returning to their land after 2,000 years in exile. The Nazis were crafty enough to tell the 350, if they were successful, they would return to the land of their forefathers.

The scene "thrilled the men, but also filled them with dread. After all, they were marching toward a threatening and unknown future."

Julius Siegel, their Jewish military trainer, did not join them in this mission.

Now Bella, for the first time in the paper, mentions my dad. "One of the departees was Dr. Leitner, (sic) the group's physician, who would play a role of the highest importance in determining the men's fate." This was followed by footnote 47, the one my sister, Barbara, was most likely talking about.

"Dr. Leitner, who was placed in the group to be its physician, played a key role in determining the men's fate. Before he headed to the East, he had served as a physician at the Eichtal camp, where he was not overly liked by the prisoners because of his strictness and reticence in offering assistance. By virtue of his devoted care for the men in the transport, the Jews in the camp were grateful to him."

The second sentence in the paragraph smacked me in the face. My eyes flared and my stomach tightened as I digested each and every word.

My father, too strict!

My dad, too reticent in offering assistance!

On his tapes my dad commented on how many times the guards had beaten him. Had the Nazis beaten him for his failing to be too strict? Did the Nazis threaten to harm his family if he offered too much assistance?

My dad didn't know the meaning of strictness. He never struck his children. He hardly ever yelled or punished us. Our mother was our disciplinarian. My dad offered assistance to everyone in need.

I found it hard to believe that my father was not willing to communicate or talk freely or reveal all the facts about something! What facts could he reveal? My dad, unwilling to do something for his fellow prisoners. I wanted examples but there were none. I wanted the names of his accusers, but they were not in the footnote. I wanted to bring him back so I could interview him, but he and his version of this story were long gone. And, I doubted if I would ever get any more details.

What I feared most as a youth, that someday I would hear a story about my dad's wartime experiences, and it would ruin my heroic image of him and it had happened. I paraphrased what he said on the tapes, "Every man looked out for himself first. That was every prisoner's rule of survival."

Now, my brain mandated a second break. I needed some fresh air, a walk and time to think. The paper could wait until my nerves calmed down. I had waited for over two months for it. What harm would occur if I waited one more night to finish it?

I needed and wanted to speak to my sister. A more positive side of Dad's story was coming up but I decided to wait until the next morning to finish the article.

"Hi Barbara. Sorry for calling so late but I had to ask. Did you *read* the Gutermann article about Dad?"

"Mort, not really. I scanned it. I saw the footnote that mentioned Dad's name and said to myself I'll read it later when I have more time."

"Well, Sis, I recommend you make the time. It says some rather unflattering things about Dad.

"Like what?" she asked.

"Like at one of the labor camps where he worked as a doctor, prisoners thought he was too strict and too reticent in offering assistance."

"Does the article give any examples?" she asked.

"Well I'm only on page 20 and I have not yet seen any. I'm going to finish it in the morning. I had to take a break. I've had enough to think about for one day. I'll call you tomorrow after I'm done reading it. We can then hash over our thoughts."

"Mort, thanks for the call. I'll start reading the article tonight. We'll talk in the morning. Love you. Bye."

"Bye. Sis. I'll call you tomorrow."

In bed, I tossed, turned and woke up every two hours. I found little comfort on my mattress as if it was stuffed with the hair of camp prisoners. I kept picturing Dad in a German uniform with a swastika armband. I pictured him training as if he were a conscript. I pictured him jumping off of moving trains.

I shut my eyes and kept wondering what I knew about this man I adored. I knew he was a guy without a mean bone in his body, a father who never laid a hand on me. He was a man who hardly ever raised his voice in anger. Could he have been too strict or too reticent to assist Jewish prisoners? What did they mean by "too strict?"

Could the doctor I watched care for his patients as if they were his own family be reticent in offering medical care to slave laborers? Did he have to make Hobson-choice decisions as a medical doctor in the camps? Of course he did. I pictured Meryl Streep in *Sophie's Choice* deciding her life or the life of her child. Would Sophie have been considered too strict or reticent.

By 6:00 A.M., returning to sleep became impossible. Half of my body pulled me back toward the Ph.D. paper. When I finally awoke at dawn, I felt like I had not slept. If I had a dream, I could not recall.

Turning on the lights, I found myself back at my desk with my yellow marker, ready to read the rest of the story.

After the roll call, The German officers left and the group of Jews were surrounded with *Volksdeutsche* guards armed with heavy machine guns and escorted by dogs. One guard was posted for every ten Jews.

They marched 12 kilometers to the town of Breslau to catch an eastward-bound military freight train. The 350 made an intriguing sight for the residents of the town. How unusual: men in uniforms with shaved heads and swastika armbands under the guard of dogs and machine guns.

Survivor Hornung said, "We marched like soldiers; after all we had been trained to do so."

For five days the 350 were locked on that military freight train, with limited seating and 30 to 40 men per car with the only means of relieving the bodily waste being one exposed latrine bucket. I tried to imagine the smell in that car.

During the train trip, the 350 were guarded by Romanian soldiers. The guards determined that the group were made up of Jews, so they beat and abused them. They claimed the abuse was justified as it was a proper reprisal for the treatment rendered on them by their former Jewish bosses in Romania.

They travelled east for about two weeks until they arrived in the town of Sebezh, a town located 200 kilometers from Leningrad. During the trip, some of the men bathed their bodies in the cold snows of Russia. Upon arrival, the 350 in deep snow were put to work transferring cargo from German trains to Russian trains, clearing snow and laying rails.

Now for the third time Gutermann referenced my Father's activities:

"The cold and the brutal labor soon began to take a toll on the prisoners, and many of them simply sat down and let themselves freeze to death. The doctor of the transport, Leitner, pleaded with them to keep moving at all times in order to maintain blood circulation, since only intensive physical effort could spare them from freezing."

This sounded like the man who raised me.

Now Bella's story included one that my dad told on his tape. It was his memory of a hastily abandoned Jewish town where he found warm food and coffee in the empty homes.

As they progressed along the tracks, the men came to a town whose population had obviously been deported very shortly before their arrival. They entered homes that had *mezuzot* on the doorposts and prayer books on the tables. On a table in one home, they found a bundle of letters of a son serving on the Leningrad front. In a doctor's home they found leftovers of food that had just been prepared. For lack of choice the men of the transport used furniture that they found to stoke the fireplace and ease the chill to some extent."

I wondered if my father or any of the 350 could have imagined that the whole population of this town were marched to a ravine or a man-made ditch and slaughtered en masse. I pictured Bar Bari and the SS troops shooting Jew after Jew in the head as the explosion from their pistols forced their bodies to fall in the gaping hole.

I returned to reading. On page 27, Gutermann entitled a new section of her paper, "Typhus Epidemic." My mind raced to my dad's story on the tapes about hiding typhus patients on the upper floors of a building in hopes that the German doctors would not walk all the way to the top floors. Would I now get a new version of the story?

As a result of the harsh living conditions, terrible cold, food, overcrowding, filth, and poor sanitary conditions, the prisoners contracted various diseases. The most debilitating was a typhus epidemic that broke out among the Jews. A young man from Klubock was the first victim. However, his illness was not diagnosed at once since the symptoms resembled colds and influenza which were routine matters.

Again I saw my father's name.

"Several days had passed before Dr. Leitner made the correct diagnoses. He then decided to conceal the diagnoses from the Germans."

I thought," He was a risk-taker."

I remembered what my father said on the tapes, "I was a risk-taker, a risk-taker with alert eyes and ears."

If he was caught covering up the typhus epidemic, the Nazis would have shot him on the spot. On the other hand, if he advised the Germans of the presence of the communicable disease, they would have just murdered all the remaining Jews to stop the spread of the epidemic. Here was an example of a Hobson's choice. My father was required to do a risk-benefit analysis, weighing the odds of deceit and possible capture versus his knowledge of the history of Nazi mass murder of Jews to prevent Germans from becoming ill.

He decided to conceal the information from the Germans, and buried the now-deceased victim in the snow. When another prisoner, from Sosnowiec, came down with the disease, Leitner tried to move him to a hospital in Idritsa, claiming he had come down with pneumonia. The German supervisors acceded to Leitner's request and assigned another prisoner to escort the patient. As they made their way to a military truck, the patient died, and his comrade buried him at the side of the road.

I pictured my father, blanketed with fear of being caught, with his bare hands digging through ice and snow to bury the man. I scanned to the footnote and upon seeing Dad's name I read: Weinreich was a relative of Dr. Leitner's who assisted him as an orderly. Yosef Ansel remarked in the interview with the author that he had watched Dr. Leitner being collected in the mornings and taken to patients in the vicinity.

I realized that Dad had a much better chance of survival as a doctor traveling on a sled going from one patient to another than a prisoner shoveling snow every day of the week from dawn to dusk.

As I continued reading I learned that within a few days many of the 350 had contracted typhus. Bella wrote: Dr. Leitner did his best to stem the epidemic and separate the sick from the healthy. He placed the patients behind a partition at the end of the hall, but the disease took such a toll and spread so rapidly that half of the group was no longer fit for labor. The camp commander, an OT official, threatened to shoot them all if they did not report to work, considering their behavior an act of evasion and attempted sabotage. This is when Leitner earned his place in Heaven in the prisoners' eyes.

Those words burned into my memory, "a place in Heaven in the prisoners' eyes." The agony of the night before turned into morning ecstasy. As a smile ran across my face I continued.

"The prisoner's had not cared much for Leitner when he was an inmate in the slave-labor camps of Silesia, but, on the journey East, he had proven to be the transported men's defender, an uncrowned leader who toiled indefatigably to aid and treat the ill."

I was riveted by Bella's descriptive words, "defender, uncrowned leader, who toiled indefatigably." Dad became a man destined to be a heroic leader.

"Even the OT supervisors, whom he had treated frequently, appreciated him. Here, however, he labored with empty hands, for he was given no medications.

"As the Jewish men continued to die, he summoned the chief military physician and described the situation to him – albeit without disclosing everything. His intention was to ask the military physician to persuade the commander to return the men to Germany. Leitner prepared for the physician's visit by placing the less ill in the front of the hall and the serious cases in the back, hoping that the physician would not reach them. He also tried to remove the filth and stench that pervaded the area. The military physician realized at once that an epidemic was at hand and agreed to recommend the men be sent back to Germany, but the camp commander vehemently disagreed with this idea and threatened to shoot them all.

The Trip Back

"The rumor about the epidemic that had broken out in the Jewish transport eventually caused panic among the local supervisors and *Wehrmacht* people in Sebezh, and the prisoners heard from the workers that the sector command had ordered the healthy prisoners to be returned to the authority of Organisation *Schmelt* in Silesia. An OT representative came the next day and ordered Dr. Leitner to prepare to evacuate the healthy workers and to abandon the typhus workers to their fate: ... All this s...t back to Germany, but only the travel worthy." Dr. Leitner protested this order to the commander, reminding him that when the transport left the East, OT representatives had promised that the men would be under military authority and within a military framework. Therefore, he argued all of them – sick and healthy alike – must be returned to Germany. His request was met."

The word "guts" jumped into my mind. My dad was a risk-taker with guts. My father had *chutzpah.* He protested and argued with Nazis. And he got his way. He remembered their promises and knew of their obedience to the code of military honor. He realized that military code might even take prescience over their hatred of Jews.

"At the railroad station, after receiving small quantities of bread and jam, they were taken to the cars. The healthy men were skeptical. Fearing a trap, they did not believe they would be returned to Germany and repressed all hope until the train actually began to move. In the cars, Dr. Leitner arrayed the men in pairs, one ill and one healthy, and warned them that they must continue to conceal the epidemic from the *Wehrmacht* soldiers who escorted the transport."

My father was a strategist. He figured out to keep the survivors alive.

As they traveled, they were given cold but edible food, which sufficed for the healthy men since the ill were unable to eat. The trip westward was no less difficult than the trip eastward. The cars were sealed; the men became increasingly thirsty and pleaded for water at stations where the train stopped. Even though compassionate civilians and soldiers were sometimes helpful, more prisoners died during the trip, and their bodies remained in the cars. Whenever the surviving men were allowed to step out, they mixed jam and snow and fed it to the ill, and buried the dead in the snow. Their first stop was Vilna, where the authorities decided to take them to a large disinfection facility used by the *Wehrmacht*. Here, too, they had to conceal the fact that they were carrying typhus, and Dr. Leitner ordered all of them, including the ill, to stand for roll-call.

At the facility, the men had their first warm baths in four months. Their wounds and frostbitten limbs were treated. Their scalps were deloused. After receiving this care they were taken back on the train. However, as the dying continued, one small consolation arrived for the living, the German guards were now allowing the Jews to throw the corpses off of the train and not have to wait until the next stop.

On the fifth day of the journey in the city of Konigsberg, 50 of the Jewish prisoner's bodies were received by representatives of the Jewish community for transport and burial.

I wondered how many Jews were left on the train .

After 10 harrowing days, their trip ended in Breslau. This was the same town where it had all started. The contingent had lost somewhere between 230 and 200 men. The 350 had been decimated on this venture into the frozen reaches of a Russian Hell, decimated by being made to live in filth, without proper food or sanitation.

My Dad was one of the 'lucky' ones.

Then the men were taken by truck back to Camp Gross-Masselwitz were they were quarantined and where the typhus resurfaced and took more lives.

The article continued: Several days later, the transport men were placed aboard a train and taken to Annaberg camp, where they found their relatives' letters. All other Jews had already been removed from this camp, and Dr. Leitner demanded that additional doctors be brought to help eradicate the epidemic."

Was this true? He "demanded?" I found it hard to believe my father demanded anything from the Germans. From his tapes,

I sensed the most he would do is make a polite request with no eye contact given to his Nazi captors. Here was another facet of the man I did not know. He had one set of big balls.

Several days later, a Jewish doctor named, Shmuel Mittelmann, arrived at the camp having been ordered there by Heinrich Lindner of Organisation *Schmelt.* The name, Lindner, rang a bell. I had read about his surprise visits to the camps where he watched the slave laborers work. If displeased at what he saw, he beat and shot, or let his dogs attack the laborers.

"Lindner asked Mittelmann, 'You're a doctor? In Anneberg I have people who have come down with the flu; they have to be cured. You will go there today, under guard. Do you know the meaning of Auschwitz?"

Upon his arrival Mittelmann realized the men had typhus and not the flu.

Mittelman went straight to work. He had no medicines and, apart from Dr. Leitner, no medical personnel. Quickly he dispatched Dr. Leitner to the sanitation Department of the *Judenrat* in Sosnowiec to ask for assistance, and he decided to tell the camp commander, an OT official, the truth about the disease.

My father was back in a city which he knew in his youth. How that city must have changed in the hands of the Nazis.

"Despite the difficulties, Mittelmann managed to save most of the patients within four weeks. The twelve who had died were given a full Jewish burial at a nearby cemetery."

They stayed in Anneberg until July of 1942, until a German official, named Henschild, ordered the young men back to work. I wondered if my father was included with the contingent. Then I read Bella's footnote. "Dr. Leitner and the team of medics remained in the Anneberg camp. Dr. Leitner survived and emigrated to the United States after the war."

I finished reading the story. There were no more mentions of Dr. Leitner in the article. I would have to go back to his tapes to possibly find out what he did in Anneberg and how long he stayed there. But the article laid out the rest of story of the remaining 105 prisoners. When Organisation *Schmelt* was disbanded in 1944, the 105 were sent to Auschwitz and Gross-Rosen concentration camps. How many survived the camps is unknown.

Thirty-Two

Slave Labor

Back in the car, Blake said, "Before this road trip comes to an end, I have a bunch of questions about Grandpa Wolf's life in the camps."

"Son, I'll try my best to answer them."

"What was Grandpa's life like as a slave laborer?"

"He was a doctor and as such he had privileges. He was allowed to go from camp to camp to render medical care to prisoners.

"Let me give you a History 101 lesson on the subject of Jewish slave labor. In the mid 1930s, the Nazis persecuted Jews by not allowing them to work in their chosen fields. Then the Jews had to do any work the Nazis ordered them to do. To earn a salary was the only way a person could get a food ration. Slave labor was also called forced labor or compulsory labor. More than one million Jewish slave laborers were required to toil for the Germans. Your great grandfather, Toby, and your great grandmother, Rose, as well as Grandma Henia, Aunt Renia, and Grandpa Wolf were all slave laborers.

"Nearly seven million people from the lands Hitler had conquered were shipped to Germany to work as slaves in factories. This group of workers freed up Germans to fight in the war. The Germans set up segregated labor camps for the Jews. In these camps they were abused and given minimal amounts of food in what can be called the Nazi policy of 'destruction through work.' Many Jews couldn't take the hard labor and the poor conditions; they committed suicide. In a way, these slave laborers were the lucky ones because those Jews who did not participate in forced labor were usually made part of mass deportations to the death camps.

"In *Sala's Gift,* Ann Kirschner wrote that your grandfather was a member of an 'elite' group of prisoners in the camp."

"Dad, what do you think she meant by elite?"

"I think she meant Grandpa, as a German-speaking doctor in many *Schmelt* Camps, had privileges and information the others prisoners did not get."

"What kind of information? What kind of privileges?"

"Sala considered your grandfather one of her protectors. She said that sometimes when your grandfather received advance warning of inspections of the barracks, he alerted her. Those prisoners caught with contraband during those inspections were severely punished. This type of information was valuable; it meant the difference between life and death. I read the 'elite' sometimes received tins of canned meat, a pack of cigarettes, and better sleeping quarters, like the *kapos* who were assigned by the Nazis to police the ghettos. The most surprising thing to me is that Grandpa was allowed to have a girlfriend.

"Sala said Grandpa used to bring her cigarettes in the Gepppersdorf Labor Camp. She had a crush on him and loved his good looks.

"In the Gross Paniow, another *Schmelt* Labor Camp, Sala considered your grandfather an influential camp elder."

"Like what kind of privileges or information?" Blake queried.

"Son, on the positive side, Kirschner said Gramps saved her mother's life by hiding her from the Nazi doctors who were experimenting on Jewish women. He hid her in a makeshift operating room. They wanted young women to do surgical experiments on. Kirschner added, 'Not all the women in the camp were so lucky.' "

"Is there a negative side?" Blake asked.

"You bet. If you save one female prisoner from surgical experiments and another prisoner gets experimented on, and the victim's relatives find out, they will always ask, 'Why didn't you save my daughter?' If those family members find out about your activity, you have made an enemy for life.

"Blake, what do you know about the Nazi doctors who experimented on Jews?"

"I know that Josef Mengele did genetic experiments on twins. He injected dye into the eyes of twins to see if it would change their color. He sewed twins together in an attempt to make conjoined twins. I always wondered what scientific value there was to this type of experimentation. It sounded like these sadist doctors got off torturing Jews."

"After Hitler came to power, German doctors sterilized the mentally infirm. From there they went on a euthanasia kick using phenol injections, which led to the use of carbon dioxide gas. The use of poisonous gas came straight from a Nazi memo. 'One does not fight rats with guns but with poison and gas.' Of course the final step in their killing process was the large-scale gassing of Jews in the camps."

"Dad, did Jewish doctors ever cross the line in order to save their own necks?"

Some Jewish doctors made the selection in the camp hospital as to which sick patients were unable to go back to work. Those patients were put on trains and transported to Auschwitz.

"I've heard of Jewish doctors who performed abortions on women in the camps on the theory that they were saving the life of the mother. If the Nazis found out a woman was pregnant they would send her to the gas chamber. I have read that some Jewish doctors even put newborns to death under the same theory. At Auschwitz, lethal injections of phenol were given to thousands of prisoners. They were administered by German medical doctors, their assistants, or sometimes prisoner doctors. So, the answer to your question is, 'yes.'"

I paused to think about my dad while wondering if Blake was having similar thoughts.

"On the other hand, I read a story, which I cannot verify as true, about a group of about 300 Jewish doctors imprisoned in concentration camps, who were given the choice of being battlefield doctors for the German army during the Barbarossa campaign in the Soviet Union in exchange for getting out of the camps. At this time the German causalities were so high and the Nazis so desperate for doctors that they would even allow Jews to practice medicine on German soldiers. They were told that they would be treated as if they were German soldiers and all they were required to do was disguise the fact that they were Jews. Most of those physicians refused the offer and were immediately executed. Each of those doctors had to make a Hobson choice: provide medical care to their known enemy, or most likely face an immediate death sentence. They faced the ultimate ethical question, that very fine line between right and wrong."

"Dad, did Grandpa Wolf ever encounter any 'good' Germans or Nazis during the war?"

"He mentioned four Germans who acted positively in his presence. The first one was an Austrian Nazi doctor who knew

Grandpa was taking care of slave laborers who had contracted typhus. The Austrian looked my father in the eyes and said, 'You know you have patients with typhus in this building?' My father kept silent fearing his acknowledgement would lead to the murder of all the Jews in his group. Normally the Nazis executed all groups of Jews infected with typhus. This Austrian kept his mouth shut and avoided a massacre.

"The second one was a German doctor who kicked a bag of medical supplies to your grandfather, which helped him save a number of people.

"The last two were Nazi guards at the last camp he was in at the time of his liberation by the American Army. The interviewer on the Holocaust tape asked Gramps what the survivors did to their German guards. And, Gramps said they left them alone because, relatively speaking, those two Guards did not abuse of the Jews."

"Did Grandpa ever talk about any bad or evil Jews he encountered during the war?"

"On the tapes, he talked about a Jew who brought the Nazis to his parent's house to arrest them."

"Did Wolf Grandpa ever mention the word swastika on his tapes?"

"Blake, I think he only referenced the swastika once. He called it the *hakenkreuz* or the broken cross. The swastika had been stamped on one of his official documents.

"Blake, did you know that the swastika has been used by early cultures around the world, from Hindus to Native Americans?"

"Yeah, Dad. I even read that early German aviators wore swastika pins as good luck symbols. Many German soldiers in World War I wore them in the battle fields. I bet Hitler wore one when he ran messages in the trenches. Hitler incorporated its use as a Nazi symbol in his book *Mein Kampf*."

Blake dropped his voice an octave. "Dad, you're pretty obsessed with your parent's wartime experiences, aren't you?"

"Son, you're right! And, just because I'm obsessed doesn't mean there isn't a basis for my obsession. The criminal acts the Nazis perpetrated on millions of Jews did not end in 1945. Their deliberate attempt to annihilate us wormed its way into our psyches and our souls. I suspect that even the grandchildren of *Shoah* victims, your generation, are unconsciously infected with this burden.

"As a child of two camp survivors, my fixation is multiplied by at least a factor of two. Having uncles, aunts, and grandparents who were survivors, and equal numbers of relatives who were murdered exponentially compounded my obsessive behavior. It stuck to me like a pit-bull for nearly forty years before loosening its grip. Today, I no longer buy every book I see on the Holocaust; my Holocaust literary shrine of over a hundred books has stopped growing. I avoid watching TV programs on the subject by quickly hitting the foreword button on my remote. My Holocaust cup overflowed with the details, the photographs, the words, the images of the tragedy. Now, I shed very little light on the subject. I had temporarily shut the shed door on the subject of the Holocaust until I decided that a good father-son relationship is grounded on family history.

"Son, my mantra became 'enough is enough.' That was until I read the article about Grandpa in the occupied Soviet Union. That article rekindled my eternal Holocaust flame.

Now I turned the table on Blake asking, "Did you ever feel your grandparents' holocaust pain?"

"Of course I did. But, my feelings are far from the level of your obsession.

Dad, after all the reading and watching of those holocaust documentaries you've done, did you ever dream that you were in a death camp?"

"I do not remember any such nightmares. I haven't given a great deal of thought to it. I don't recall even one dream where I confront a Nazi or a Kluxer, let alone find myself imprisoned in a camp.

"Grandpa Wolf, six months before he passed away, mentioned dreaming about his time in the camps. He said to the interviewer on his tapes, 'Sometimes I dream of it now.' He also admitted to having a breakdown at Auschwitz."

"Wow! I didn't know Gramps had a breakdown."

"I studied Freud's theories on dreams when I was in college. I read his book, *The Interpretation of Dreams.* Freud might have speculated that my obsession is so out in the open, that it is only housed in my conscious mind. The other possibility is, I erased those nightmares before I awoke making them impossible to remember. It's like we have a finger in our head that pushes down on our video recorder erase button. Freud might have said that all of my Nazi dreams were censored in my preconscious and not allowed to pass into the conscious."

I paused and Blake jumped in.

"Wasn't Freud the shrink who was heavily into symbolism and sex; a cigar represented a penis, and any box represented a vagina?"

"Yup that was Freud. He wrote the classic punch line which made fun of his theory: Sometimes a cigar is only a cigar."

"Dad, wasn't he the genius who came up with the idea that dreams were, 'The royal road to the unconscious.' He called our unconscious minds something like wish-fulfillment machines, tools which attempt to resolve our inner conflicts? Based on some of my dreams about my girl friends, he hit the nail right on the head."

"Son, sometimes a nail is only a nail."

We both let out our best manly laughs. I glanced down at the speedometer as my brain raced on.

"Blake, dreams are one of G-d's most creative miracles. Almost every night, your brain writes a short story, casts all the actors, pens the dialogue, sets up the scenery, plots the story and directs the players."

"Dad, well said. Did you just come up with that?"

"Yup." I replied as I turned the car into the Holiday Inn parking lot.

That night in my hotel bed, I had my first remembered Holocaust nightmare. The dream scene appeared in black and white as if coming from my family's old television set. In the dream it was early fall and a chill filled the air. I walked the crowded Warsaw Ghetto streets. I observed a seated Jewish vendor who looked to be in his mid-thirties. He handled some documents. He seemed at ease as did all the bustling shoppers. Everything seemed normal, except Nazi soldiers strolled in the background with rifles slung over their shoulders.

I thought about this relative calm, the lack of fear on the faces of these Jews. Two Nazi soldiers approached me. One was short and the other tall. The short unkempt soldier wore a three-day-old beard and a swastika-emblazoned uniform. I watched as his nose twitched. He sneezed and failed to cover his mouth; he made no attempt to. Out of that orifice came the loudest, wettest, most disgusting sneeze, I had ever heard or felt. My face was the target; my face was covered in Nazi spittle. Before I had a chance to respond, I awoke.

How would Freud interpret this dream? I would ask Blake for his opinion in the car as the trip continued.

At eight o'clock in the morning, my hands rested on the wheel, my eyes rested the on the road, and my mind rested on being interviewed. My son had taken on the role of interviewer. I flashed back to my dad. I never interviewed him and it still bothered me. But all these years later, I have not changed my mind on that decision. If he did not want to open that bottle, that was his decision. I, the good son, would not pull out the plug.

"Dad, how do you think the Holocaust affected your life?"

I paused for a few seconds to gather my thoughts.

"Great question; I have given that one a good deal of thought. If my parents were not survivors, would my behavior or life have been different? On the positive side, I am a much more compassionate person, rooting for the underdog, the minority, the downtrodden, the picked on and the bullied.

I protested and picketed for civil rights and equality in the admission process for Blacks on the University of Miami campus. Come to think of it, my essay for admission to the University of Miami was entitled , 'Man's Inhumanity To Man.' Of course, it was about Nazis and Jews and Grandpa Wolf's and Grandma Henia's experiences during the war. Of course, the essay's theme was the dehumanization of my parents, my family and my people.

When we lived in Louisiana, I criticized bigots to their faces when they spat out the "N" word.

I punched Iraqi students in their heads when those Arabs attacked protesting UM students. The Jewish UM students were protesting against Iraqi Jews being hanged in Baghdad. Dictator Saddam Hussein alleged that a number of Iraqi Jews were Israeli spies. He had them hanged in front of a crowd of thousands of cheering Iraqis." I paused to catch my breath.

"Son, of course it messed me up psychologically. I am tainted with post Nazi Hebraic paranoia, a paranoia that knows that the next Hitler is just around the corner, or that my family will all end up in camps. My paranoia has led to obsessive behavior which took up great quantities of my time and energy. Who knows how many thousands of hours? How many days spent studying, fantasizing and talking about the *Shoah?* Could that time have been put to more productive projects and causes? Probably. But who knows what replacement obsessions would have filled the void?

"Would I have taken more risks in my life? Probably. But I owed my parents the comfort of not having a "bad son." While I lived at home, my life was consumed by doing well in school and making them proud. They had suffered enough. They deserved no more pain. I gave them the unconditional love and respect they deserved."

My vocal chords tightened as a rant flew out of my mouth.

"Like most survivor's children, I'm tasked with the responsibility of passing on the 'Never Again Syndrome' – making sure young Jews like you do not forget what their families experienced. Be vigilant. Be prepared so no such events will ever occur again. That's why Grandpa and Grandma made their tapes.

"Grandpa said it loud and clear, 'The Jews cannot depend on anybody for their protection. They have to be able to protect themselves.' "

I coughed to clear my throat.

"You will hear some Christians and even some Jews say, 'Enough is Enough'; no more talk about the Holocaust; it happened so many years ago. Forget about it. Move on. Too many books and movies have been made on that subject. That is all in the past. It can never happen again, not in this great land, not in a land where a Black man was elected president. No one's telling Blacks to stop talking about the Klan."

"Dad I know what you're talking about. They even have a term for it. It's called Holocaust exhaustion."

Son, don't listen to them. Do not remain silent. Don't be afraid to tell them in a loud, clear voice to shut the fuck up. Tell them to get lost. They are idiots. They watched *Schindler's List, Life is Beautiful* and *The Pianist* and now they are experts on the subject matter. Their tolerance for Holocaust info has ended. They know it all.

"Never again!' is not only the motto of the Jewish Defense League, it's the motto of the Jewish people.

"I may be paranoid, but you need to remain vigilant. You need to keep our eyes and ears opened. As Joseph Heller said in *Catch 22*, 'Just because you're paranoid, does not mean they *aren't* after you.' There are millions of people out there after us.

"Don't be naïve and downplay this fact. Just watch CNN and see the hatred painted on the faces of European and Arab bigots as they burn Israeli flags. Remember that on May 10, 1933 the Nazis and the German Student Association burned over 35,000 books in one night. This cleansing by fire took place in 34 different German universities. First, the students marched in torch-lit parades and then accompanied by the music of live bands, they ignited 'purification bonfires.' They cheered as these so-called 'subversive Jewish ideologies' went up in smoke. These students forgot or never learned the words of the German Jewish poet who wrote in 1820, 'Where they burn books, they will in the end also burn people' or maybe they cheered the thought of genocide.

"Watch CNBC and see the racists deface Jewish cemeteries and synagogues with swastikas.

"Your grandfather emphasized it on the tapes. He stressed it as his most important message. 'Even in this great country, things can turn sour on the Jews in a minute. Israel needs to be protected at all costs. Without Israel, Jews will have no safe haven to escape to. It is our island of last resort, a safe haven left on earth in times of crisis.'

"Blake, do not forget you are now a messenger for the six million. This burden now rests on your shoulders. It is your sacred duty to pass it on. The story must be told."

As I pulled into the Jacksonville Embassy Suites, our last hotel of this trip, Blake replied, "Dad, I understand."

Thirty-Three

The Trial Transcript

The next morning, I joined Blake at the Embassy Suites' breakfast lounge. I grasped a freshly printed copy of a six-page, post World War II trial transcript.

As Blake sipped his coffee and munched on a bagel, I babbled about the email I had received a half hour earlier.

My voice rose as each sentence left my mouth. "You won't believe what I received today. It's an email from my cousin, Mel Laytner. He's writing a book on his father's experiences surviving the war. Grandpa and his father were both internees at Blechhammer Labor Camp."

"Dad, slow down you're gulping your words. Take a deep breath."

"Okay, he sent me a summary transcript of Grandpa's testimony at the American military trial of SS *Kommandant* Erich Walter Fritz Hoffmann. Hoffmann was the first *Kommandant* at Blechhammer."

Blake stopped chewing, swallowed a mouthful of bagel and gave me his full attention.

"Dad, what did you learn?"

"First, that grandpa's testimony helped get Hoffmann extradited back to Poland where he was hanged in 1948."

"Well that's great news," Blake clamored. "Dad, I don't remember ever reading, or you talking, about Blechhammer or Hoffmann on this trip."

"You're right. All this is new to me. I didn't know that Grandpa testified at any military trials. The transcript summary is only six pages long. But it answers a bunch of questions I never thought I'd get answers to."

My words leapt out of my mouth.

"Here is some history Cousin Mel said about the bastard Hoffman. He was a member of the SA. When he was in charge of operations at the camp, Blechhammer was part of Organization *Schmelt.* He was replaced in 1944, after a reorganization and consolidation which placed administrative operations under the control of Auschwitz personnel."

"Dad, slow down. I know you're excited. Catch your breath. How far away was Blechhammer from Auschwitz?"

"Blechhammer was about 30 to 35 miles from Auschwitz."

"You said it was a military trial. How was it conducted?"

"It was held on July 23, 1947 in Munich under the auspices of an American Military Government Liaison and Security Office. There was a chairman and two assessors, a prosecutor, and a defense counsel. Thirteen witnesses testified on behalf of the prosecutor. Hoffmann was not there. He was tried *en absentia* because he had been arrested and mistakenly released. Then he fled into the English zone."

I picked up the curled transcript and read the charges against Hoffmann:

Respondent was camp commander at Camp Blechhammer (Silesia) where Jews were interned. He whipped them to death, is responsible for the killing of Jews, sent Jews to the gas chambers at Camp Auschwitz.

I handed the transcript to Blake. "Son, read the witness statements I have highlighted.

Witness Palluck: Hoffmann whipped internees daily at Blechhammer, mostly over the face. Hoffmann induced the camp physician Dr Ritter (also a former internee) to send certain internees to "Convalescent home – Auschwitz; decided himself which people will be transferred to Auschwitz; sent for example a Jewish girl to Auschwitz after he raped her repeatedly and she thus became pregnant; had beaten another girl (14) until she fainted; told the members of the ambulance corps they shall not change the bandages for the sick people being transferred to Auschwitz with the remark "They will come into the stove anyway."

I watched Blake's face tighten as he continued to read.

Witness Mrs. Palluck declares the expression "sadist" for the defendant is but a very slight expression. He refers to the case of Lewy. Mr. Lewy died after enduring mistreatment by Hoffmann. Palluck refers to Dr. Ritter, former camp physician, who had been sent to Auschwitz by Hoffmann; Hoffmann disliked him and had the intention to separate him from his wife, a beauty, whom he wanted to gain for his sex-life. He explains a cold water treatment procedure at camp Blechhammer; internees were bespattered with cold water until they perished. In some cases the victim's abdomen was filled with water by leading in of a hose into the mouth. Mrs. Palluck also verified death injections at Blechhammer.

Blake's pallor turned to a whiter shade of grey. I saw questions flying across his blinking eyes. I knew he wanted to stop reading.

"Son, you have got to read two more testimonies; each one is only a paragraph in length."

He continued reading.

Mrs. Ellert: "I was in Blechhammer for only four weeks, but during that time I was forced to act as secretary to Hoffmann. In that period Hoffmann ordered 350 people to be sent to

Auschwitz, knowing that they would be killed in the gas chambers. I saw him beating three Jews; all of them died within a day or two. Also he once put his bloodhound on to a Jew. The Jew was terribly torn and bleeding. After four weeks, I myself was sent to Auschwitz and was with the people being forced into the gas chambers when I managed to persuade an SS officer to release me. I heard the cries of the people as they perished in the gas chamber.

I looked at Blake as tears formed in his eyes. "Son, now read your Grandfather's testimony."

Dr. Leitner: "I was a physician in the sick room at Blechhammer. One day Hoffmann came and told me that two of the sick girls were to be killed before 12:00 o'clock. I refused to do this and the next day Hoffmann himself shot the two girls. As a result of my refusal to obey the order, I was sent to Auschwitz. I was with Mrs. Ellert, almost in the gas chamber, when we managed to persuade an SS officer that we were not sick at all, that they had been sent to Auschwitz by Hoffmann for personal reasons, that he hated them. The SS officer felt mercy on them and released them. This verifies the statements of Mrs. Ellert concerning the mistreatment of 3 Jews that resulted in their deaths.

Blake's eyes met mine. "Dad, you finally got some answers to your story The 'Stairs,' where you as a ten year old, sat on the top step in the Woodridge house, listening to your father tell his story to many people and in many languages; how he was forced at gunpoint to strip, stand at attention and almost marched into the gas chamber; how he thought it was a miracle that he was ordered out of the group and found his bundle of clothes in seconds."

"Yup." I replied as I thought about the differences between the two stories.

"Son, he failed to mention some significant portions of his story, like his own verbal behests for removal from the group to the SS guard, his girl friend's naked pleadings as part of the throng, the words they both said that separated them from the crowd, and hearing the sounds of the thousand gasping for air in the gas chamber. He was a selective story teller, as we all are, and he did say he was only giving the listeners one thousandth of a percent of his story. He gave us the shadow or the skeletal remains of his story."

Blake continued, " I remember wondering what his girlfriend or lover said to the Nazi guard. I remember thinking about the miracle of him finding his clothes in a split second. How he managed to escape the crowd as the remaining poor souls were forced into the gas chamber where they inhaled their last breaths of Zyklon B. Now, I know Grandpa heard their screams of agony. Dad, I can see why he neglected to tell you parts of his story. "

I sat quietly absorbing my son's words.

"Dad, it's hard to believe that fifty-four years after you sat on the top of the stairs, eavesdropping on Grandpa's tale, you now know the rest of the story, why Grandpa was sent to Auschwitz and what he and his girlfriend said to the Nazi guard to get themselves out of the gas chamber line."

Blake picked up his coffee cup, took a long, slow sip and then carefully placed the cup back onto the saucer.

He looked straight into my eyes and muttered. "Life is one fucking miracle."

About This Book

A Hebraic Obesession was written, designed, and typeset to meet or exceed the highest standards of the publishing industry.

With the advent of mass-marketed books, book design – especially with respect to typography – declined. The business risks associated with enormous print runs demanded the use of smaller type packed tightly inside narrow margins. But today's production technology allows single books to be manufactured to order. Why not return to an aesthetic characterized by the glorious days of hot metal typesetting? This edition of *A Hebraic Obesession* is cloth-bound, foil stamped, printed on creme stock, wrapped in an attractive dust jacket, and priced affordably. The additional pages required to accommodate its classic margins and legible type add negligibly to its cost.

If you would be kind enough to post an honest review of your reading experience in the online bookstore or readers' forum of your choice, I would be most grateful.

– Mort Laitner, May, 2014

www.ingramcontent.com/pod-product-compliance
Lightning Source LLC
LaVergne TN
LVHW011216080426
835509LV00005B/151
* 9 7 8 0 9 9 6 0 3 6 9 2 4 *